Action and Consequence
in Ibsen, Chekhov
and Strindberg

ALSO BY ZANDER BRIETZKE

The Aesthetics of Failure:
Dynamic Structure in the Plays of Eugene O'Neill
(McFarland, 2001)

Action and Consequence in Ibsen, Chekhov and Strindberg

ZANDER BRIETZKE

McFarland & Company, Inc., Publishers
Jefferson, North Carolina

LIBRARY OF CONGRESS CATALOGUING-IN-PUBLICATION DATA

Names: Brietzke, Zander, 1960– author.
Title: Action and consequence in Ibsen, Chekhov and Strindberg / Zander Brietzke.
Description: Jefferson, North Carolina : McFarland & Company, Inc., Publishers, 2017 | Includes bibliographical references and index.
Identifiers: LCCN 2017033380 | ISBN 9781476672236 (softcover : acid free paper) ∞
Subjects: LCSH: European drama—19th century—History and criticism. | European drama—20th century—History and criticism. | Ibsen, Henrik, 1828–1906—Criticism and interpretation. | Chekhov, Anton Pavlovich, 1860–1904—Criticism and interpretation. | Strindberg, August, 1849–1912—Criticism and interpretation. | Characters and characteristics in literature.
Classification: LCC PN1851 .B75 2017 | DDC 809.2/034—dc23
LC record available at https://lccn.loc.gov/2017033380

BRITISH LIBRARY CATALOGUING DATA ARE AVAILABLE

ISBN (print) 978-1-4766-7223-6
ISBN (ebook) 978-1-4766-3089-2

© 2017 Zander Brietzke. All rights reserved

No part of this book may be reproduced or transmitted in any form or by any means, electronic or mechanical, including photocopying or recording, or by any information storage and retrieval system, without permission in writing from the publisher.

Front cover image: August Strindberg (1849–1912),
The Avenue ("Allén"), 1903, oil on canvas, 94 × 53 cm.
Thielska Galleriet, Stockholm, Sweden. Photography: Tord Lund.

Printed in the United States of America

McFarland & Company, Inc., Publishers
  Box 611, Jefferson, North Carolina 28640
    www.mcfarlandpub.com

In memory of

Trij Brietzke (1927–2015)
Milton Brietzke (1922–2015)
Robin MacAskill (1944–2015)
Martin Gerry (1943–2016)

Table of Contents

Acknowledgments ix

Introduction: The Super Objective 1

PART 1
Ibsen: The Buried Secret and the Big Surprise 21

A Doll's House (1879) 38
The Wild Duck (1884) 47
Hedda Gabler (1890) 57
The Master Builder (1892) 67

PART 2
Chekhov: Life in the Subjunctive Mood 77

The Seagull (1895) 93
Uncle Vanya (1896) 101
Three Sisters (1900) 111
The Cherry Orchard (1903) 121

PART 3
Strindberg: Isles of the Dead 131

Creditors (1889) 149
The Dance of Death (1900) 159
A Dream Play (1906) 167
The Ghost Sonata (1907) 177

Conclusion 188

Notes 191

Works Cited 193

Index 197

Acknowledgments

Martin Puchner, the brilliant professor now at Harvard, invited me to teach modern drama at Columbia University in 2006 and I can never sufficiently express my gratitude to him for that opportunity. I bundled Ibsen, Chekhov and Strindberg together on two occasions over the next seven years and had the privilege to teach extremely interesting students, none more so than Kate Clairmont, whose current pursuit of a doctorate at Princeton makes her old professor very proud. The diverse questions and curiosities of many students inspired the initial impulse and subsequent development of ideas in this book.

I often say that while I like to *study* drama, I don't like to *live* it. Most plays come into being as a result of the bad choices and wrong decisions made by the leading characters. No bad choices, no drama! In class, students seemed particularly keen to explore the social, political, psychological, economic, sexual and racial dynamics that created or forced such bad decisions. Drama offers a vicarious method to examine and test the mistakes of others and to question or hypothesize about what one might do in similar situations. The plays of Ibsen, Chekhov and Strindberg present three distinctive, compelling and contrasting ways to inhabit the world, each with a seductive and myopic vision that adheres too closely to an outdated one-point perspective. I intend for an analysis of their plays to encourage readers to re-examine their own steadfast positions, to step back from overzealous prescriptions for living and to broaden horizons about what is possible and desirable to do.

The antecedent for this book harkens back 30 years to my own graduate school training and a dissertation on Chekhov that I never published. I clearly outkicked my coverage with that effort, despite heroic guidance and direction by Alice Rayner, but I tried to show (over and over again!) how recurring patterns in Chekhov's plays produced particular meanings. I did not much care at that time for the motives or relationships between characters. Despite my criticism of young Konstantin in *The Seagull*, I fear that my quest echoed his overwrought and fervent calls for new forms of drama! Over the years I have learned something, perhaps, and I now sympathize with such critics as Emma Goldman, known more for her political views than her dramatic criticism, who nonetheless argued that the new modern drama of Ibsen and Chekhov had more to do with subject matter and progressive ideas than innovations in form. With a tip of the cap to the old Communists, I would like to think that my book presents formalism with a human face.

The successive deaths of my mother and father in 2015, followed closely by the passing of my wife's mother and then her father—four deaths in 14 months—sobered my outlook as I tried to wrap up a book on doing things. I began to think that the action within the plays had to be viewed with the endgame, death, in mind as the ultimate destination. Having been inspired by students to start the book, the deaths of family members spurred a not-so-subtle reminder about the stakes in the game and how it all ends. Life intervened to delay completion of my little work on dramatic fiction, but I am hopeful that time to mourn infused my prose with a seriousness of purpose.

Nothing would ever have been completed, though, without the emotional and financial support of Carol Brooks, who has made all things possible for 25-plus years.

Introduction
The Super Objective

In these days of terror, where, even nestled comfortably in a little academe one may speak of interrogating a literary text, the opening lines of *Hamlet* dramatize an accepted mode of critical inquiry: "Stand and unfold yourself" (1.1.2).[1] Like the ghost in that tragedy, a text also resists and remains mute to those of us who are not the famous Dane. Later in the play, Rosencrantz and Guildenstern spy upon their childhood friend in order to learn his motives for what he has done and plans yet to do. Hamlet reacts angrily to this betrayal of trust and decides to make a teaching moment of the situation by offering a musical recorder to his friends. They refuse, naturally, claiming that they lack the necessary skill to play the instrument. Why, then, Hamlet retorts, do they have the audacity to think that they can play upon him? Is he not more complicated than a simple pipe? Why, he asks, do his dear old chums readily presume to pluck out his mystery (3.2.296–372)? As Tom Stoppard later brought the Shakespearean supernumeraries to center stage in his modern comic masterpiece, I intend to take Rosencrantz and Guildenstern's critical approach seriously in order to define and contrast the distinctive dramatic actions of three early modern masters in the late 19th century: Ibsen, Chekhov and Strindberg. My ultimate goal is not to reduce each playwright to one convenient objective, however, but to explore the diverse costs and consequences of clinging too tightly to what amounts to pathological ideology.

The birth of modernism in drama started by Henrik Ibsen (1828–1906) and furthered by August Strindberg (1849–1912) and Anton Chekhov (1860–1904) gave rise to plays that did not break along melodramatic fault lines of good and evil, right and wrong, black and white, and high and low, but fractured in complex and contradictory ways. Their best plays, covering a 30-year period between 1877, the year in which Ibsen produced the first of his 12 prose plays, *The Pillars of Society*, and 1907, the year in which the other great Scandinavian playwright, Strindberg, wrote *The Ghost Sonata* for his intimate chamber theater, defy easy explanations for what happens or does not happen in the stage action. Is Hedda Gabler a victim or victimizer? Why don't the Prozorovs go to Moscow? Why doesn't Madame Ranyevskaya heed a reasonable plan to save the beloved cherry orchard? Why does Miss Julie pursue an affair with her servant? Why cannot the men and women in Strindberg ever seem to get along? The number of yearly productions of plays by these authors suggests that there are many possible answers to such questions and that audiences look forward to the variety of interpretations—as if each production were a part of some platonic whole that offers a unique perspective on a newly-discovered facet of an old dramatic text. Still, though, there remains at root a fundamental drive, the thing done, the action, that informs the possibilities within the work and I plan to identify and define that drive as it manifests in a selection of representative plays from each playwright.

Without getting dogmatic about definitions, at least three important aspects distinguish modern drama: rebellion against the past and prevailing representations of contemporary life; the use of experimental methods and techniques to create new forms of expression; and a unique worldview that manifests such formal innovations. At their best, Ibsen, Strindberg and Chekhov combat melodramatic appeal and suffuse their plays with heavy doses of irony, ambiguity and further provocations. Strindberg's preface to *Miss Julie* (1888) overtly prepares his audience for a new kind of drama and theater and Konstantin's diatribe against his mother's kind of theater in Chekhov's *The Seagull* does much the same thing, though Chekhov positions his stance in the guise of an immature young writer. Ibsen's banquet speech to the League of Women Voters in 1898 in which he outrageously and disingenuously claims not to have consciously written dramas in support of women's rights, thus liberating himself from a specific cause, also attempts to avoid a melodramatic taint in favor of a deeper and more profound project in service of all humanity. Just as it is possible to identify a distant figure on the horizon through familiar patterns of rhythm and movement, different styles and thematic concerns identify each playwright with an adjectival tag as Ibsenian, Chekhovian, or Strindbergian.

Ibsen adapted the prevailing structure of the well-made play to a new serious purpose, though this credit often diminishes him as a true theatrical innovator who collapses time in order to write exposition that simultaneously fills in the past, brings the story up to the present moment, but also drives the plot forward. In particular, Ibsen's use of one particular trope from the well-made play, the buried secret from the past that comes to light in the present, allows his overt plot to run parallel with the unfolding psychological development of human will and consciousness. If Ibsen is the master of plot, Chekhov's pervasive use of the subjunctive mood on a rural estate makes time the implicit subject as characters talk endlessly about the past and future and the wish to be elsewhere, anywhere else. Meanwhile, the relentless ticks and tocks drain the present of vitality and leave the residents lonely and lacking. Strindberg, finally, an accomplished visual artist, creates a drama of the future that anticipates later theatrical developments and challenges even the theater technologies of today to invent the theatrical means to stage his plays. The call to stage his plays in a manner that does not yet exist keeps pace with his persistent complaints about the toil of daily living and his conviction that death represents an escape and relief from worldly concerns.

At the end of his massive Ibsen biography, Michael Meyer, who also published a similar tome on Strindberg, summarized the achievements of Ibsen in terms of the other two playwrights and their dramatized subjects:

> Ibsen's two great successors in the realm of tragedy explored fields that he did not. Strindberg, like no writer before him, mapped that no-man's-land where reality and fantasy, sanity and insanity abut; and he wrote of sex with a frankness which Ibsen, being Ibsen, could not match, especially of sex divorced from love and riding hand-in-hand with contempt or hatred. The only other dramatist since Ibsen who is his peer in stature is Chekhov, and to argue whether he or Ibsen is the greater is like arguing whether Bach is superior to Beethoven [814–815].

Ignoring the sketchy classification of all three writers as tragedians, Meyer differentiates between Ibsen and Strindberg according to the choice and handling of specific subjects: madness and sex, particularly. While I might agree that Ibsen understates these matters, certainly with respect to Strindberg, plays such as *Rosmersholm*, *Hedda Gabler* and *The Master Builder* intricately mix sexual desire with insanity. With respect to Chekhov, Meyer suggests that perceived superior or inferior qualities are simply a matter of taste and temperament and overlooks the fact that the two playwrights appeal to different sensibilities through their remarkably different plays—not only in terms of subject (though they do draw upon vastly different subjects)—but more importantly in terms of radically dissimilar dramatic styles and constructions. Quite simply, their plays do different things and affect audiences differently.

Critical studies invariably mention Ibsen, Strindberg and Chekhov in that order as the founders of modern drama. They are the first three playwrights that Peter Szondi considers in *Theory of Modern Drama* (1965). After Büchner, whose plays of the 1830s were not discovered until the end of that century, Robert Brustein and Richard Gilman treat the three dramatists successively in their respective books, *The Theatre of Revolt* (1964, 1991) and *The Making of Modern Drama* (1972, 1999). As fellow Scandinavian artists, Ibsen and Strindberg wrote as rivals. If one visits the Ibsen Museum today in Oslo, one can see Ibsen's apartment in which he lived the final 11 years of his life and the study where he wrote both *John Gabriel Borkman* and *When We Dead*

Awaken. Above Ibsen's writing desk hangs, surprisingly, a large portrait of Strindberg that the Norwegian had purchased for that particular spot on the wall.[2] To those who raised eyebrows about the placement of such a choice, Ibsen reportedly explained that it helped him to write with "that madman staring down at me" (Meyer 732). The two never met, but Strindberg, at least, was very aware of Ibsen's work. He references *Ghosts* (1881) in *The Father* (1887) by having the character of the doctor refer to lines from Mrs. Alving that he heard at the theater. Strindberg hated *Hedda Gabler* and felt that Ibsen created the title character after Laura in *The Father*. He also thought that Eilert Løvborg was modeled upon himself. He had previously expressed that Hjalmar Ekdal in *The Wild Duck* (1884) was a representation of himself. How could such distinctly different characters, Løvborg, the author of the future, and Ekdal, the inventor of nothing, be patterned after the same man? In general he felt that Ibsen stole his work through some strange, sexual and genetic manipulations: "Do you now see that my seed has fallen into Ibsen's brainpan—and fertilized! Now he carries my seed and is my uterus!" (Meyer 732). Of course, Strindberg made such wild comments at a time when he was fast approaching what he called his inferno crisis in which he endured a period of tortured madness.

Despite the personal antipathy between the Scandinavians, Chekhov is the playwright more at odds with Ibsen than Strindberg. Chekhov, who liked Strindberg's *Miss Julie* very much and even sent Maxim Gorky a copy of that play, never had much good to say about Ibsen.[3] Chekhov's first stage success, *The Seagull*, takes a clear shot at *The Wild Duck* through repetition that effectively empties the symbolism from the play. After having flopped on stage for almost all of Act 2, the bird takes a trip to the taxidermist and makes a final stuffed appearance in Act 4. Chekhov saw productions of *Hedda Gabler*, *When We Dead Awaken*, *An Enemy of the People*, and *The Wild Duck* and expressed enthusiasm for none. Michael Meyer points out that Chekhov would have seen such productions and read the plays in poor translations (815). Stanislavsky, the actor and director and co-founder of the Moscow Art Theatre, who played in and produced all of Chekhov's major plays and brought fame to the theatre organization and to Chekhov, opined that poor productions may have been responsible for Chekhov's dislike. Chekhov, according to Stanislavsky in his autobiography, *My Life in Art*, thought Ibsen was a "dry, cold, a man of reason" (345).[4] Stanislavsky insisted that he and his players tried to play Ibsen as they played Chekhov, "but we were too clever when we played Ibsen to reach the results of Chekhov's simplicity and depth" (345). Chekhov routinely disapproved of Stanislavsky's theatrical interpretations and always displayed ambivalence regarding the Art Theatre's productions of his works.[5] But, in a particularly Chekhovian reversal, Michael Meyer concludes his section on Chekhov's regard for Ibsen by quoting Chekhov's letter to actor V. I. Vishensky in which the playwright confides: "You know Ibsen is my favorite writer" (815).

The impulse of Strindberg and Chekhov to distance themselves from Ibsen reflects the fact that the playwrights pursue very different objectives and use different means to accomplish them in their works. All of the experimental techniques and methods of the playwrights ultimately serve the third aspect of modern drama, the unique worldview of the artist. With Ibsen, it has to do with the imposition of individual will and consciousness and desire in relation to the standards and dictates of contemporary society. Characters in the Chekhovian world search for significance within the boring routines of everyday life. They often model themselves after literary figures or literally even think of themselves as dramatic characters and behave as if they were acting in a play. Strindberg, finally, depicts the dirty hardships of daily living and existence in order to show that death and the afterlife provides the only promise of happiness and release from pain.

These objectives are analogous to the theatrical term—"super-objective"—that Stanislavsky explains in *An Actor Prepares*.[6] The master teacher Tortsov, Stanislavsky's alter ego and literary stand-in, opens the chapter on the super objective by defining thematic concerns as dramatic actions: "Dostoyevski was impelled to write *The Brothers Karamazov* by his lifelong *search for God*. Tolstoy spent all of his life struggling for *self-perfection*. Anton Chekhov wrestled with the *triviality* of bourgeois life and it became the *leit motiv* [sic] of the majority of his literary productions" (256). Action verbs distinguish the grammar of the super objective from thematic and literary statements about a work. To "search" for God, to "struggle" for self-perfection, to "wrestle" with triviality are phrases that describe an event in physical terms that can animate human behavior on stage. While Stanislavsky in the examples above applies the technique to Dostoevsky and Tolstoy's narrative efforts, an actor might state a super objective to determine motivation and psychological make up of a character in a role. One of the primary tasks of the theatrical director, too, is to identify and name the action, or super objective of a dramatic text. In the grammar of stage direction expressed succinctly by Harold Clurman, dramatic action is the verb that ignites an interpretation and gives the production a spine upon which to grow and develop (28).[7] While there are usually many things that happen in a given drama, dramatic action states the most important thing from which all other action and activity follows. This reductive device forces a director to choose what is most important in the play and separate the main action from subsidiaries in order to provide a focal point for a production.

Recurring patterns in the works key subsequent, subjective decisions about the action of a particular play. In Ibsen, a lone protagonist tries to make events in the world accommodate and correspond to his or her own perceptions and desires. The world may be one way, perception of it may be entirely different, but the Ibsen hero attempts to treat subjective experience as wholly and entirely objective regardless of any outside or competing views. While the Ibsen lead character is willful, Chekhov, conversely, presents an array of characters in such a way that precludes identifying a single protagonist. A group convenes in the country and proceeds to talk endlessly about the past, the future, and what might have been. It is a mistake to say that nothing happens in Chekhov—Konstantin becomes a writer; Nina pursues Trigorin and has her baby; the battery comes and goes in *Three Sisters*; Lopakhin buys the cherry orchard—but characters self-dramatize their lives in an effort to heighten their importance in the routine of everyday life. It is as if they think of themselves as dramatic characters in a very serious play about the meaning and importance of life. No wonder, then, that Chekhov considered his works comedies! The same cannot be said for the last playwright of the triumvirate, Strindberg, who pits man and woman together in intractable relationships of love and hate. Ironically, compared to the other two, Strindberg is the most optimistic and hopeful about the human condition because of his devout Christianity. The possibility for life after death in his plays redeems the terrible pain of daily living and the inevitability of death. This trajectory becomes more explicit over the course of Strindberg's career as his stylistic move from realism to expressionism mirrors his shift in preoccupation from the purely physical and material to the spiritual and ethereal. For all the received opinions about Strindberg's misogyny and his madness, he delivers the voice of salvation.

Ever since Aristotle defined drama as an "imitation of an action," critics have debated about what he meant and about what those two key terms even mean (61). For my purposes, with a grateful nod to Stanislavsky and his theatrical mindset, imitation refers to acting and action refers to a goal for human endeavor. The super objective is nothing more than the ultimate goal of the artistic work. Just as Stanislavsky urged actors to define a super objective for their individual roles in the plays, I seek to identify a super objective for each playwright's body of work. Stanislavsky's method for actor training unlocked the unconscious and creative talents and abilities through conscious and analytic steps and techniques. In no way do I presume that Ibsen, Chekhov, Strindberg or any other writer ever consciously pondered the super objective of his or her work. It is a task for the critic, here masquerading as a stage director, to name a super objective that informs a playwright's creative vision and releases the plays to a wide range of imaginative possibilities. In the three parts of the book that follow, I will ascribe a dominant action to the dramatic efforts of each the three playwrights and will proceed to discuss and interpret individual plays in light of their overriding super objectives, the hook upon which the interpretation hangs. And, while it is traditional to discuss the playwrights chronologically according to author's birth date and thus list Ibsen first, followed by Strindberg and Chekhov, the contents of this book shall lead with Ibsen, counter with Chekhov, and conclude with Strindberg. In this fashion, Ibsen, in Part 1, pioneers as the dramatist who writes the thesis of modern drama: to impose the will upon the world. Chekhov presents the antithesis of seeming non-action in Part 2: to dramatize the scene of boring, everyday life. Strindberg, the most stylistically diverse of the three playwrights, offers synthesis in the final third of the book: to transcend the brutality of human existence.

Ibsen is the easiest of the three playwrights to read because he seems to be the most direct. The entire first act of *Ghosts*, for example, is mainly expository in which Mrs. Alving talks about the history of her marriage on the eve of opening an orphanage in honor of her late husband. It turns out, however, that Captain Alving was dissolute and debauched and that Mrs. Alving is simply trying to put a shine on what had been a bleak and sad situation. The play goes into full gear when her son Osvald, who looks exactly like his father, returns home from Paris and his mother hears him fondling the maid, Regina, just offstage, just as Mrs. Alving was recalling her husband's affair with Regina's mother. Unbeknownst to Osvald, the target of his affections is his half-sister. Unbeknownst to his mother, Osvald has returned home at this time because he has contracted syphilis that is certain, in time, to drive him mad. In the unfolding action, Mrs. Alving discovers that her son has inherited the disease from the father and Osvald realizes the truth about Regina, whom he wanted because she would give him the drugs to kill him rather than tend him as an invalid when the inevitable disease struck. The climax of the play occurs at the end of the second act with the burning down of the orphanage in a case of arson, a fire that is also a metaphor for the burning up of Osvald's own mind and also the purification of the past and all the lies that propped up the dedication to such an enterprise. In the final act, after Regina leaves, after everyone leaves, Osvald is left alone with his mother and as the play ends it is clear that the disease has struck and that Mrs. Alving faces a difficult choice of what to do. The real action of the play focuses on Mrs. Alving and her reflections on her life choices and how she regrets what she did in the past and how she feels that she betrayed herself and sold herself in marriage and even was responsible thereafter for her husband's wayward behavior. What she has learned during the course of the play will be put to the test at the end when disease incapacitates her son and he begins to speak incoherently. What will she do? How will she act? Has she learned anything through what she has discovered about the past actions and can she put her new knowledge to use? The probing of the past and, more importantly and emphatically, Mrs. Alving's evolving consciousness are the real actions in the play, despite the theatrics of the orphanage fire and the shenanigans of Engstrand, the Machiavellian carpenter who ignited it.

The play follows what Brian Johnston described in his interpretive study: "The invariable action in an Ibsen play is that of the spirit awakened from its spiritual sleep to a terrible awareness of the *unreality* of the world it finds itself in (a world from which it has derived its identity), and its unnerving exploration of dimensions of reality more authentic but more demanding" (50). Johnston's great study of Ibsen's prose plays sees all 12 as a conscious playing out by dramatic means of Hegel's *Phenomenology of Mind*. Here, my goal is less lofty to identify the major drives of the play, drives that the protagonists consistently make in order to prove their points and defend their interpretations of the world and its events. Protagonists such as Mrs. Alving may not like what they discover. But, like Oedipus, nothing can stop them from their pursuits. Invariably, self-knowledge and self-awareness come at a steep price, but the search astonishes the protagonists and their onlookers or readers who follow their journeys. Mrs. Alving wants to build an orphanage, not to honor her late husband, but to provide closure on a painful chapter in her life. She believes that she will be able to start a new life for herself. But, over the course of the action, she learns that the past has come alive in the shape of her long-absent son, and more significantly, that the past as she interpreted it was not entirely accurate. She lied to herself and she discovers the lie in the unfolding of the present plot. She is able to articulate her transformation but her narrative still unravels as she makes more discoveries about the motivations for her prior actions. The Ibsen worldview marvels at human determination but dramatizes the limits of self-knowledge and self-discovery in the presence of a world in which the variables remain unknown. Again and again, characters try to make the world conform to their own desires, but discover, often too late, that the world does not obey the laws that they construct for it. The secrets that they dig up and divulge from the past do not provide the answers to the questions that they asked, but remind them rather that the world remains mute and mysterious.

In contrast to Ibsen, Chekhovian characters skirt the surface of things. The rural setting for Chekhov's plays reveals quite a different kind of dramaturgy at work than in Ibsen. One never quite knows where one is in the country of Chekhov. Moscow always looms; the Ragoulins are down in Kharkov; an aunt lives in Yaroslavl; Nina travels to a third-class venue in Yelets. But where does the action take place? In the country, the actress Arkadina observes in *The Seagull*, where no one does anything, or says anything interesting. All the characters sit around and philosophize about this and that. The rural inhabitants dream of life in the city; the city folk come out to the country and admire the scenery and view their time as a welcome retreat. No surprise, then, that the professor from Moscow decides that he cannot retire for life at such a place! The writer, Trigorin, claims, however, that he would do nothing but fish if he were to live near such a lake as exists in *The*

Seagull. He insists that he loves fishing more than anything. Nina, with stars in her eyes, cannot believe that he would love such a boring, mundane activity. She dreams every night of going on the stage in Moscow. Of course, the Prozorovs in *Three Sisters* say that they want to go to Moscow and they state their desires repeatedly, but, comically, they do not go. Chekhovian characters rarely express contentment regarding their present situation. The city folk escape to the country; the country folk aspire to the urban center. No one really wants to inhabit fully the actual space where the action takes place.

Why doesn't Madame Ranyevskaya listen to Lopakhin and make plans to save the estate by subdividing the property and cutting down the cherry orchard? The answer, in part, has to do with the fact that she does not want to be there and that the memories of the estate are painful to her. The play opens in the nursery of the house and reminds Ranyevskaya that her son, Grisha, drowned on the estate years ago. In an Ibsen play, the facts around that event and all the guilt surrounding it would be explored and expiated. In Chekhov, however, Ranyevskaya dramatizes her guilt and the pain of losing her only son, but she never must relive and confront it. Instead, her entire flight to Paris years ago was her means to cope with personal tragedy. And now she wants to leave the estate and return to Paris as quickly as possible. Staying among the ghosts of her past is never an option. As David Mamet astutely observes, she doesn't want to save the orchard; her love lives elsewhere (118).

The few characters that do act forcefully in the plays are not necessarily more attractive because of it. Arkadina and Trigorin are professional artists, but Trigorin refers to his occupation as an obsession and a habit that he cannot break. Arkadina is a successful actress, but her son's accurate critique of her career casts her accomplishments as trivial. Serebriakov, the retired professor in *Uncle Vanya*, had a long and distinguished academic career, but his lasting contributions to scholarship or society appear nil. Lopakhin, the new owner of the cherry orchard at the end of that play, remains extremely sympathetic and even a good man, but his plans to chop down the orchard and subdivide the estate to build summer houses for the affluent are tasteless. If he is the harbinger of the new world to come, then the future does not seem very bright. None of these characters approaches Natasha in *Three Sisters*, however, in terms of vulgarity and even villainy. Initially an outsider, Natasha marries into the Prozorov family and immediately begins to take over the household, gives birth first to Little Bobik and then Sophie, then pushes Olga and Irina out of their rooms to make room for the little ones, emasculates her husband Andrei, browbeats the old retainer Anfisa, and all the while carries on an affair with the local bigwig bureaucrat Protopopov. At the end of the play, she rules the house and sisters watch from outside as idle spectators. While they focused their attention upon Moscow, Natasha displaced them from their family home. On the one hand, her action warns of the perils of not taking action and defending one's property and rights. On the other hand, Natasha's craven greed and selfishness give forceful action a bad name. If she is a representative of the future and an example of what it will take to survive in the 20th century, then it is no wonder that other characters try to ignore her threats of a materialistic and ghastly world.

There is a sense, then, that the Chekhovian aristocrats, long on cultured taste but short on ready money, are part of a dying class that needs to turn over in order for the world to progress. The bourgeois takeover of the world is necessary, perhaps, and an historical fact, yes, but Chekhov does much more than chronicle and mourn the necessary changes in society of a particular historical moment. Natasha is a crass little creature, as Andrei finally describes her, devoid of empathy and compassion for other human beings, but she stands out as a wonderful anomaly and exception in the Chekhovian world. Most characters do not attain or even pursue their heart's desires. Better, they reason, to ask for less and receive less, but never to feel too poignantly the lack of what one most wants in life. Change, loss, death may be the nature of things in the world, but awareness of that makes characters less likely to make themselves vulnerable in terms of what they want and to whom they choose to confide such admissions. There is a lot of feigned emotion in Chekhov's plays; there is a lot of talk of love. There are very few interactions suffused with committed love and passion. Chekhov builds his plays, however, around such rare moments and where they break out, however briefly and tentatively, to show what's at stake and why characters strenuously avoid confrontation, love, and emotional involvement, will receive particular attention in Part 2.

If meaningful moments of contact between characters remain sparse, the majority of stage time allocates to thoughts of the future, or the past, longings to be somewhere else and even to be someone else. Indeed, in the Chekhovian worldview, the search for significance on the part of characters leads them to dramatize their own mundane lives and see themselves as dramatic characters (Masha as tragic heroine in *The Seagull*; Solyony as Lermontov in *Three Sisters*; Vanya as Schopenhauer; Madame Ranyevskaya as a tragic heroine in *The Cherry Orchard*). Searching outside oneself and adopting literary/dramatic models of behavior, even thinking of oneself as a dramatic character and living in the world of Stanislavsky's "magic if" (what would I do if I were this character in these given circumstances), forestalls any urgency for action in the real world. Worse, the heightened sense of life as a literary drama obscures the dull and routine actions of daily life that actually enrich a sense of community among people and add needed comfort. The dramatization of life within the dramas tempts Nina to run off to Moscow in search of Trigorin; prevents Vanya from appreciating the quiet beauty of his rural routine; idealization of work and love, in the absence of real love and work and connections with daily life, leads Irina to sentence Tuzenbach to death in *Three Sisters*; and Lopakhin's lifelong infatuation with Madame Ranyevskaya, whom he has no chance of marrying, blinds him to the possibilities of a reciprocal partnership with Varya in *The Cherry Orchard*. Everyone, including especially Ranyevskaya and even Lopakhin, assumes that they will marry, but, at the last moment of the dramatized action, he still does not propose to her. And so it goes, and time passes, and while characters dream and imagine a future that is not possible, real life intervenes and people come and go and time goes by and characters let moments pass and leave things unsaid and little by little they lose their chances for happiness in search of something, some phantom happiness, that seems to be more grand.

The torment of emotion between men and women is the great subject in all of Strindberg's plays. He is the first dramatist to depict the conflicting emotions of love and hate that flow not alternately but concurrently in romantic relationships, particularly married couples such as the Captain and Laura in *The Father*, Adolf and Tekla in *Creditors*, as well as Tekla's previous husband Gustav, and Edgar and Alice in *The Dance of Death*. The ravages of time take their toll upon all of these couples. They say terrible and hurtful things to one another but they stay together, anyway, out of more than habit but affection and even a kind of enduring love. The opening scene of *The Dance of Death* comically presents a couple trapped together and planning to celebrate their 25th wedding anniversary, what Alice calls their 25 years of misery together. Yet there they are, trading barbs, finishing each other's sentences, comfortably aware of everything about the other. Edgar counters about their many years together: "miserable they may have been, but we've had our fun—now and then. Time is short and we've got to make the best of it. Time has an end" (*Selected Plays* 2:187). Marriage may be painful, Strindberg suggests, but it is the only treasure that mortal times afford.

Strindberg's most famous play, *Miss Julie* (1888), equally influential because of the accompanying preface that lists the objectives and contributions of the modern theater in compact form, does not depict a married couple but instead a man and woman separated by class but drawn together by circumstance and biological need. It is no surprise that this play is the most naturalistic of Strindberg's plays and deliberates on the disastrous effects of genetics and environment upon a relationship. At the center of the play, though unseen and offstage, is their sexual act—impulsive, improvisational, quick, and possibly violent. With it, Strindberg suggests that neither man nor woman is in control of sexual desire and that sexual need trumps all rational decision-making. Instinctual desire, natural perhaps, unavoidable perhaps, inevitably leads also to disastrous results. Strindberg carefully extracts love from sex in the play. Julie says that she loves Jean at one point, but she only voices this sentiment after the sexual act in Jean's room, in a vain attempt to recover her respectability in his eyes. By the end of the play, though, she freely admits that she hates him and would like nothing more than to splatter his brains.

Less well known than *Miss Julie*, but written immediately after, *Creditors* is a better play that entwines love and sex and hate in such a way that depicts the awful pain of human existence in which one gives one's heart to another to the extent that such offering makes one weak and vulnerable. Here, the triangle between a wife and her current and former husband reveals the quintessential pain in human, sexual relationships and the fragility of marriage and all intimate relationships. The current husband, Adolph, fears that he loves his wife, Tekla, too much and that this vulnerability makes him weak. His wife, however, married him precisely because of his capacity to give himself freely. Her marriage to him is successful largely because she has learned to love herself as a result of a prior marriage that ultimately failed. Her former husband is everything that her current man is not: strong, proud and controlling. Gustav, however, the former husband, cannot reconcile himself to losing his wife to another man and he destroys the new husband by filling him with doubts about the faithfulness and love of his wife. An artist and sensitive by nature, Adolph crumbles and dies when faced with the prospect that his wife has been unfaithful and loves someone else more than him. Tekla's first marriage prepared her for the second, but the first husband cannot let go and wrecks them all, including himself, rather than allow the new couple to move on without him.

Strindberg's late plays, written in the first decade of the 20th century, after what may have been a mental breakdown, during which, at any rate, he wrote no plays, continue to dramatize the devastating havoc of sexual relationships between men and women. But, as Strindberg ages and approaches death, hastened by painful awareness of his growing stomach cancer, the plays embrace Christian spirituality and death as a release from the heartbreaks of intimate, human bonds. The form of the plays, too, softens from the early naturalism and realism of the first plays to a subjective surrealism (*A Dream Play*) and expressionism (*The Ghost Sonata*) that physically manifests a freedom from the rules of everyday life. The dreamer is none other than Strindberg himself and while he still presents a world that is petty and corrupt, in which men and women are terrible sinners, the best of them are aware of their sins and wish that they could act better, a saving desire that translates into a beautiful benediction at the conclusion of *The Ghost Sonata* with a vision of eternal peace and grace after death.

Each part of the book includes an introductory essay on the playwright and analysis of four representative plays. With Chekhov, the task for selection was quite easy—he only wrote four major dramas. Ibsen and Strindberg required more discretion in terms of final choices. None of the excellent verse dramas that Ibsen wrote prior to his exclusive turn to prose in 1877 gets any notice in these pages. Inclusion of *Brand*, *Peer Gynt* or *Emperor and Galilean* would have expanded the narrative of the book. Indeed, Ibsen regarded the latter play as his most important work. Still, the role of the ego, conscience and consciousness is unmistakable in those messianic dramas and Ibsen states virtually the same message in a much more subtle form when the plays come down to earth in the later bourgeois dramas.[8] Within the oeuvre of Ibsen's 12 prose plays, chosen plays span the scope of his career from the domestic and social scene of *A Doll's House* to the life and temperament of the artist in *The Master Builder*. Performance frequency in today's repertory also factored into the selection process. The reader is much more likely to encounter a production of *Hedda Gabler* than *The Lady from the Sea* (although that play fascinates because of its unusually surprising and very happy ending!), and would sooner have a chance to see *The Master Builder* before *Little Eyolf*, *John Gabriel Borkman*, or *When We Dead Awaken*. *Hedda Gabler* represents the height of Ibsen's dramatic powers, in which he seamlessly integrates his dramatic vision and structure. His next and final plays, beginning with *The Master Builder*, question what the artist is to do after he has done all that he can do, and, interestingly, the lofty ideals expressed by the hero outstretch the ability of the playwright to execute them.

Strindberg, predictably, posed the greatest challenge in terms of picking only four plays to represent his vast body of work. Initially, *Miss Julie* was one of them, as it seems to be the only Strindberg play that is ever anthologized, in part because of the famous preface attached to it. *Creditors*, written immediately after *Miss Julie*, also seemed like a good choice, especially after the late Alan Rickman directed a brilliant production first at the Donmar Warehouse and later at the Brooklyn Academy of Music in 2010. It did not seem right to include both of these similar plays at the expense of Strindberg's later work, but the Red Bull Theater in New York solved the dilemma with a very fine production of *The Dance of Death* in 2013. That play substitutes for Miss Julie and represents an interesting transition from the early naturalistic plays to the late surrealistic/expressionistic dramas, the height of which Strindberg captures in *A Dream Play* and *The Ghost Sonata*, the latter of which stands as his greatest play.

Discussion of each individual play begins with the fable that tells the story of the play and reveals the interpretive bias of the writer. As a diagnostic tool, the fable reveals and makes public what the critic thinks is most important, but also shows what the critic misses or fails to see and relegates as trivial or unimportant. The fable, then, catches a glimpse of the play from the perspective of the critic in the same way that a theatrical production reveals certain aspects of a play in performance that had remained mysterious and unexplored in previous efforts. The fable provides a concise slant on the action, but the bulk of analysis on each play will explore key scenes that convey the action. Ibsenian scenes, usually long and with only a couple of characters, contrast greatly to the Chekhovian scenes that are generally very short and often have many characters in them. Ibsen masterfully builds one scene on top of another, while the fluidity of a scene in Chekhov constantly changes the stage picture as one group of characters leaves and another enters. Ibsen stacks his narrative; Chekhov constantly deflates narrative sequence. Strindberg, as his career progresses and as he moves away from realistic style, defies the conventions of narrative in order to create dream sequences of his imagination.

Scene analysis exposes the vital contradictions that pervade and resonate with meanings throughout the entire play.[9] "Drama equals conflict" is a familiar mantra that students learn with their first exposure to the genre. They look for opposing forces to understand and to articulate the conflict: between nations, between men and women, between the old and the young, between a mother and a daughter, between two sisters, brothers, etc., etc. Here, vital contradictions may not be as overt as in melodrama but they are no less in opposition. Chekhov, as critic Northrop Frye observed, is intensely ironic and the differences between how characters would like to project themselves and the reality of those characters as perceived by the reader/audience creates a good bit of the humor as well as conflict, or contradiction, in the plays (178). The gap between perception and reality may well have been why Chekhov thought of his plays as comedies. Ibsen, though no comedian, stages contradictions in his scenes, as well, that often create rich humor. Given that the little girl dies in the end, *The Wild Duck* can hardly be called a comedy, but there is a lot of humor in it. Hjalmar Ekdal, for example, thinks of himself as a noble inventor, but spends most of his time eating, sleeping or drinking. The audience and the other characters in the play view him quite differently than the way that he fashions himself and the awareness of that difference produces a comic reaction. Humor, naturally, is only one possible outcome that results from the recognition of a contradiction between two or more things. The many contradictions in a scene, between language and action, thought and deed, give life to the scene and propel the action in interesting, surprising and provocative ways.

The overt blackmail plot in *A Doll's House*, for example, and the suspense that builds around the letter in the mailbox, contradicts the primary action that unfolds in the expanding consciousness of Nora Helmer. In fact, as an examination of an early scene in that play will show, Nora's real problem exists independently of Krogstad's intrigues and machinations. In *The Wild Duck*, Ibsen cleverly changes perspectives within the drama. In the first act, the audience views the central conflict as father against son and likely sympathizes with the son's point-of-view. Subsequent acts, however, call Gregers' idealism into question and the scene shift to a photographic studio creates images of doubt in an audience's collective imagination. Ibsen's dramaturgy loads events of the past into the present in an economy of construction that simultaneously makes the past the subject in the present. The most important scene in *Hedda Gabler* occurs when the heroine actually replays a scene from the past as she sits with the former object of her affection and they recall how they used to behave. The repetition affords an opportunity for Hedda to choose a different course of action and change the direction of her life and destiny, and offers the one moment of vulnerability in the play, but Hedda quickly covers up and regains her steely poise. Finally, in *The Master Builder*, Ibsen again creates perspectival shift from the conflict between youth and age to the robust argument between the protagonist's ego and conscience and consciousness brought on by the unexpected arrival of Hilda Wangel. In this play, too, Ibsen undermines his own strategy of uncovering a buried secret in the past by exposing it as a lie. As in *A Doll's House*, the barriers to freedom lie within the protagonist's moribund conscience and consciousness.

In the Chekhov section, the elliptical space between the pivotal third and final fourth act of *The Seagull* that characters fill with narrative rather than dramatic speech threatens to collapse the drama completely and the image of the empty theater where Konstantin staged his little play in the opening act comments on the poverty of the genre and art's inability to provide any kind of meaningful relief for spiritual distress. The map of Africa in *Uncle Vanya* serves as the exotic, out-of-place and unnecessary property that comments on the unrealized aspirations and hopes of the estate's inhabitants. The beauty of the final scene with its silences and repetitions and sound effects counter the stoically grim expressions of Sonya and her uncle. In *Three Sisters*, the staging at the start of the play offers a perspicuous example of Chekhovian irony that shows, unequivocally, that the Prozorovs will never go to Moscow. The "breaking string" scene in *The Cherry Orchard* occurs twice in the play, once in the middle and again at the end, in order to comment on symbolism and show, quite conversely, how the hyper-realism of the sound effect creates the very opposite condition—a weird existential moment that highlights the artifice of theater.

Strindberg spotlights the relationships between men and women and the antipathy that threatens to ruin any alliance. In the life and death contest of *Miss Julie*, Julie proves victorious over Jean even though she walks to her death at the end. *Creditors* dramatizes the fragility and vulnerability of love and lovers and as such shows the apparent winner of the revenge plot as the biggest loser in the play. While *Creditors* examines a young marriage, *The Dance of Death* follows Edgar and Alice to the brink of their 25th wedding anniversary. They bicker and trade brutal insults constantly in an attempt to gain the upper hand with one another, but also as part of an elaborate and accepted game that they enjoy together immensely. So much so that they invite a guest to watch and for whom they perform in a manner that reminds a contemporary audience of *Who's Afraid of Virginia Woolf?*. Like Albee's great play, Strindberg's love story flickers under time's relentless melt, but flourishes with the advancing prospects of old age and imminent death. Further along death's continuum, *The Ghost Sonata* presents a remarkable contrast between what things seem to be and how they truly exist. A young man seeks love, but finds corruption and death draining vitality from the beautiful young woman whom he adores. An earlier image of the old people gathering at the dinner table to partake of their "ghost supper" dramatizes the decomposition of the physical body and the corruption of the spirit. Death poses as relief from the tortures of daily living over years and years and promises to bring peace for the ravaged spirit that does not die.

Ibsen's protagonists try to impose their will upon the world, but they do so in very different ways that do not simply restate the same old thing, but explore different aspects and ramifications of the same basic drive. Young and naïve, Nora Helmer in *A Doll's House* knows that the world of experience does not accord with the world of ideals to which she holds fast. She tries desperately to prove that her hopes, dreams and fantasies are true, but discovers in their falseness that she cannot continue to hide behind her husband and children in the safety of his home. *The Master Builder*, on the other hand, explores a different realm of experience as the mature artist, Solness, tries to overcome his guilt over what he has done to others in order to advance his own career. With the aid of a young woman who functions as his conscience and alter ego, he releases the "troll within him" in order to climb to greatness and overcome all his fears of falling. This play has routinely been interpreted as Ibsen's self-portrait of the aging artist, but if that is really so, it is an unflattering picture of a maniacal old man who hogs all the glory (and money) of artistic success and disregards the mandate for old age to give way to youth. Solness may transcend his human limitations at the end on his ascent to the heavens, but the graphic description of his crushed skull against the rocks in the quarry below cancels any romantic idealization of the artist. The titular heroine of *Hedda Gabler*, by contrast, refuses to act for herself in the way of Nora or Solness, but retreats from the world in favor of action by proxy: she tries to accomplish her life's work by motivating her unrequited lover to do her bidding. Worse, Hedda actually misses the opportunity to redress her former mistakes in the past. Given the choice, she does the same thing again and the action demonstrates the ramifications of not taking responsibility for one's own life. Finally, *The Wild Duck* presents a protagonist, Gregers Werle, who doggedly pursues the truth of what happened years ago and destroys a family in order to appease his own guilty conscience concerning his past actions. This play issues a cautionary warning about assertion of the will as it critiques the nature and value of truth. Go softly, proceed cautiously, the action suggests, for one does not know what one does.

The Chekhovian response to the problem of action, particularly with respect to Gregers Werle and *The Wild Duck*, is to do nothing. Characters bask in images of themselves as dramatic characters in order to create some sense of significance. It is astonishing, for example, how many of them, especially the supporting characters, exhibit theatrical tics and eccentricities that distinguish them from each other: Carlotta's magic tricks, Pishchik's pill popping, Yepikhodov's melancholy, Telegin's complexion, Yasha's aristocratic yearnings, Dunyasha's affectations of sensitivity, Masha's snuffbox, Sorin's prescriptions, Solyony's cologne, the doctor's newspapers in *Three Sisters*, and Gayev's billiards. As Dr. Dorn says to Sorin in *The Seagull*, when you add such affectations you become someone else—and that is exactly what the Chekhovian characters long to do. Making a drama out of their lives, they think, is a way to give them significance that they lack in everyday life. A more insidious implication for this tactic exists, however. By thinking of themselves as dramatic characters, by pretending to be someone other than who they are, they render all real action as impossible and negate the possibilities of personal change and development. The fictive life, the imaginary life is the perfectly safe setting for these characters to thrive. They may wish for things to be different, but that never changes the way things are. All the while, time passes by and the refusal to deal with things results in lost opportunities. Worse, in their search for happiness outside themselves in the external poses of other people, grand and successful people, writers and actors, Chekhovian characters regularly overlook the everyday occurrences around them and the natural beauty of their surroundings that might bring them real contentment. They cannot see these things, but the audience does and therein lays the comic pain of true perception and false reality.

There is no need for pretense and dissembling in Strindberg: the world is a horrible place that inevitably dooms men and women to love and hate each other in ways that they cannot control and can seldom correct. *Creditors*, for example, demonstrates the fragility of relationships and marriages. The second marriage of Tekla and Adolph promises to be successful based in part on what Tekla learned from the failure of her first marriage to Gustav. Unfortunately, Gustav cannot let go and sees no advantage in allowing Tekla to benefit in her second marriage from the things that he gave to her and taught her in the first marriage. Gustav ruins his own life in pursuit of the destruction of Tekla because he refuses to move on and grant her also the chance to grow and develop in her subsequent relationship with Adolph. *The Dance of Death*, by comparison, features Edgar and Alice who have endured 25 years of marriage and stayed together the entire time. Despite the awful things they say to each other, despite also the terrible things they do to each other, they also love each other and need each other—it is possible that they say/do such vile things to each other in proportion to how much they need one another. At the same time, made very clear in a relationship play with a mature couple, death serves as the real subject of this and all Strindberg's plays. And while it is initially feared, Edgar undergoes a near-death experience in *The Dance of Death* that changes him and seems to project a new view in the rest of Strindberg's plays. In that play, Edgar realizes that death grants release from life and that, ironically, it affords, perhaps, the first opportunity to live (in some sort of afterlife). Certainly both *A Dream Play* and *The Ghost Sonata* present the everyday life on earth as one of repetitive toil and unending hardship. Death, however, might bring an end to suffering and the beginning of peace in an afterlife that promises to surpass anything known in the earthly life.

Today's scholars and students alike accept the playwriting form that Ibsen perfected almost for granted, as if Ibsen's particular innovations have become *de rigueur* for typical play structure. Such critical ambivalence erodes his contributions other than in the realms of important subject matter (e.g., the role of women in society). Chekhov remains beloved, but often for only vague reasons of atmospheric indolence and with only a faint and respectful nod that stems from the feeling that one ought to like Chekhov in the same way that one ought to like broccoli for dinner. Yet certainly the existential crises that the principal characters endure in his plays foreshadow, say, the bare-stage metadramas of Samuel Beckett in which the theater serves as a vehicle for experiencing and reflecting upon the ironic vicissitudes of mundane life. Strindberg, the least performed of the three, at least in the United States, appeals to the contemporary director more than the actor because of the stylistic range and imagination of his works that invite a creative team to invent methods of performance in order to stage the plays.

Still, Strindberg's interest in science and his study of human behavior and his stated enjoyment in the theater that stems from learning something anticipated, if not inspired, the epic theater of Bertolt Brecht in the age of science in the 20th century. In the United States, Strindberg irrefutably influenced America's only Nobel Prize-winning playwright, Eugene O'Neill, whose acceptance speech for that award in 1936 praised Strindberg as the Master (428). When O'Neill opened his own avant-garde theater in 1924 he chose *The Ghost Sonata* as the inaugural production and voiced similar praise for the Swedish playwright in "Strindberg and Our Theatre," included in the program. Several of O'Neill's plays owe a direct debt to Strindberg, including, most famously, *Long Day's Journey Into Night* in which the four Tyrones equally hate and love each other so much. Some of O'Neill's early plays pay homage to Ibsen as well, but Arthur Miller most inherits Ibsen's critical acumen for social hypocrisy and the dangers of idealism. Miller's version of Ibsen's *An Enemy of the People* reveals differences between the two stalwarts to be sure, but it also shows the bias of Miller toward social reform and critique as opposed to a Strindbergian/O'Neillian focus on the individual. The other important American playwright in post-war mid–20th century, Tennessee Williams, who adapted *The Seagull* in a version he called *The Notebook of Trigorin*, riffs on Chekhov's pervasive theme of time and time passing and analogies can be made between aristocratic life in rural Russia at the end of the 19th century and southern life in the United States in the 20th century. Williams at his best dramatizes the cost of progress in the 20th century and laments the loss of grace and charm even as he looks unblinkingly at the agrarian past funded by racism and the sins of slavery. Similarly, Chekhov is aware that the feudal past of Russia is morally unacceptable, but the prescient look to the future and the revolutionary times that lay ahead provide little reason for hoopla.

Together, Ibsen, Chekhov and Strindberg form the primary triad of modern dramatists that continues to stock the theatrical repertory of today. On one side of the footlights, audiences cannot see enough productions of their plays, in part, because they can only see a few facets of a complex play in any given setting of a single production. Each subsequent production of a play carries the potential to uncover and explore new territory within the text even as it adds to the history of the play's interpretations. One of the phenomenal aspects of playgoing is the opportunity to see more of the play (a physical, material production of a dramatic text) and less (a single interpretation favors certain aspects over others) simultaneously. On the other side of the footlights, actors want to play in substantial roles that test their skill and training and that establish their bona fides as performers among their peers and critics. The number and quality of opportunities for actors, especially for women, distinguish all the plays. In Ibsen and Chekhov, for example, outstanding female roles include Hedda Gabler, Mrs. Alving, Nora Helmer, Rebecca West, and Hilda Wangel; for Chekhov there is Arkadina, Ranyevskaya, the Prozorov sisters, Yelena and Sonya in *Uncle Vanya*. Strindberg creates Miss Julie, of course, but also Tekla in *Creditors* and Alice in *The Dance of Death*. Performances in such roles set a comparative standard to measure and evaluate past and future performers and performances.

Good actors like to play the roles in Ibsen, Chekhov and Strindberg, but, audiences, too, like to envision themselves in the roles that the playwrights create. Whether they are reading the play or watching a star performer in the theater, audiences imagine themselves in the roles and ask, à la Stanislavsky's *magic if*, what they would do if they were those characters in similar situations. Characters, to be sure, invariably make the *wrong* decisions: Nina runs after Trigorin to Moscow; Hedda refuses Løvborg again;

20   Introduction

Gregers needlessly rescues his friend from a domestic situation in which his friend was completely happy; Gustav destroys the lives of his former wife and her new husband, but robs himself of any chance of future happiness as well. If characters did not make bad or wrong decisions, there would be no drama. The characters in Ibsen, Chekhov and Strindberg all make wrong decisions, in part, by sticking too ardently and steadfastly to their super objective. The dominant drive hardens and calcifies into a single-minded ideology that accepts no compromise. In the stakes of "all or nothing," characters in these plays lose almost every time.

Characters make bad decisions or decisions that turn out badly, but the audience does not have to act similarly on its own outside the theater. Instead, an audience gets to see how choices play out on stage, evaluate the consequences, and then *not* do the same things that lead to devastation. An audience can reflect upon the consequences of a single drive through life, evaluate the cost and, above all, see what the characters in the plays miss. Brecht famously objected to the linear construction of most drama because it implied, if not directly stated, that certain human outcomes were inevitable. He wanted to show in his plays that human destiny was never inevitable but always the product of specific choices that could produce different outcomes if characters made different choices (71). An audience member should be able to object at any juncture, and not just in a Brecht play or in a cheap melodrama, when a character is about to make a big mistake. The three playwrights in this study may not state what the characters miss, but they do show what they miss. By comparing the action in a play to what might happen in real life, audiences develop empathy for the characters that perform for their sake and in their stead and learn through the sufferings of those onstage that there are no easy answers, that life and living are difficult, but that the struggle defines humanity. Wisdom gained through suffering, even vicarious suffering, increases the human capability as well as the need for understanding and forgiveness of all.

PART 1

Ibsen
The Buried Secret and the Big Surprise

In his oft-cited speech in 1898 at the Festival of the Norwegian Women's Rights League in Christiania, Ibsen, the famous playwright of plays such as *A Doll's House* (1879), *Ghosts* (1881) and *Hedda Gabler* (1890), claimed that he had never consciously worked for the women's rights movement. He emphasized his point by adding that he did not even know exactly what the women's rights movement was. "I have been more poet and less social philosopher than people generally seem inclined to believe," Ibsen began, prefacing this assertion with another pronouncement that he had never written anything with "any conscious thought of making propaganda" (*Letters and Speeches* 65). While he allowed that it was indeed desirable "to solve the problem of women's rights," he argued that his primary task as a writer had been "the *description of humanity*" (italics his). Before an audience of women, Ibsen concluded his short speech by saying that it was up to them "to solve the social problem" (66). This would prove to be a great task for women and mothers, he said, but they were certainly up to the challenge and he thanked them for their efforts and wished the Women's Rights League great success.

Biographer Michael Meyer encouraged all critics to memorize this little speech by heart before interpreting *A Doll's House*, presumably to cut short any ideas that the play might concern issues of women's rights (774). For Meyer, and for many more mostly male critics, the poet and the social philosopher stood on opposite banks of the artistic divide. Reviewing a contemporary production of *A Doll's House* by the Royal Shakespeare Company, Richard Hornby defends Ibsen as not "some cranky pamphleteer but a profound poetic dramatist, the best since Shakespeare" (685). Similarly, Robert Brustein assesses that "Ibsen's revolt is poetic rather than reformist or propagandist" (40). For these critics, then, any aspect of a social issue that Ibsen may have addressed in his plays adversely taints their opinion of his art and his achievements as a playwright. Hornby links *A Doll's House* to Ibsen's early explicitly poetic, epic, mythic, and historical plays by saying that it retains the "symbolism, mysticism, and poetic atmosphere from his earlier period [*Brand, Peer Gynt, Emperor and Galilean*], which are not to be found in the oeuvre of the French social problem playwrights like Augier, Scribe, or Dumas *fils*" (685). Brustein, on the other hand, sees *A Doll's House* as a social play that is much less good than the early works but that eventually leads to the much better messianic plays of individual (and male) will and ego that mark the end of Ibsen's career, beginning with the *Master Builder* (1892), and followed by *Little Eyolf* (1894), *John Gabriel Borkman* (1896) and ending with *When We Dead Awaken* (1899).

There have been plenty of critics, to be sure, who have championed Ibsen more as a social philosopher than a poet. *The Quintessence of Ibsenism* positioned him as primarily concerned with issues such as marriage and equality among the sexes, but the book revealed as much if not more about George Bernard Shaw's thoughts on these subjects than it did Henrik Ibsen's. Emma Goldman, the American anarchist and feminist, published *The Social Significance of Modern Drama* in 1914 in which she argued, naively, perhaps, by today's standards, that Ibsen's greatness as a dramatist could be measured to the extent that he sympathized with women's issues and championed them in his dramas.[10] For her, *A Doll's House* is about the harmful effects of the marriage contract upon women and speculates about what changes might be necessary to create more loving and mutually beneficial relationships between men and women (8–12). Unlike an avowed modernist critic such as Brustein many years later, Goldman eschews the late Ibsen plays in order to study the social issues, including women's rights, moral hypocrisy, and inherited ideas in four early prose plays: *Pillars of Society, A Doll's House, Ghosts,* and *An Enemy of the People.*

With respect to the history of *A Doll's House* and its critical reception, Joan Templeton has questioned whether it is really possible to say that Ibsen is not concerned with women's rights in that play. Can form and content separate so easily? Probably not, but after picking apart various attacks that dismiss the serious issues of the play, or that condemn the play for espousing those same issues, Templeton concludes by showing rather convincingly that Ibsen did campaign for women's issues during his career and that "he was passionately interested in the events and ideas of his day. He was as deeply anchored in his time as any writer has been before or since" (38). Most recently, Toril Moi, in her brilliant book, *Henrik Ibsen and the Birth of Modernism* (2007), persuasively argues that Ibsen's interest in women's rights in his work establishes him as a modern writer. The saturation of the everyday in his works provides the grounds for his modernity, she writes, and the seriousness and purposefulness and complexity with which Ibsen immersed his plays in the world of everyday life marked a new stage, modernism, in the history of drama.[11]

To resolve the conflict between the "poet" and the "social philosopher," I propose a theatrical and directorial model based on dramatic action, the thing done in the play, in order to show how Ibsen embeds characters within an historical and cultural situation in which individual conscience and consciousness battle against the self and society in pursuit of a personal goal or mission. In this view, Ibsen neither describes humanity in terms of universal truths nor identifies the perceived holes in the fabric of society, but dramatizes the attempt to reconcile individual needs and desires with those of the surrounding community. Plays unfold as contests between the one and the many in which protagonists rebel against the crowd to live according to what they think is a more honest way, but that sometimes proves to be a matter of their own distorted perceptions. Either way, their actions isolate them from others and force them to reconsider their positions in the world. Ibsen, unlike Chekhov, whom I'll discuss in Part 2, presents protagonists that try to impose their will upon the world and bend the community to their liking, or according to how they see the world, or how they would like the world to be. This wreaks havoc on others and often leads to deadly endings for the hero. Almost always, too, the Ibsen seekers find that which they did not expect. Believing that the world is one way, they direct their actions accordingly, only to discover ultimately that things are radically different than they had supposed.

The dramaturgical device that Ibsen utilizes in each of his prose plays is none other than that of the "buried secret" that he dug up from the intrigue dramas of Eugène Scribe (1791–1861). The connection between Scribe and Ibsen is unequivocal according to Maurice Valency in *The Flower and the Castle*: "Ibsen's realistic plays are, in a sense, the end-product of the French school: he represents its perfection. All his realistic plays are well made; none is free of some degree of contrivance. He worked strictly within the traditional frame of 'le theatre,' and even his best and freest plays have that epigrammatic neatness which is the mark of good Scribean craftsmanship" (149). This is not to say that Ibsen merely copied or imitated the commercially successful dramatic formula of Scribe without adding a distinctive and unique twist of his own. He did, and that turn is the specific focus of my interpretation of Ibsen's prose work. As Raymond Williams points out, by the time Ibsen was writing his plays, the conventions of intrigue drama, while they still held sway in the commercial theater, had already worn out. The form remained the same, but the content no longer compelled an audience. Ibsen inherited the forms of Scribe, perhaps, but he found himself writing in a new age, the modern age, and the old forms needed to retrofit for the new content and serious concerns of everyday life. In *Drama from Ibsen to Brecht*, Williams writes: "New conceptions of destiny and responsibility, new feelings of relationship and personality, new attitudes to psychology and motivation, needed new conventions to emerge as drama, and were merely compromising and sentimentalizing when applied externally, to the conventions still running in the theatre" (28). Ibsen transformed the intrigue drama and *pièce bien faite* into something entirely new, entirely modern, by his new conception and configuration and manipulation of the old "buried secret" device.

Still, Michael Meyer insists that there is no evidence that Scribe "ever exerted the slightest influence upon Ibsen" (117). The nature of influence, of course, is quite difficult to estimate and determine. Meyer voices shock that a great dramatist such as Ibsen might follow as shallow a playwright as Scribe. I certainly do not mean to suggest that Ibsen admired Scribe, who produced more than 350 works for theater, including 35 full-length plays, but he knew his plays well, not just from having seen them, but having produced and directed them, and he knew very well how effective and popular they played in front of audiences. When Ibsen turned to prose in the 1870s and began to write about domestic and social issues concerning Norwegian daily life, it seems likely that the Scribean model and mode of playwriting would have been present in his mind as he wrote. Art critic E. H. Gombrich observed that landscape painters did not set up their easels in nature and paint what was before them. Instead, they painted what they knew in terms of painterly techniques. Similarly, when Ibsen began to write his plays, he could draw upon Scribe as his model.

Norway in the mid-to-late 19th century was a cultural and artistic wasteland. The best playwrights of the 19th century were not seen there: Büchner, obviously, since his work was undiscovered and unproduced until the early 20th century, but also fellow Germans Christian Dietrich-Grabbe, Heinrich von Kleist, and later Friedrich Hebbel; Alfred de Musset's French comedies of the 1830s didn't play in Norway until the 1860s; Gogol's *The Government Inspector* and Turgenev's *A Month in the Country* didn't reach Norway until 1890; nothing by Ostrovsky until the 20th century. Of all the plays that remain a part of the theatrical repertory today, the farces of Eugène Labiche, including *An Italian Straw Hat* (1851), which Ibsen directed a few years later, did make it to Norway! There was no classical theater to see: no Shakespeare, Greeks, or even Moliere, but only a few English Restoration comedies in bad translations (Meyer 103). Ibsen's own plays are almost enough to gauge the stifling provincialism and conservatism against which he rebelled. No wonder, then, that he escaped from his home country and lived and wrote abroad for most of his life in Italy and in Germany until 1891.

Ibsen learned his craft, according to Meyer, as a dramatist during a prolonged apprenticeship in the practical theater that lasted 11 years. In 1851 the Norwegian Theatre at Bergen engaged him to "assist the Theatre as dramatic author" (83). Ole Bull, the great musician and later infamous founder of the utopian Oleana colony in Pennsylvania, persuaded him to move from Christiania (Oslo), where he was a student, to Bergen, where, for the next six years, Ibsen performed every task except acting that can be done in the theater: writing plays and prologues to others' plays, but also directing, coaching actors in speech and movement, designing sets and costumes, as well as running the business side including the overseeing of accounts. Early in his tenure, Ibsen received a three-month travel grant to visit foreign theaters in Copenhagen, Berlin, Dresden and Hamburg (89), during which time he learned a great deal, saw Shakespeare for the first time, including productions of *Hamlet*, *King Lear*, *Romeo and Juliet*, and *As You Like It*, and quite possibly read Herman Hettner's *Das Moderne Drama* after his arrival in Dresden with its championing of Hebbel's *Maria Magdalena* as an example of a new kind of drama (95).

He encountered very little talent with which to work when he returned to Bergen. He directed an adaptation of *As You Like It* in 1855, re-titled *Life in the Forest*, but it was not successful (123). Actors had no training for such ventures and audiences preferred familiar comedies. The fact that Ibsen was charged to train actors even though he himself had no theatrical training indicates, perhaps, the level of playing. In any event, rehearsals usually numbered only between three and five for each production, so Ibsen could have inflicted little harm (106)! The playing conditions of the physical theater were equally poor and resembled the Continental and English theaters of the 18th rather than the 19th century. Painted, two-dimensional scenery consisted of wings and drops depicting stock images of town and country. Changes in scene occurred through a chariot and pole system mounted underneath the stage that transformed the scene, pushing one set of wings on, pulling another one off, via a manual cranking device also underneath the stage. A combination of chandeliers, footlights, and lamps placed vertically behind the drops produced general lighting as well as special effects (105). Bergen did not install gas lights, which first appeared in Philadelphia in 1816 at the Chestnut Theatre and which had been installed in the two principal London theatres, Drury Lane and Covent Garden, the following year, until 1856, the year before Ibsen left.

Both Raymond Williams in *Drama from Ibsen to Brecht* and Richard Gilman in *The Making of Modern Drama* stress the significance of Ibsen's work in the practical theater as a major influence on the prose plays he would begin to write over a decade later. And what did Ibsen produce in the theater at that time when he had neither the physical stage and artistic talent nor audience demand for either a classical repertoire or serious contemporary plays? He staged Scribe or plays of the Scribean variety. Of the 150 plays he directed at Bergen, half of them were French "intrigue dramas," 21 by Scribe himself, but the rest from the Scribean mold (Gilman 53, Williams 26–27). In 1857 the Norwegian Theatre of Christiania appointed Ibsen as stage instructor and artistic director and beckoned him home to a position that he held until June 1862. Despite the change in locale, the job proved to be about as desolate and despairing as the one in Bergen. He produced another nine plays by Scribe during his five-year tenure at Christiania (Meyer fn 152).

Who is this Scribe? No one reads his plays anymore and few people see them on stage. He is not alone by any means with his pronouncements that the theater is a place for relaxation and entertainment rather than engagement and edification. He is not forgotten, exactly, but certainly more read about than actually read. In the introduction to his still-in-print volume of well-made plays, Stephen Stanton remarks about Scribe: "It is curious that a playwright with so tremendous and varied a talent [considering the tremendous volume of output] should be remembered today rather for his impact on the modern theatre than for his own plays" (xii). In assessing his influence related to Ibsen, Stanton's structural outline of the well-made play clarifies Scribe's dramatic formula and shows how the Norwegian playwright poured his new wine into old bottles. A summary of one of Scribe's most popular plays highlights the differences and similarities between the two playwrights.

At Bergen in December 1856, shortly before Ibsen assumed a similar position in Christiania, he directed Scribe's *Le Verre d'eau* (*The Glass of Water*, 1840), "perhaps the only comedy by him that stands revival today" (Meyer 133). Indeed, Stanton includes it in his anthology as a representative work by the author in a 1936 English version by DeWitt Bodeen along with *A Peculiar Position* in addition to plays by Dumas, *fils*, Augier, and Sardou. Still, if *The Glass of Water* is Scribe's best, the play provides ample evidence to show why a once prominent playwright has not survived the age in which he once prospered. It is a very silly play, an historical drama set in early 18th-century England during the reign of Queen Anne, with no basis in actual fact or history. Bolingbroke, the male protagonist, announces the theme: "[Y]ou must not despise little things; it is they which are responsible for great effects" (46). Metadramatically, given this theme, the play holds some interest for the modern critic who might wish to see the drama commenting upon its own gratuitousness as the real stuff of drama.[12] Within the play, the private and competing passions of the Duchess of Marlborough and Queen Anne threaten to undermine the peace accord between France and England. All hell breaks loose when the queen spills her glass of water, an action that reveals the secret that she has long loved young and handsome Masham, the very same man after whom the duchess lusts as well. Masham, naturally, loves someone else entirely, and the romantic stalemate between political rivals creates the opportunity for world peace.

Stanton outlines seven aspects of the well-made play, the first of which, involving a secret, is the most important, the plot driver of the entire play mechanism, and the element that is most salient in relation to Ibsen's plays. The rest of the list adheres to an Aristotelian bias that favors plot as the most important element of drama: (2) a pattern of increasing suspense set in motion after lengthy exposition and facilitated by properties (e.g., letters, revolvers, handkerchiefs); (3) a series of ups and downs in the hero's fortune, made possible by (4) a pattern of peripeteia (reversal) and anagnorisis (recognition) that culminates in the *scène à faire* (obligatory scene); (5) a central misunderstanding between characters that is obvious to the audience; (6) a logical and credible denouement; and (7) the reproduction of the overall pattern within each individual scene and act (xii-xiii).

Ibsen's handling of exposition in his opening acts is comically direct, usually involving the entrance of a familiar character to a household, but one who has not appeared for some time prior and therefore has occasion to inquire about new events. In *Ghosts*, for example, Pastor Manders asks Regina after a brief introduction in the act, "[H]ow's it been going for your father out here?" (*Complete Prose Plays* 210). Headmaster Kroll asks the same question of Rebecca West at the beginning of *Rosmersholm*: "So, how are things going out here?" (500). Gossip between women fills the backstory of *Pillars of Society*: "You don't know about his wicked past?" Mrs. Rummel asks Mrs. Lynge almost rhetorically before supplying her and the audience with the necessary information (24). Two old friends, Mrs. Linde and Nora Helmer, reunite in the opening act of *A Doll's House* after "nine—ten long years" and proceed to tell each other (and the audience) what has happened to them in the intervening time (130). Similarly, Mrs. Elvsted reintroduces herself to Hedda Gabler after many years absence and proceeds to tell her (and the audience) everything that has happened to her and Eilert Løvborg (708–715). In *The Wild Duck*, Gregers Werle greets his childhood friend, Hjalmar Ekdal, in the opening scene: "Yes, we two old classmates, we've certainly drifted a long way apart. You know, we haven't seen each other now in sixteen—seventeen years." This gives him reason to ask next, "How's it going for your father now?" (396). Twin sisters reunite in *John Gabriel Borkman* to review the past: "Well—Gunhild," Ella Rentheim begins, "it's nearly eight years now since we saw each other last" (945). Mayor Stockmann provides the exposition himself in *An Enemy of the People* by discussing his brother's business: "I hear my brother's become a vary active contributor to the *People's Courier*" (285). Solness, the eponymous protagonist in *The Master Builder*, initiates the exposition of that play by speaking in confidence to a family friend: "Dr. Herdal—let me tell you a strange story. That is, if you don't mind listening" (796).

It is easy enough to make fun of Ibsen's expository phrases above, but he gets done with them quickly by virtue of his loaded props. Richard Gilman notes in *The Making of Modern Drama* that Ibsen's use of props resembles the mechanics of well-made plays: letters in *A Doll's House*; the father's pipe in *Ghosts*; Løvborg's manuscript in *Hedda Gabler*. Such devices, he claims, hem in Ibsen's imagination (71). Andrew Sofer takes a much different and more nuanced view of these things in his wonderful *The Stage Life of Props* by giving them a purpose beyond mere appearance and apparent functionality. Such properties propel the plot, certainly, but they also "embody the past" and give it a dramatic shape that helps to avoid lengthy expositions. Sofer explains: "While Ibsen's dramatically charged objects—such as the incriminating letter in *A Doll's House* (1879)—outwardly resemble the plot devices that crowd the well-made plays of Scribe and Sardou, Ibsen's props embody the decisive influence of the past on the present: they externalize his characters' internal (and hence ethical) characteristics, which emerge as damning evidence in the forensic anatomizing of the psyche that is Ibsen's project" (173). Aunt Julie's hat in *Hedda Gabler* is a perfect example of a fully exploited prop. Tesman comments on his aunt's new hat at the start of the scene and the hat rests in view of the audience for an extended time until Hedda makes her entrance, notices the hat and, knowing full well whose hat it is, pointedly comments on its ugliness as a way of telling Aunt Julie to back off and make it clear that she is not welcome in the house. The double life that Sofer brings to props agrees with Robert Brustein's much earlier assessment that Ibsen's plays have a double level: the "drama of ideas coexists with a drama of action" (48). The plot, the mechanics of the play, allows the drama of ideas, the psyche in Sofer, the drama of consciousness and conscience in this study, to flourish.

The contrast between an Ibsen scene and one by Chekhov could not be more dramatic. Props, in Chekhov, often appear out of nowhere, such as the pistol in *Uncle Vanya*. The pistol-packing Vanya pursues the professor throughout the house in an out-of-the-blue comic, almost farcical moment (complete with rapidly timed entrances and exits). The gun is not "loaded" with the past and future in the way that General Gabler's pistols are in Ibsen's play. The gun only exists to express Vanya's pent-up frustration and it disappears after Vanya shoots as if it were a violent exhalation that, once released, disappears forever. The map of Africa that hangs in Vanya's study in Act 4, too, is a perfect contrast to Aunt Julie's hat. The map calls attention to itself by its presence and incongruence to the situation. Astrov looks at it and even comments that it must be hot in Africa at this moment. But that is as far as the map stretches. It is no symbol. It is no device that a character can use to voice aggression or want or desire. While Ibsen uses everything up in his scenes, Chekhov employs a strategy of incongruity and superfluity. Such differences between the playwrights suggest the drive in Ibsen to reveal all things and the opposite intent in Chekhov to deflect an emphatic interpretation and create ambiguity.

According to Stanton, the well-made play, including of course all the plays of Scribe and his ilk, exhibits a "plot based on a secret known to the audience but withheld from certain characters (who have long been engaged in a battle of wits) until its revelation (or the direct consequence thereof) in the climactic scene serves to unmask a fraudulent character and restore to good fortune the suffering hero, with whom the audience has been made to sympathize" (xii). Ibsen, too, takes his audience on a dramatic ride with changes in fortune of the protagonist, ups and downs marked by recognitions and reversals that build to a final climax that satisfies because of its logical outcome based upon everything that has previously occurred. The mechanics of the play that seem so obvious are an intentional part of the enjoyment. Stanton observes that the overall plot of the well-made play repeats in every scene, as if the construction metaphor for such plays might be a series of Chinese boxes. Ibsen's plays pick up at a point in which the central characters resume a battle that started prior to the start of the play. I am thinking here about Krogstad and Helmer in *A Doll's House*, Rebecca West and Kroll in *Rosmersholm*, Thea Elvsted and Hedda Gabler, and Old Werle and his son Gregers in the opening scene of *The Wild Duck*. Unlike Scribe, Ibsen regularly misleads the audience regarding the true and fraudulent characters. The hero at the start of a play such as *The Wild Duck* turns out close to a villain at the end. Similarly, the handsome couple of Nora and Torvald ultimately breaks up, while the struggling Krogstad and Mrs. Linde may set the foundation for a solid, lasting and loving relationship in a "true marriage." Ibsen regularly inverts relationships, roles and expectations in his plays.

The movement in the well-made play brings that which is hidden to light, answers all the questions raised by the action, and disposes properly of all things: the good, though they have suffered, will be rewarded; the bad, though they have prospered, will ultimately be punished. Richard Gilman defines these plays in terms of visual clarity and ocular perception:

> The well-made play was one of almost entire visibility, which is to say it possessed almost no dimension beyond what was literally placed before the audience's eyes and ears; figures of inflated physical and deprived moral or spiritual status, at their extreme points the stock personages of melodrama and farce, its characters moved through dramas whose values were wholly corporeal, or else abstractions for corporeality—myths of love, power, social prowess, etc.—which its audiences uncritically accepted as the reflected truths of their own lives [*Making of Modern Drama* 69].

Ibsen's dramaturgical method in his prose plays manipulates the "buried secret" device, borrowed from the well-made play formula of the 19th century, to reveal the essential action: something in the past comes to light, but it is not what the Ibsen protagonist expected and the surprise jolts the character or the audience/reader or both to make new realizations about the nature of the world or experience. Ibsen, of course, was not the only 19th-century playwright to manipulate the buried secret device. Oscar Wilde's "trivial comedy for serious people," *The Importance of Being Earnest* (1895), pokes fun at conventional dramatic play structure and highlights the artificiality of the leisure class as it joyfully celebrates art and the invention of lying as the prime creative human force that makes life interesting and worth living. Wilde satirizes the well-made play by making a joke of the buried secret, the paternity of Mr. Earnest Worthing, who, in the hilariously climactic scene discovers that he is the very person he had always pretended to be. Just as spectacularly, a poet, to Ibsen, is one "who sees" (Gilman 64), but Ibsen, in play after play, presents characters that are blind to anything or anyone beyond their personal desires. Ibsen's development of the "buried secret" device over the course of his prose playwriting career reveals his maturation of skill but also highlights the change in focus from play to play, from the most transparent use in his first plays, to an untethered and then almost inconsequential use of the device at the end, a dramatic shift that signals his preoccupation with the limits of the ego to apprehend reality.

Pillars of Society (1877), the first installment of Ibsen's relentless prose cycle of a dozen plays in which he published a new drama almost every other year for 22 years, offers the most conventional use of the "buried secret" device among any of the plays, yet it still displays a distinctive Ibsenian twist at the end. The protagonist, Bernick, has built his career success upon a lie by allowing his best friend to take the blame for an affair that Bernick had with a married woman. Unbeknownst to his friend, though, Bernick also created the impression that his friend left town after having robbed him. Bernick turned his back on the woman he loved as well, marrying instead another woman who offered him the money he needed to save his business. Over the years, Bernick became a big success, a "pillar of society," as a shipbuilder and leading businessman and his secret past remained hidden, even as his hypocrisy continued to grow. As the play begins, he has recently purchased land around a proposed railway line that will increase his personal wealth considerably if the deal can be executed. He claims that he acts for the benefit of the town, but no one will benefit more than him if the deal passes muster. His former friend, Johan, who has returned after many years' absence, threatens to expose Bernick's past, and Bernick, in retaliation, does not warn him from booking passage to America on a ship that he knows is unsafe and will sink before it can complete its transatlantic voyage and thus bury his secret at the bottom of the sea. Quite independently, Johan decides on his own that the ship is unsafe and he books passage on an alternative voyage. But also unknown to Bernick, his little son Olaf sneaks aboard the defective vessel in hopes of traveling to America. Fortunately, Bernick's wife discovers the boy's whereabouts and the ship returns to port. Bernick is saved, not by his own volition or turn of conscience, but by the rational thinking of others. Luck, too, turned out to be on his side. The family is reunited at the end and Bernick makes a public confession of his initial crime (but not the business about the railroad or the ships) and his wife feels that they can start over in a true marriage. Uplifted, Bernick claims that the women, his wife and also Lona, his former lover, are the true pillars of society, but Lona's concluding lines correct him by stating that "the spirit of truth and the spirit of freedom—*those* are the pillars of society" (*Complete Prose Plays* 118). Bernick is left to grapple with his own conscience regarding the deadly fate that his best friend, his only son, and many others aboard that vessel narrowly escaped.

Ibsen nuances the "buried secret" in *A Doll's House* (1879). Ostensibly, Nora's forgery is the big secret in that play, accompanied by the justification that she did it in order to save her husband's life. However, the deeper secret, one that Nora already suspects at the play's outset but cannot act upon, is her rising fear that her husband does not love her as an equal partner and that she must find the courage to live independently in order to discover the nature of her true identity and that of the world. That twin process forms the subject of the initial play discussion in this study.

In *Ghosts* (1881), the revelation that Captain Alving was not the virtuous man whom most people perceived appears to disclose the secret. But in the second act his widow admits to herself for the first time that she may have been responsible for his debauched behavior by preventing him from experiencing the "joy of life." Helene Alving devoted her life to polishing her late husband's reputation and the opening of an orphanage in his name is the final monument built in his honor. In conversation with Pastor Manders, however, the man to whom she fled from her husband after only a year of marriage, she reveals that Captain Alving did not reform and remained dissolute and degenerate until his death. The news shocks Manders. Helene wanted to run away with him but he convinced her that it was her duty to stay with her husband. Afraid of what people would think, Manders refused to flout the conventions of a tightly knit and ultra-conservative society. In response, Helene bowed to his wishes and pledged to uphold a lie about her husband: that he changed his sinful ways and became a good husband and father. To further protect the reputation of her husband and to protect her child, she sent her only son Osvald away at an early age so that he would never be aware of his father's true nature. Unfortunately, Osvald's return years later, as a young man in his twenties, spurs Helene to rethink all of her previous actions and her motives behind them. Osvald, a painter, complains that the environment in Norway is not conducive to creative work because of the rain and darkness and mood of the environment. In Rome and Paris, his fellow friends and artists possessed and created the joy of life in their work. Here, in Norway, Osvald finds nothing. Helene realizes now that her husband, too, Captain Alving, had the "joy of life" and that he could find no outlet for his passions in such a dull environment. He destroyed himself out of despair, and Helene recognizes in hindsight that she did nothing, even hindered, his desire for such joy. And Helene also realizes that it was a mistake for her to accede to Manders' advice about remaining with her husband. She and Manders turned their backs upon love. Instead, Helene admits that she allowed herself to marry a man for his position and money and remained with him in order to avoid scandal. Conformity to such dead ideals prevents Osvald from relying upon his mother to help him when his own debilitating disease strikes. His homecoming ends with his mother's fateful and fatal decision very much in doubt.

Like many Ibsen protagonists beginning with Brand in *Brand*, Dr. Thomas Stockmann in *An Enemy of the People* (1882) is "All or Nothing" to the end and his final declaration seems to sum up or even define the meanings of the play: "the strongest man in the world is the one who stands most alone" (386). Unlike Brand, though, and unlike any other Ibsen hero, Stockmann is uncomplicated and almost comic in his egocentric nearsightedness. The small town in which he lives stands on the brink of a financial boon as a resort town that boasts of a health spa. Dr. Stockmann, the director in charge of the municipal baths, has conducted experiments, however, that show conclusively that the tanneries upstream have polluted the water supply. Naively, Dr. Stockmann believes that the town will thank him for saving future lives. Instead, he discovers that they brand him an "enemy of the people" for exposing a situation that will ruin the town economically for years to come. Dr. Stockmann realizes that the real secret is not the polluted water but the moral pollution and corruption that would deny the truth of his research for the sake of monetary profit. Dr. Stockmann's ego, however, is partly to blame for the problem. His idealism, a function of his enormous pride and ego, prevents him from considering the impact of his discoveries and what it will mean for the community. His failure to present the case in such a way that would compel the community to take preventive action brings about his own status as an outcast and town pariah. Certainly, he is right, but he fails to consider the vested interests of others before issuing his own edicts and proclamations about the situation. As much as the action of the play demonstrates the hypocrisy and selfishness of the town's leaders, the majority that is always wrong, Dr. Stockmann is hardly in the right as the lone, minority figure. Narcissistic ego and self-righteousness negate his cause.

Gregers Werle, the protagonist in the following play, *The Wild Duck* (1884), is another unpleasant idealist, but his self-serving actions lead to tragic results. He attempts to reclaim the former greatness of his best friend, Hjalmar Ekdal, by exposing the lie at the heart of his friend's relationship with his wife and child in order to establish a "true marriage." Unfortunately, he completely misreads and misinterprets the domestic situation of his friend, who is not the great man whom Gregers assumed him to be. He tries to assuage the problems of others in order to avoid what he has done and not done with his life. His idealistic zealotry, which is really just a lofty cover for him to salve his guilty conscience regarding his mother and father, leads to heartbreak and senseless death.

Beginning with *Rosmersholm* (1886), the rest of Ibsen's plays deal explicitly with sensuality and sexuality and death at the end often substitutes for the sexual act. Rebecca West and John Rosmer live at Rosmersholm as two true companions after the suicide of Rosmer's wife. Together, they plan to change the world by advocating freethinking and liberal learning and abandoning the traditional thoughts and teachings of the Christian Church. Rebecca confesses in Act 3, however, that her motives were not pure in coming to Rosmersholm—that she had designs on marrying Rosmer. She became a confidant of the late wife, Beata, whom the husband deemed crazy for her wild passion and sensuality that was a direct response to Rosmer's sexual restraint. Rebecca did nothing to relieve her of her intense feelings of inadequacy. In fact, she intimated to Beata that she was pregnant with Rosmer's child. Beata made way for her husband and Rebecca to marry by committing suicide. But over time, too, Rebecca transformed and renounced her sexual desires, but also realized that she could not be happy with Rosmer. Ennobled, perhaps, but never happy. And she finally realizes that Rosmer would never be able to do the kind of good work they dreamed about unless he could have the innocence of a child. He insists that he'll never have that now. To prove her love and devotion to him, Rebecca volunteers to give up her life, just as Beata gave up her life for Rosmer. Fascinated and attracted to the idea, sick as it may be, Rosmer questions whether Rebecca has the courage to do that for him, then declares that he will go with her and they consecrate their marriage in a mutual suicide pact by hurling themselves into the millrace at the very same spot from which Beata leapt.

The Lady from the Sea (1888) follows *A Doll's House*, *Ghosts*, and *The Wild Duck* and *Rosmersholm* in its critique of modern marriage and a portrait of what a "true marriage" might look like.[13] Ellida Wangel, Dr. Wangel's second wife, has not slept with her husband since their son died three years prior. The son reminds the wife of the former lover. That she promised herself to another before Wangel appears to be the buried secret in the past that comes to light. Wangel, who senses that something is wrong with his wife, suspects that she may have had a prior relationship with his old friend Arnholm. But this is not the case. In Act 4 of this five-act drama, Ellida confesses that her real crime against herself, and the buried secret that threatens to destroy her and her husband's life, is the fact that she "sold" herself in marriage to Wangel in order to make an easier life for herself. "I never should have sold myself! The meanest work—the poorest conditions would have been better—if I'd chosen them myself, by my own free will!" (*Complete Prose Plays* 663). Her description of marriage is not unlike Mrs. Alving's description of the terms of her marriage to Captain Alving in *Ghosts*. Of course, Wangel is a sweet and docile physician, a loving family man, and not the debauched Alving. Still, Ellida did not marry Wangel for the right reason; she did not marry him freely. Now, a few years later, her former lover, the Stranger, reappears and beckons her to run away with him in a true marriage of equals that has nothing to do with the legal and societal mores regarding matrimony. Wangel, at first, forbids her from leaving and threatens to prosecute the Stranger. Then, however, he recognizes that he can only reclaim his wife if he lets her go and allows her to depart freely of her own will if she elects to do so. Given this sudden freedom and the power to choose between her husband and the romantic Stranger, Ellida reverses course and elects to stay with her husband and in fact they vow new devotions and save their rebuilt marriage at play's end.

The next two plays, *Hedda Gabler* (1890) and *The Master Builder* (1892), receive extended attention in individual sections that follow this introduction. The former play marks the last of Ibsen's critiques of contemporary society, what Robert Brustein labeled as the "modern phase" of Ibsen's oeuvre.[14] Hedda Gabler does not even contemplate running away with a romantic stranger from her past in the vein of Ellida in *The Lady from the Sea*. Terrified of even a hint of scandal, Hedda refuses to admit her love for the brilliant Eilert Løvborg. When that secret comes out and given the chance to run away with him again, she refuses him a second time and instead tries to empower him to greatness in the exalted image of a Greek god. Unable to have him herself, she convinces him to take his own life in a beautifully romantic gesture that fails pathetically, and she ends up shooting herself in a shocking manner that is neither romantic nor beautiful.

Ibsen's final four plays, beginning with *The Master Builder*, exhibit, according to Brustein, a combination of Romantic freedom and Classical restraint that elevate them beyond all of his previous work (50). They are his favorites in part because they are the most modern in the sense that the social critique of contemporary society fades in favor of an exploration of the individual psyche particularly as it pertains to a mature male artistic protagonist who has reached a point of impasse in his career and searches for a way to give his final days meaning.[15] The metatheatricality of these plays, featuring self-consciousness about art and artists, is likely one of the distinctively attractive features of these plays that critics such as Brustein admire. It is impossible not to consider that Ibsen surveyed and assessed his career as a playwright as he dramatized the final days of an architect/builder, author, Napoleonic capitalist, and sculptor. The titular hero in *The Master Builder* contents himself with building ordinary houses in guilty recompense for his belief that he willed his house to burn down in order to collect the insurance money that established his career. He knows rationally that the home did not burn down from the crack in the chimney that he had seen but purposely not repaired, but he believes that he nonetheless "willed" the destruction of the property that destroyed his wife's happiness and ultimately killed his two little boys as well. The buried secret, at this late juncture in Ibsen's career, reduces to nothing more than the protagonist's desires. The arrival of young Hilda Wangel, however, prompts him to let go of his guilty conscience and unleash the troll within him to transcend traditional morality about good and evil, right and wrong, and to dream of castles in the air with her inspiration and goading. Such idealistic flights of imagination lead him to climb the tower of his last house to place the wreath at the top, from which he ultimately plummets and dies, the horrific image of which complicates any desire to romanticize the role of the artist.

Rita Allmers tries to hang on to her husband in *Little Eyolf* (1894) and interrupt the bond between him and his half-sister, Asta, a younger woman, who, it turns out, is not really his half sister at all. This revelation, however, does not constitute the buried secret in the play. Eyolf, the Allmers' son, was crippled from a fall when he was just a baby. The shared secret between husband and wife is the fact that the child fell when he wasn't being watched, when in fact Allmers and Rita were making love instead. As part of his guilt, Allmers turns away from his wife sexually and tries to atone by devoting himself first to his work, he is writing a book called *Human Responsibility*, and then to the exclusive devotion to his son's development and happiness. He must abort the plan at the end of the first act, however, when Eyolf slips out of the house and drowns in the sea. The grief and guilt of both husband and wife continue to threaten the marriage. The play turns when they realize that they cannot continue to focus exclusively upon each other but must direct their attention to others. In this way they are able to expiate their guilt, change, and redirect their lives in a positive direction that breaks the bonds of obsessive and compulsive behavior. Specifically, Rita realizes that she has never paid any attention to the lot of poor boys who live in hovels below them near the water and she decides that she will devote herself to helping them. Allmers, too, realizes that in helping others he might best serve the memory of his dead son and save his marriage as well. Surprisingly, then, the couple learns a way out of their morass and the final image has them standing together looking forward to the future.

The buried secrets in *John Gabriel Borkman* (1896) are literally natural resources in the ground that the hero can never tap. Ella, the woman Borkman forsook in order to pursue his millions, prophesies just before his death in Act 4: "John Gabriel Borkman—you'll never win the prize you murdered for. You'll never ride in triumph into your cold, dark kingdom!" (*Complete Prose Plays* 1022). The murder she refers to is her capacity for love, which he killed when he gave her up to another man in exchange for power and glory. Borkman, a Napoleonic figure of finance, rose to bank president on the cusp of reaching all of his goals when a "friend" turned him in to the authorities for fraud. He had used people's investments as collateral to make his financial conquests and his arrest came before he could make proper restitution of all the funds he had diverted for other purposes. His grand scheme failed, he was imprisoned for five years and he spent the last 8 years in solitude waiting for his chance to return to action. He felt, unequivocally, that the citizens would visit him and beg him to take his old position again. But he waits in vain. He lives on the upper floor of the house that Ella bought for him while his wife, Ella's twin sister, lives apart on the first floor. Mrs. Borkman does not speak with her husband and blames him for ruining her life and holds on to the notion that their son, Erhart, will do great things and restore the family name and erase John Gabriel's name from the public record. Ella, too, has returned with hopes that Erhart will comfort her in her last days of terminal illness. For his part, Erhart declares that he will side with neither sister and will not try and restore the name of the father. He has taken up with an older woman seven years his senior, and much to his mother's horror, he elects to travel with her abroad in pursuit of happiness. Borkman never regrets the choices he made in pursuit of wealth and power; fortunately, his son takes a different path and for once the past does not repeat in the present.

The simplest of all his plays in terms of fable and action is Ibsen's last, *When We Dead Awaken* (1899). Rubek, a sculptor, encounters the beautiful model Irene, the inspiration and subject for his masterpiece, *Resurrection Day*, at a mountain retreat after a prolonged absence. She claims that she is dead now because he destroyed her soul in the name of art and refused to admit that he loved her. For his part, Rubek claims that he had to remain detached and professional as an artist in order to create his best work. Still, their mutual passion rekindles (re-awakens) and they elect to climb the mountain together despite the warnings of an impending winter storm. In the end, Rubek calls her his "sanctified bride" and they climb together through the mist toward the light at the top of the mountain above the storm (1091). The buried secret is the revelation that Rubek's artistic masterpiece came at the price of Irene's soul and Rubek's personal happiness as well. In the end, triumphantly, they reclaim their lost lives in a spiritual marriage in which they literally try to transcend the earthly limitations of gravity and common sense with a highly sexualized resolution: "Then let our two dead souls live life to the full for once—before we go down in our graves again!" Rubek exclaims. "Up to the peak of promise!" Irene answers, "in an ecstasy of passion" (1091). The avalanche that buries them in the play's final image recalls not only the end of *The Master Builder*, but more emphatically the messianic *Brand*, and, as such, caps Ibsen's entire career.

Given the nature of Ibsen's last plays, in which realism gives way to symbolism, in which a critique of modern society and social problems fades in favor of a more introspective study of the individual artist, with perhaps a self-reflexive or metadramatic assessment of Ibsen's own career dramatized in the portrait of the artist figure, in which the familiar drive of the Ibsen plot borrowed from the structure of the well-made play gives way to a static drama of ideas, epitomized by John Gabriel Borkman's eight-year self-interment in the upstairs apartment of his home, in which the "buried secrets" that created mystery and suspense in early works become sites of a spiritual abyss in the late plays, is it any wonder that Ibsen, about to finish his last play, *When We Dead Awaken*, stood before the League of Women's Rights at Christiania in 1898 and claimed that he was an artist rather than a social philosopher? In the practical speaking situation of that event he may have had his latest work in mind as he encouraged his audience to respond to his "description of humanity" rather than any ideas he might have regarding "women's rights." Ibsen suffered a stroke shortly after completing that play and never published another before his death five years later in 1905. There's really no way to authenticate anything Ibsen said at the banquet as his dire conviction. He could have been deliberately provocative, given the speaking occasion, in order to attract attention and publicity to his new work. As an artist, though, in addition to promoting his new play, one that probably consumed him emotionally and psychically, he might have wanted to discourage an interpretation of his work based on subject matter. Or he might have wished to separate the subject matter of the plays and the characters' actions within them from ideas he might have actually held as a private citizen in society. Even if the two were one, and there is plenty of evidence to suggest that Ibsen the man was vitally interested in the subject of women's rights, he still might have wished to encourage audiences to interpret the plays for themselves.

In a less-quoted passage from his little speech to the women's group, Ibsen does offer a model of interpretation that plays well with the kind of study this critical volume tries to represent. After Ibsen defines his oft-repeated phrase about his intentions as an artist, "My task has been the *description of humanity*," he goes on to define the task of the reader/audience:

> To be sure, whenever such a description is felt to be reasonably true, the reader will insert his own feelings and sentiments into the work of the poet. These are attributed to the poet; but incorrectly so. Every reader remolds it so beautifully and nicely, each according to his own personality. Not only those who write, but also those who read are poets; they are collaborators; they are often more poetical than the poet himself [*Letters and Speeches* 65].

Perhaps Ibsen merely patronizes the gathering of females. Perhaps he says, too, that what they see in his works is not really there, but only figments of their wild imaginations. On the other hand, what he says above matches the gist of reader response theory of interpretation in the 20th and now 21st centuries. Indeed, the directorial model of interpretation endorsed by this volume remains, at best, a model for reading and reconstructing the play as it unfolds, theoretically, in time and space. Any production of an Ibsen play or any other for that matter interprets the text in a way that may or may not correspond to what the playwright had in mind when he or she first penned the play. It is successful to the extent that it appeals to and challenges the imaginations and expectations of the audience at the time of performance. In that regard, Ibsen needs an audience as much as any of us do and remains always our contemporary.

A Doll's House (1879)

> "Ah, I was tired so often, dead tired. But still it was wonderful fun, sitting and working like that, earning money. It was almost like being a man."

Nora Helmer harbors a secret regarding what she did to save her husband's life when he was gravely ill: she forged a note in order to secure a loan that would pay for him to convalesce in a warm climate and regain his health after an extended rest. She tells herself that one day she will tell him what she did and that he will be proud and grateful and recognize her as his equal partner in a true marriage. That would be a miracle, Nora recognizes, and the fact that she has never said anything reveals that she has genuine doubts about his ability and willingness to accept and appreciate her sacrifice. The revelation of her buried secret at the climax of the play in Act 3 destroys all of her illusions about Torvald Helmer and her ideal marriage. Nora finally realizes what she has always known but refused to admit: her husband does not love her and has stunted her development as a human being. In leaving her home at the end, what has been little more than a doll house, she willingly and bravely steps out into the world and graduates from childhood to adulthood.

Ibsen sets the scene at Christmas when the Helmers stand on the brink of success. Nora has almost paid off her loan through years of tireless effort. Torvald, too, has just been promoted to bank president and all the perks of bourgeois success appear imminent for the happy family. As Linda Loman laments her husband's suicide in *Death of a Salesman* by noting the irony of the situation in which the last mortgage installment has just been paid and that the Lomans are finally "free and clear" after 30 years, the Helmers find themselves in a similar situation.[16] Arthur Miller modeled much of his dramaturgy after Ibsen and juxtaposes the height of success and happiness with the lowest depths of despair and failure. Nora is positively giddy in the first few scenes about the prospects of getting out of debt and all the economic and social benefits that her husband's professional rise will offer. At her most exuberant moment, Nora confides to her confidante Mrs. Linde: "To know you're carefree, utterly carefree; to be able to romp and play with the children, and to keep up a beautiful, charming home—everything just the way Torvald likes it!" (*Four Major Plays* 56).[17] At this precise moment an intruder calls to introduce the blackmail plot that will drive the rest of the action.

Nora fears that Nils Krogstad, the man from whom she procured the loan, has come to reveal her secret. He assures her, however, that he merely wants to keep his job at the bank now that his old classmate Torvald Helmer is scheduled to be his new boss. He urges Nora to exert her influence on his behalf and assures her that it is not just about the money, but that the job represents a first step back toward respectability. He committed a crime years ago and now works to restore his reputation, a task even more important now that his sons are old enough to hear rumors of scandal in town. Krogstad tells her that he won't tolerate Helmer kicking him down again after he has labored so hard to climb up. Nora's naiveté astounds him when she confides that her primary fear is that her husband will discover from where the money came. The issue to Krogstad is not whether Torvald knows about what Nora did, but the fact that what she did was a crime (not unlike the crimes that Krogstad once committed). She borrowed the money from Krogstad to save her husband's life, but she forged her father's signature as the guarantor of the loan on the promissory note. Nora would have done anything to save her husband's life. She is ignorant of the law but aware of the moral imperative to "take in the sick." Krogstad warns her: "Laws don't inquire into motives," to which Nora replies, "Then they must be very poor laws" (67). Moral law versus civil law introduces the "Antigone" plot that, similar to the Greek tragedy, pits a lone woman of conscience against men in power who stand behind the laws that they created to rule society. Krogstad leaves with a final threat: "if I get shoved down a second time, you're going to keep me company." Nora asserts, with less confidence than she earlier boasted: "I did it out of love" (67).

Nora fails spectacularly with her bid to sway her husband's resolve to sack Krogstad at the bank. He does not believe that his former classmate is capable of rehabilitation. The worst part of Krogstad's offenses, according to Torvald, beyond the crime of forgery, was that he never came clean and admitted his mistakes. Torvald's diatribe against Krogstad strikes Nora as if he were speaking about her: "Every breath the children take in is filled with the germs of something degenerate" (70). Lies year after year poison the family home and Torvald claims that the mother is usually to blame: "Almost everyone who goes bad early in life has a mother who's a chronic liar" (70). Krogstad previously asserted that he and Nora looked alike in the eyes of the law. She now wonders if she has corrupted her home by keeping secrets and telling little lies to her husband during the past few years. Torvald tells her that it would be impossible for him to work with Krogstad now: "I literally feel physically revolted when I'm anywhere near such a person," (70) he says. If he knew her secret, Nora wonders, would he feel the same way about her? Alone on stage at the end of Act 1, Nora wrestles with the questions of her motives and actions and what they mean. She professes that she would never hurt her children, but her decision to keep them away from her despite their pleas, casts doubt upon her convictions of innocence. She comforts herself with the thought that, if necessary, Anne-Marie, her nurse, who functioned as a mother to Nora and who left her own child to care for her, would be a good mother for her three children if she were to leave for any reason.

In Act 2, after Christmas, Nora regularly checks the mailbox to see if any letter from Krogstad to her husband has arrived. She has been unable to convince Torvald to change his mind about Krogstad, but Krogstad has not made any move yet. Torvald refuses to reinstate Krogstad because he thinks that giving in to his wife's request and reversing his prior decision will make him look weak to his superiors. In further dialogue with Nora, however, he reveals that his chief reason for letting Krogstad go has nothing to do with perceived moral failings. Torvald readily admits, too, that Krogstad is quite good at his job. But the two of them knew each other as boys growing up and Torvald resents the familiarity between them. That Krogstad calls him by his first name is intolerable to the new chief of the bank. He wants to get rid of him and start with a fresh slate. When Nora accuses him of pettiness, he calls for a maid to deliver Krogstad's termination notice immediately. Moved by his wife's emotional distress on his behalf and her fears of how Krogstad might retaliate, Torvald assures her of his desire and ability to defend her from any subsequent attack: "Whatever comes, you'll see: when it really counts, I have strength and courage enough as a man to take on the whole weight myself" (79). Terrified, Nora implores that he mustn't do that—she thinks of the crime that she committed and the punishment that might ensue from it. She completely believes that Torvald will try to save her, but she refuses to tell him what she did and contemplates suicide as an escape (80).

Upon his next visit, Krogstad applies leverage to restore his position at the bank. He expresses contempt for Torvald that he could care so little about the scandal to which he might expose his wife. The fact that she has not apprised her husband of the situation signals to Krogstad that Nora has little faith that Torvald will protect her. He holds a letter that he has written to Torvald that explains everything. He is no ordinary blackmailer—he does not want money from Nora's husband—he just wants to get on in the world. It is no longer enough for him to keep his old job; now he wants a new position, a better one, from which he can continue his ascent to prominence. "Inside a year," Krogstad claims, "I'll be the manager's right-hand man" (88). He anticipates Nora's desperately romantic suicide plan and informs her that it will not work because he'll be in control of her reputation and the scandal would only hurt Torvald and the children. "One doesn't do these things, Mrs. Helmer," he says (88), voicing the similar boast of Judge Brack in *Hedda Gabler*. He leaves, but after Nora endures a few tense moments of waiting, the fateful letter drops into the mailbox to which only her husband has the key.

The letter, with its weighty portent, a staple of drama since the Elizabethans at least, heightens the drama as it builds to its climax. Convinced now that Torvald will find out everything, Nora confides in her friend Mrs. Linde: "It's the miracle now that's going to take place" (89). Torvald only recently swore to protect Nora from the threat of any danger, and Nora feels that his stepping up to shield her from scandal would constitute the miracle for which she has always longed in her marriage. Such a romantic gesture, she thinks, would prove his love for her and verify their ideal marriage. In keeping with that romantic theme, Nora does not plan to allow Torvald to carry out his noble pledge to her. She will hurl herself into the fjord and end the matter once Torvald manifests his love and devotion. Before these theatrics can take place, however, Mrs. Linde plans to visit Krogstad and convince him to demand his unread letters from Torvald. "There was a time once when he'd gladly have done anything for me," she adds, referring to their past relationship in sunnier days (90). In the meantime, Mrs. Linde urges Nora to stall her husband from retrieving his mail until she can return.

Nora and Torvald have plans to attend a costume party at an upstairs apartment on the following evening where Nora will dance the tarantella. She convinces Torvald on this evening that he must give up everything, including reading his mail, in order to help her because she is frightened and nervous about dancing at the party. This interaction between the couple, the most extended thus far in the play, defines their relationship with Torvald exerting the male prerogative in the dominant position and Nora in the weaker role as the submissive female. Slyly, however, Nora uses these roles to her advantage as she plays to her husband's vanity: "Oh, sit down and play for me, Torvald. Direct me. Teach me, the way you always have" (91). After Nora dances violently with a tambourine and a shawl, Torvald chastises her for forgetting everything that he has ever taught her. He realizes that he has a lot of work to do with her before she will be ready to impress others at the party and reflect well upon him as her husband. Nora's plan works splendidly, then, as Torvald completely forgets about his pile of unread mail. During a break, Mrs. Linde appears in the doorway and reports privately to Nora that Krogstad has left town and will not return until the following evening. Nora orders champagne and macaroons in advance of the party to come, but also to celebrate the miracle that she senses is now on the brink. Mrs. Linde left a note for Krogstad, but Nora replies evenly: "You shouldn't have. Don't try to stop anything now. After all, it's a wonderful joy, this waiting here for the miracle" (93). Nora informs Mrs. Linde, who possesses no trace of romanticism, that she could not possibly understand the miracle. Anticipating her suicide, Nora proclaims: "Thirty-one hours to live," and then flies into Torvald's open arms as his little lark and songbird.

The third and final act opens with a scene between Mrs. Linde and Krogstad that is remarkable not only because it is the only prolonged scene in which Nora does not appear, but more importantly for what it shows: a man and woman coming to terms with the past in a mature conversation. It is the night of the costume party and Mrs. Linde sits in the Helmers' apartment, listens to the music above and hopes that Krogstad will read her note that she left for him and arrive at the Helmers' before it is too late. He does come, eventually, and the couple sits down to talk and trace events of the past in which he accuses her of heartlessly throwing him over for a man with more means. "When I lost you," he says, "it was as if all the solid ground dissolved from under my feet" (95). Now, Mrs. Linde, a lost soul in her own right, reaches out to him: "I need to have someone to care for; and your children need a mother. We both need each other. Nils, I have faith that you're good at heart—I'll risk everything together with you" (96). Suddenly, she hears the tarantella from above and knows that the Helmers will return imminently. Initially, she wanted Krogstad to demand his letter back. Now, though, as a result of an honest exchange of thoughts and feelings, Mrs. Linde changes her mind completely: "Helmer's got to learn everything; this dreadful secret has to be aired; those two have to come to a full understanding; all these lies and evasions can't go on." Krogstad agrees, but says that there is one thing that he can do immediately to right things. "I can't believe it," he says as an exit line, "I've never been so happy" (97). Krogstad, along with his past and future partner, Mrs. Linde, serves as a foil for Torvald and Nora. Whereas the young couple represents a handsome ideal, Krogstad and Mrs. Linde actually form a mature partnership that is based upon honesty and equality. Ibsen's dramaturgical sleight-of-hand becomes apparent as the melodramatic villain slips away and transforms effortlessly into a sympathetic hero. The fact that Krogstad committed a crime similar to Nora's also reflects well upon him and valorizes the motive behind the deed rather than the deed itself. The overt conflict essentially disappears at this point and sets the stage for Nora's miracle to happen.

The whole business with Krogstad merely brings into focus a problem that Nora has avoided for her entire life: that she has allowed others, particularly men, particularly her father and then her husband, to treat her as a child and not grant her respect. Nora hopes and dreams that Torvald will acknowledge his debt to her at some point and that he will be grateful to her when he discovers all that she has done for him, but she is afraid to find out for certain if his devotional pledges have any truth behind them. Indeed, it would be a miracle if it were true, though Nora does not see that. She does not want to give up the security of a successful marriage and strong social position and all the material comforts that have come with the bargain that she made with her husband. At the same time, the start of the play shows Nora in doubt and in a crisis that is completely independent of what Krogstad will later do. His machinations merely expedite Nora's process of self-discovery and personal revelation. Even if Krogstad were never to appear, Nora would eventually have to face her problem of identity and autonomy in her social network and the very first scenes of the play, prior to the entrance of Krogstad, make this fact abundantly clear.

Humming happily, Nora enters her home in Act 1 with a lot of wrapped packages and she tips the delivery boy generously for carrying the Christmas tree. Certainly the holiday season sparks Nora's innate generosity, but she is also giddy because her time of hardship, when she has been scraping for money to pay off her secret debt, is almost at an end and this gives her cause to celebrate much more lavishly than usual. At the same time, however, this period of intense struggle has provided her the greatest joy in her life. She has for the first and only time in her life earned her own way and felt "almost like being a man" (55). Nora takes pride in the fact that she has earned the money to pay back the debt incurred by her husband's illness and she takes exception to Mrs. Linde's assertion in an early scene that she is "just a child" (52). Nora fights back and claims that she can do things for herself and she spills her secret to Mrs. Linde that she alone saved Torvald's life by raising all the necessary funds herself. "A wife can't borrow without her husband's consent," Mrs. Linde reminds her (53). Nora teases her by suggesting that she charmed an admirer for the money, but Mrs. Linde is even more disturbed that Nora could have gotten the money without Torvald's knowledge. Nora maintains that her husband must never know that she saved his life: "Torvald, with all his masculine pride—how painfully humiliating for him if he ever found out he was in debt to me. That would just ruin our relationship. Our beautiful, happy home would never be the same" (54). She softens her stance a little and says that she might tell him someday, when she grows old and loses her looks and he no longer enjoys her dancing and dressing up for him. Then, she indicates, she might need this old debt as a chip to keep Torvald's attention. Nora calls it having "something in reserve" (55). Krogstad's intervention, then, with his letter that explains everything, speeds up Nora's timetable and forces her to put her "reserve" in play.

While Torvald has no sense, really, of what Nora is really like as a person and calls her any number of belittling and unpleasant little pet names such as "lark," "songbird," and "squirrel," it is also true that Nora deceives him in order to wheedle money to repay her illicit debt. Torvald enjoys gently reproaching her as a spendthrift, when in fact Nora uses every available resource not to buy more and more things, but to pay Krogstad. Torvald alarms her by suggesting that her excessive spending habits have been handed down through heredity. "It's in your blood," he opines with certainty (46). At the same time, he seems to be aware that Nora withholds something from him, but he cannot admit to himself that it might be vitally important and an opportunity for a serious discussion quickly vanishes. One of the most telling signs of the unacknowledged split between Torvald and Nora is the attitude that each displays on the subject of Nora's work. Torvald recalls how just one year ago the family Christmas was dull and boring because Nora shut herself away from the family for three weeks in order to make the ornaments by hand out of financial necessity. (This was a time when she also did extra sewing and such to make additional money.) "Ugh, that was the dullest time I've ever lived through," Torvald allows. In response, Nora says quietly: "It wasn't at all dull for me" (47). Nora took pride in her ability to earn money and felt useful as a person and also enjoyed the autonomy and freedom of working alone in her own space—a space similar to Torvald's study to which he retreats and from which he emerges from time to time to join the rest of the family. Ironically, Torvald announces that the hard times are at an end for the family and that Nora will never have to work like that again. Nora knows that this will be a problem. The business with macaroons is another telling gesture that reveals Nora's quiet rebellion against her husband's dominion. In the opening scene, Nora sneaks a few of the confections before Torvald can issue a reprimand from his offstage study. Nora lies and says that she is not eating them. Later in the act, Nora basks in the power of her position as Torvald's wife. Both Mrs. Linde and Krogstad have approached her to use her influence over her husband. She celebrates by breaking out the contraband macaroons for a little snack and utters a surprising oath: "to hell and be damned!" (59). Nora relishes the thought that she will soon be free and clear of any obligation, yet she is most certainly under her husband's thumb.

Revelations in the middle of Act 2 expose the final crack in Nora's ideal marriage to Torvald. Earlier, she joked with Mrs. Linde about getting the necessary funds she needs from a male admirer and benefactor, and now she considers asking Torvald's best friend, Dr. Rank, for the money. Rank informs her that his deteriorating health will rapidly become terminal within the month. Nora pursues her objective and wonders aloud if there might be a favor that he could bestow and begins: "You know how deeply, how inexpressibly dearly Torvald loves me; he'd never hesitate a second to give up his life for me" (83). Rank responds a bit too quickly that Torvald is not the only one who would give up his life for her. His frank admission that he loves her, too, stops Nora from further divulging any secrets. She could plausibly accept his offer as a friend, but not as a rejected lover. Although she has surely known how Dr. Rank felt about her for some time, love has never been named and she could deny its existence. She *knows* that Rank would do anything for her. She *pretends* to believe that Torvald's proclamations and protestations on love carry the same conviction. Nora would do almost anything not to put them to the test because she knows, deep down, that they are false and that her husband would always value his reputation more than his love for her. Back to Rank's offer, Nora changes tack and refuses his help and claims as well that he misconstrued her meanings and intentions. Confused, Rank counters: "So many time I've felt you'd almost rather be with me than with Helmer" (84). Nora admits that this is true and makes an analogy to her childhood in which she loved her father most of all, but had more fun when she went downstairs to play in the maids' quarters because they "never tried to improve me" (85). Nora never questioned the fact that the people around whom she spent time might also be the same ones for whom she held great affection, even love. She never imagined that she might be in love with Dr. Rank because she never associated love with friendship and companionship.

The miracle Nora tries to stage in Act 3 to preserve her ideal marriage does not happen. Torvald reveals himself as not the man that he said he was or that Nora hoped. After Krogstad and Mrs. Linde confess their hearts, the following scene with Torvald and Nora reveals them as little more than very attractive strangers. Late at night after the costume party upstairs, Torvald sweeps Nora into their apartment intent upon sexual intercourse. Mrs. Linde's greetings interrupt his plans and force him to describe how well Nora danced and what a success she made at the party, though he adds that the "performance may have been a bit too naturalistic" (99). By that he means that it may have been a bit too sexually provocative: "it rather overstepped the proprieties of art" (99). A triumph nonetheless, Torvald removed Nora from the party as soon as the dance ended and after they made a farewell tour around the ballroom. Watching Nora perform for others whetted Torvald's sexual desire and he is eager to get Nora alone. While he lights candles in an adjoining room, Mrs. Linde informs Nora that Krogstad no longer poses a threat, but that she should tell her husband everything. "I know now what's to be done," Nora answers, no longer thinking of Krogstad as her primary adversary. She considers her miracle and the possibility that she will commit suicide in order to preserve her ideal marriage. Finally, Mrs. Linde leaves and Torvald expresses relief that such a "deadly bore" has finally left them alone (100).

Torvald prizes his wife as his dearest possession and discloses his fantasies of her as a young virgin and how he imagines sweeping her off her feet for the first time. When she fully realizes her husband's sexual intent, Nora rejects him impulsively and reflexively: "Go away, Torvald! Leave me alone. I don't want all this." Incredulous, uncomprehending, Torvald responds: "What do you mean? Nora, you're teasing me. You will, won't you? Aren't I your husband—?" (101). He simply cannot believe that his little spendthrift can refuse his sexual advance. Dr. Rank appears at the door next to say goodbye for the last time. He jokes to Nora that his scientific research regarding his health has yielded conclusive and certain results. Nora bids him to sleep well and asks for him to wish the same for her. She thinks that she will die this evening just as surely as Dr. Rank. Pointedly, Helmer pays no attention to this conversation and shows no interest or compassion for the fate of his best friend. Torvald retrieves his mail, finally, and notices a death notice from Dr. Rank along with Krogstad's letter. Again, Torvald reveals his shallow feelings for his best friend by dismissing the dark news as something good for him and Nora because they will be now "thrown back on each other, completely" (104). Embracing her, he elaborates: "You know what, Nora—time and again I've wished you were in some terrible danger, just so I could stake my life and soul and everything, for your sake" (104). Hearing that, Nora directs him to read his mail. Torvald objects—he wants to have sex! "With a dying friend on your mind?" Nora chides, incredulously, and a chastened Torvald retreats at last with his letters to his study. Nora paces about the room and contemplates the end and suicide by drowning that she has envisioned as her next step after the miracle occurs.

Suddenly, Torvald throws open the doors and grabs hold of her. Nora screams and struggles to break free of his grip: "Don't try and save me, Torvald!" (105), but saving her is far from his mind at this moment. Stage directions describe Nora's face as "hardening" as she gauges her husband's reactions to Krogstad's letter. Pacing to and fro, Torvald refers to his wife as a hypocrite, a liar and a criminal. Nora "says nothing and goes on looking straight at him" (105). Torvald reads only the implications for himself in the letter and nothing about Nora's heroic efforts to save his life: "Now you've wrecked all my happiness—ruined my whole future" (106). Torvald decides that the whole mess must be hushed up as quickly as possible and therefore they will continue to live in the same residence in order to maintain appearances, but they will no longer live as man and wife (despite Torvald's persistent sexual desires). And Torvald bans Nora from any contact with the children: "I don't dare trust you with them" (106).

The doorbell rings and another letter arrives for Nora, but Torvald intercepts and opens it. It, too, is from Krogstad, but now Torvald cries out joyfully: "I'm saved. Nora, I'm saved!" (107). In this uncanny reversal of fortunes, Krogstad now apologizes for what he has done and returns Nora's promissory note. Torvald's tone changes completely as well and he wants now to forget the whole matter as if it never happened. His ardor for his wife returns as well: "I wouldn't be a man if this feminine helplessness didn't make you twice as attractive to me. You mustn't mind those sharp words I said—that was all in the first confusion of thinking my world had collapsed. I've forgiven you, Nora; I swear, I've forgiven you" (107). Nora exits to an interior room and Torvald speaks to her through the open door. She surprises him when she emerges wearing her street clothes when he thought she was getting ready for bed. She puts his sexual fantasies about his newly forgiven wife, akin to ones about the virgin bride, once more on hold. Nora draws a chair up at the table and instructs her husband to sit down.

Nora has done more than change her clothes—her new mode of behavior baffles and confuses Torvald. Indeed, in eight years of marriage they have never once sat down together to have a serious conversation. Nora finally consciously realizes that her husband does not know her and is thus incapable of loving her. "You thought it fun to be in love with me, that's all," she says (109). Nora informs Torvald that she is going to leave him and that she must fulfill her duty to herself: "I believe that, before all else, I'm a human being, no less than you—or anyway, I ought to try to become one" (111). She means to start by examining her alleged crime. She does not believe that the law is fair: "A woman hasn't a right to protect her dying father or save her husband's life! I can't believe that." She struggles to reconcile what is legal and just with what is good and right and vows to figure things out for herself over time: "I'll try to discover who's right, the world or I" (111). The world is quite different than what she had ever imagined, but now, for the first time, she is curious and intent upon making sense of it all. As for Torvald, she tells him that she realized that she no longer loved him when the "miraculous thing didn't come" (112). Torvald objects: "there's no one who gives up honor for love," to which Nora retorts, simply, "Millions of women have done just that" (113). The gendered theme of love above honor parallels the ethical theme of morality versus law. Nora demands her wedding ring from Torvald and returns his to him as well. She will take nothing from strangers and Torvald implores if he might ever be more than a stranger to her. That, Nora says, would take the greatest miracle of all, because they would have to transform themselves to the point that their "living together could be a true marriage." Distraught, Torvald asks an open question in the final line: "The greatest miracle—?" (114). Nora slams the door shut on her way out.

The Wild Duck (1884)

> "When I look back on all you've done, it's as if I looked out over a battlefield with broken human beings on every side."

As in *A Doll's House*, *The Wild Duck* critiques the idealism of a "true marriage." Unlike Nora Helmer, however, who ultimately confronts what she has always known about her husband, Gregers Werle refuses to alter his worldview in the latter play and his persistence produces devastating consequences. The action begins with his return home after a long absence to celebrate his father's birthday. At the party, he encounters his childhood friend, Hjalmar Ekdal, who has not had the success for which he once seemed destined, and also sees that his friend's father is now a poor, downtrodden old man. Gregers confronts his own father, Haakon Werle, about what has happened in the intervening years and accuses him of taking advantage of the Ekdals. Gregers realizes, too, that his father has called him down for the occasion not simply to celebrate the birthday, but to sanction Werle's announcement of marriage to his former housekeeper, Mrs. Sørby. Considering all the philandering that his father has done and the harm that it did to his dead mother, Gregers experiences again the pent up guilt that led him to run away from home years ago. He always took his mother's part, according to his father, but he couldn't stand up for her when it was appropriate and he's never been able to forgive himself. Now he spies an opportunity to make amends with his conscience and pay a debt to the past by turning from his father to his friend and raising Hjalmar to the brilliant heights that once had seemed so certain. Gregers fervently believes that Hjalmar will reach his stature of greatness if he can reckon with his domestic situation and establish a "true marriage" with his wife, Gina. The truth, however, does not have a palliative effect upon Hjalmar. In the end, Gregers' mission in life to expose the secret of the Ekdal family assuages his guilty conscience, but tragically destroys another innocent life in the process.

Ibsen casts the misleading perspective of Haakon Werle as the villain in the expository scenes of Act 1. The servants working at the birthday party gossip about Werle as he proposes a toast to his housekeeper, Mrs. Sørby, in an adjoining room and they speculate whether or not there is something between them. "I've heard he was a real goat in his day," one says, hinting at sexual scandals that have apparently dogged Werle for years (119). Another notes that Gregers has just returned home, while a third remarks that he did not even know that Werle had a son. Collectively, they question whether the father's relationship with Mrs. Sørby and the son's homecoming are related events or mere coincidence. When Old Ekdal, uninvited to the party, slips into the room after doing some copying work as a kind of charity case, the servants have more fodder for conversation. The old man had once been Werle's partner, but committed a crime through the business and spent years in prison. They feel sorry for him. Werle, on the other hand, escaped all criminal liability. As the guests of the party pass through the study from the dining room to the large inner room upstage, Werle directs a disapproving look to his old partner's son, Hjalmar Ekdal, a gesture that makes Werle's feelings about the Ekdals very clear.

Hjalmar, it turns out, is Gregers' guest and the two old friends engage in dialogue that provides classic Ibsen exposition that reads almost as a parody of dramatic technique. Gregers observes that the two former best friends have not seen each other in 16 or 17 years and then proceeds with a series of questions and answers that further portray Gregers' father in an unflattering light. After the scandal broke involving Hjalmar's father, Werle informed Hjalmar that his son wanted nothing further to do with him. Werle instructed Hjalmar to give up his studies and sever all of his old friendships. In return, however, Werle set Hjalmar up in business as a photographer and positioned him to marry and start a family of his own. Gregers never knew anything about these events, but he grudgingly acknowledges now that perhaps his father had a "kind of conscience" (124). The scene turns, though, when Gregers learns the name of Hjalmar's wife—Gina Hansen, the housekeeper of Werle's during the last year of Gregers' mother's illness. Gregers asks his friend, with feigned innocence, how he happened to meet Gina and Hjalmar admits that Werle orchestrated the entire match. "My father has almost been a kind of providence to you," Gregers says without Hjalmar noticing any irony in this remark (125). Confident that the facts of the backstory are correct, Gregers suspects that his father is behind the fall of the House of Ekdal and informs his old friend that he might pay him a visit later at his home.

At the end of the first act, the conflict of the play between father and son seems straightforward. Indeed, the linear unfolding of events accentuates the fervor with which Gregers pursues the truth in order to help his friend. Unfortunately, the forward drive that picks up speed and momentum as the action progresses brings on tragic events before anyone can apply brakes to Gregers' unstoppable force. He stampedes through all of the cautionary signs surrounding the Ekdal family that should have given pause to his unbridled pursuit of the truth. Either he does not see them or he chooses not to recognize them, but they exist nonetheless. Gregers confronts his father about past affairs in the final scene of the first act. Werle evades the question of his part in the legal scandal by emphasizing Old Ekdal's weakness: "There are people in this world who plunge to the bottom when they've hardly been winged, and they never come up again" (131). The first of many "duck" references casts the Ekdals as wounded and lost causes. Werle maintains that he's done a lot through the years to keep the Ekdal family afloat financially and he attempts to allay his son's suspicions by saying that he invited him down for the party because he wanted him to join the family business as a partner. Werle also wants to marry Mrs. Sørby and gain his son's approval to sanction the event and silence gossip about Werle's old affair with Gina Hansen, his previous housekeeper. Gregers, though, cannot forgive or forget his father's transgressions against his mother. Pondering the bribe from his father, he muses: "What's left then of all the stories about what the poor dead woman suffered and endured? Not a scrap. Her own son ground them to dust" (135). Werle accuses his son of viewing him only through his mother's eyes, which, he adds, were "clouded" at times, a euphemism for mental instability. Gregers says that Werle's numerous affairs, capped by the one with Gina Hansen, drove his mother insane. He then considers his friend Hjalmar and how wretched it must be for him to live "plunged in deception" with "that creature." Gregers concludes: "When I look back on all you've done, it's as if I looked out over a battlefield with broken human beings on every side" (135). As he prepares to leave, he informs his father: "at last I can see a purpose to live for," a clear indication that he will try to save Hjalmar (136).

The first act takes place in Old Werle's home at night. The second and all subsequent acts of the five-act drama occur in Hjalmar Ekdal's apartment that doubles as a photographic studio. This shift in scene also offers a shift in perspective on the Ekdal family. Hjalmar and his father do not appear to be the men that Gregers imagined them to be, while Hjalmar's wife and daughter, Gina and Hedvig, have worked hard and endured much to create a loving home and family for their men. With no time lapse from the end of Act 1, Gina and Hedvig await Hjalmar's return home from the fancy dinner party at the beginning of Act 2. They lament the high cost of Hjalmar's butter and beer even as they casually and unselfconsciously disclose that they have gone without any hot food on this evening. Hedvig distracts herself by drawing, shading her bad eyes to protect them from the light, but the prospect of her father's imminent return excites her because he promised to bring her a treat and she is now a little hungry. Gina emphasizes, ironically, possibly referring to Mrs. Sørby and Werle's predilections: "Yes, you can bet there are lots of treats to be had in *that* house" (138). Gina and Hedvig speculate about what's happening at the party and they agree that Hjalmar will be in a good mood when he returns. Hedvig notes that things are "pleasanter" when there is something positive to tell Hjalmar when he comes home, and they agree that finding a boarder for the vacant room in the apartment will be good news best saved for another occasion.

Still, when Hjalmar arrives the family must rally to content him. Hjalmar at first shows off for his family as if he were the center of attention and life of the party, whereas the action at Werle's demonstrated his loneliness and awkwardness among the rich folk. When Hedvig can wait no longer and finally asks for her promised treat, Hjalmar admits that he forgot completely, but then tries to cover his gaffe by pulling out the bill of fare from the dinner and describing for her every dish that he tasted. Hedvig cannot completely hide her hurt feelings, and her father becomes angry and begins to pace and play the part of the suffering breadwinner who cannot really be expected to remember everything among his long list of cares. To settle his irritation, Hedvig offers to bring Hjalmar his flute and a bottle of cold beer. At first, Hjalmar refuses: "I want no pleasures in this world. Ah, yes, work—I'll be deep in work tomorrow; there'll be no lack of *that*. I'll sweat and slave as long as my strength holds out—" (145). But, predictably, he relents and plays a sentimental folk dance and takes Gina's hand and says "with feeling": "So what if we skimp and scrape along under this roof, Gina—it's still our home. And I'll say this: it's good to be here" (146). At this precipitous moment, the moment of greatest visible family love and affection, Gregers knocks at the door and enters.

Gregers insinuates himself among the happy family and begins his investigation immediately. Hjalmar startles him with the revelation that Hedvig is going blind due to heredity. Under veiled questioning, Gregers discovers that Hedvig's birth coincided with Gina and Hjalmar's marriage. Old Ekdal interrupts and invites Gregers to explore the hunting ground in the attic by opening a pair of sliding doors at the rear of the apartment. In the moonlight, Gregers sees a wild duck in a basket among poultry, pigeons, and rabbits. Hedvig claims the wild duck as her favorite pet and Gregers is curious to discover its origins. Werle shot her on a hunting party, Ekdal explains, but owing to his poor eyesight he only winged her, and the bird dove straight down to the bottom of the lake. Werle's dog, though, a very clever animal, dove after her and brought the duck back to the surface. Werle gave the wounded duck to the Ekdals as a gift and the bird has since prospered in captivity and seems to have forgotten its old life and has now even gotten fat. Gregers transforms the story of the wild duck into a metaphor for the Ekdal family. He then asks to rent the spare room in their house and plans to move in the next morning, an offer Hjalmar welcomes as good fortune but that Gina tries to dissuade. Undaunted, Gregers says that he hopes things go as well for him as with the wild duck. It is hard to be named "Gregers Werle," he confides to Hjalmar and Gina, and that if he had his wish, if he could choose to be someone else, then he'd be a clever dog: "A really fantastic, clever dog, the kind that goes to the bottom after wild ducks when they dive under and bite fast into the weeds down in the mire" (155). This cryptic allusion completely baffles Hjalmar.

Gregers continues his survey of the Ekdal household in Act 3, the following morning, from close range. Gina reports that Gregers has already made a mess of his room. While Hjalmar dabbles with retouching photographs, Gina scurries about to prepare lunch for the guests, Molvik and Dr. Relling, neighbors from downstairs whom Hjalmar has invited. Hjalmar's protestations about work belie the observation that he does very little. Gina and Hedvig must constantly check up on his progress and his diligence, but Hjalmar often discards his work and slips into the loft any chance he gets.

After accusing Hedvig of spying on this occasion, he persuades her to take his brush and perform the retouching herself at the table. Hjalmar cautions her about ruining her eyes, but warns her that it will be her fault if anything happens to her. He rationalizes his decision by saying that he will only stay in the loft for a few minutes.

Once Hjalmar leaves, Gregers interrogates Hedvig alone about the wild duck. Everything looks different, Gregers observes, in the morning light, to which Hedvig concurs: "Yes, it can change so completely. In the morning it looks different from in the afternoon; and when it rains it's different from when it's clear" (162). Gregers suggests that it must be a "world of its own" in the loft and concludes: "The wild duck rules supreme in there, doesn't she?" Hedvig agrees and adds that the duck is completely mysterious: "There's no one who knows her, and no one who knows where she's come from, either." Gregers corrects her: "And actually, she's been in the depths of the sea" (164). Gregers' strange choice of phrase strikes Hedvig as funny, she says, because the entire attic, with all its sunken treasures, has always seemed to her as the "depths of the sea." That is strange, she says, because it is only an attic. Gregers confuses Hedvig, as he did Hjalmar previously, by interpreting the duck and its habitat as metaphorical rather than literal. She does not understand the symbolism at this point, but Gregers' serious talk inspires her vivid imagination. In a bit of foreshadowing, her father warns her, upon his return from the attic, not to play with his pistol because one barrel remains loaded.

Peering into the loft, Gregers spies the wild duck clearly and observes its limp from where the dog bit hold and how the bird drags one wing from the shot. Gina, sick and tired of all the fuss made over that duck, calls Hedvig into the kitchen to help with final meal preparations. Alone with Hjalmar, Gregers extends his metaphor and applies the plight of the wild duck to his best friend: "You've plunged to the bottom and clamped hold of the seaweed." Hjalmar, Gregers continues, has been "wandering in a poisonous swamp" and carries "an insidious disease in [his] system, and so [he's] gone to the bottom to die in the dark" (170). Seeing himself as Werle's old dog, Gregers plans to retrieve Hjalmar from his swamp of deception. Hjalmar, however, cannot stand such unpleasant talk and begs Gregers to stop. Everything has turned out for the best, Hjalmar claims, because he's nearly finished his photographic invention that will bring the family fame and fortune and Dr. Relling has even suggested that the government might allow Old Ekdal to don his military uniform again. Hjalmar ends the scene defiantly, if not melodramatically, in defense of his contented life: "My lot is a poor one—but, you know, I'm an inventor. And I'm the family breadwinner, too. *That's* what sustains me through all the pettiness. Ah, here they come with the lunch" (170).

Beyond Hjalmar's protests, two other men intercede and try to prevent Gregers from fulfilling his self-appointed task. Dr. Relling recalls at the luncheon that Gregers once made a name for himself by producing a pamphlet called the "Summons to the Ideal." Relling hopes that Gregers learned something from that experience and does not plan to distribute such idealism again. Relling adopts counter measures to blunt the perceived threat from Gregers: he props up Hjalmar with toasts to his father (who Hjalmar does not invite to lunch); he compliments Hjalmar on his fine and capable wife; and he anticipates how grand it will be once Hjalmar brings his marvelous invention into the world. Looking around, Relling pronounces a summation: "Well, now, isn't it good for a change to be sitting around a well-spread table in a happy family circle?" Undaunted, Gregers retorts: "I, for my part, don't thrive in marsh gas" (173–174). Comically, Gina takes his remark literally, but Relling detects the intent behind the metaphor and reminds Gregers not to issue any "Summons to the Ideal" to this household.

Haakon Werle's sudden entrance interrupts the argument between Relling and Gregers and the father requests to speak with his son privately. He fears that Gregers plans to tell Hjalmar the truth about his marriage and child and asks his son to reconsider those plans. What happened to Old Ekdal can never be undone, Gregers admits, but there is still time to save Hjalmar from all the lies that threaten to destroy his life. Werle questions whether Hjalmar is the sort to appreciate what Gregers plans to do, but his son argues that this is the only way to cure his own sick conscience. Gregers cuts all ties with his father and announces that he has no plans beyond his mission of restoring Hjalmar's prominence in the world, suggesting that, possibly spurred on by Hjalmar's reported suicide attempt, Gregers, too, harbors thoughts of killing himself after fulfilling his noble task. Gregers invites Hjalmar to take a long walk and talk, both Relling and Gina beg him not to go, but Hjalmar quite innocently thinks that his friend needs him and that it would be a betrayal of friendship if he were to decline. Relling proclaims Gregers as dangerous and sick with a "national disease" that he calls "moralistic fever." No one at this point pays any attention to Hedvig, but she pointedly delivers the curtain line of the act: "This is all so strange to me" (178).

Hjalmar pledges to become a new man as a result of his consultation with Gregers. Events in Act 4 demonstrate, however, that change is not good for Hjalmar. Visibly upset upon his late return home, Hjalmar clearly does not want to give up the joys of the attic and to work full-time in the photographic studio, but, with Gregers' words fresh in his head, he feels that he must. Gina attempts to dissuade him, pointing out that he needs time to work on his invention. Hedvig adds, too, that he needs time to be free for the wild duck. He'll start a new regimen the day after tomorrow, Hjalmar concludes, because he has promised to celebrate Hedvig's birthday as usual. About the wild duck, though, he frightens Hedvig: "I'd almost like to wring its neck!" (180). He elaborates in such a way that his wife cannot miss his point: "I shouldn't tolerate under my roof a creature that's been in that man's [Werle's] hands" (181). He sends Hedvig outdoors for her afternoon walk in order to confront Gina about her past relationship with Werle. Hjalmar cannot believe that she does not "regret this spider web of deception," but Gina says quite calmly that she has had too much to think about in terms of running the household and that, in fact, after all these years, she's almost forgotten about that old affair (183). Hjalmar was not in good shape when Gina married him she reminds him and she saved him from the misery and despair that overtook him after the tragedy with his father. Now, they have finally started to turn the corner and made their house a home. Using Gregers' words, which Gina recognizes, Hjalmar refers to his cozy home as a "swamp of deception" (184). He blames the polluted environment for his inability to finish his invention and basks, melodramatically, in what he perceives as a hopeless situation: "Everything's over and done with now. Everything!" (185).

Eager to check on the efficacy of his handiwork, Gregers encounters a gloomy atmosphere instead of the transfigured faces that he anticipated. According to him, "there's nothing in the world that compares with showing mercy to a sinner and lifting her up in the arms of love" (185). Gregers wants Hjalmar and Gina to form a "true marriage," though such marriages are rare to the point that he has scarcely ever known of one. Relling, as a voice of reason, observes that the wild duck of idealism flies again. Later, in Act 5, he describes Hjalmar as a fraud who is far from the beacon of light that Gregers believes him to be. Relling explains that he spends time with Hjalmar, not because he likes him, but because as a doctor he feels it is his duty to try and help him by sustaining the life-lie of Hjalmar as an inventor. Relling defines the life-lie as the animating principle of human life: "Deprive the average man of his vital lie, and you've robbed him of happiness as well" (203). This bald statement carries thematic weight and seems to come from the voice of the playwright. Relling is more than a mouthpiece for the playwright, however. In response to Gregers' dream of a "true marriage," Relling is the first and only one to warn Gregers, Hjalmar and Gina that they must consider what they are doing to Hedvig, still a child, but also an adolescent on the verge of womanhood: impressionable, emotional, and prone to act on impulse.

Mrs. Sørby announces her marriage to Werle in a surprising visit in the next scene that alters the view of the entire play. Shocked by this news but anxious to cover his reaction, Relling comments that Werle at least is not likely to beat her as her former husband did and, at any rate, Werle is likely worth a great deal more than old Mr. Sørby. Mrs. Sørby rejoins quickly and directly: "At least he hasn't wasted the best that's in him. Any man who does *that* has to take the consequences" (188). Her jab at Relling undercuts any notion that the "life-lie" offers a viable alternative to Gregers' philosophy. In fact, the inference that Relling is capable of directing other lives but not his own suggests that he has something in common with Gregers the idealist. Gregers notices the interplay between the two of them and wonders what his father would say if he were to disclose their past liaison. Mrs. Sørby surprises him by saying that she has told him everything. Just as Mrs. Linde and Krogstad emerged late in *A Doll's House* as an admirable couple, so, too, do Mrs. Sørby and Werle evolve from the apparent villains to the most unlikely heroes. The reversal of perspectives and inverse of values, of course, makes Ibsen's subtle point. Speaking to Gina and everyone present, Berta (Mrs. Sørby) makes it clear that honesty is the most important thing in relationships and then confides that she will be able to care for her new husband when he becomes infirm. She innocently elaborates to the group that Werle is going blind. "Lots of people do" is all that Gina can add by way of explanation of the coincidence that both Werle and Hedvig are going blind at the same time (190). Oblivious to this revelation but still thinking of Gina's former liaison with Werle, Hjalmar vows to repay the "debt of honor" that consists of all the money that Werle has given him through the years. Mrs. Sørby departs after noting the significant change that seems to have taken place in the Ekdal household. It is no longer the happy home that it was prior to Gregers' arrival.

The "true marriage" of Werle and Mrs. Sørby rankles Hjalmar and violates his sense of justice, yet he places divine retribution in the fact of Werle's looming blindness. He reflects: "It's useful sometimes to go down deep into the night side of existence" (192), at which point, Hedvig returns from her afternoon walk with an announcement that Mrs. Sørby has given her an early birthday present, an actual letter addressed to her in Werle's hand. The gift turns out to be a monthly stipend for Old Ekdal, but one that will pass on to Hedvig in perpetuity after Ekdal's death. Hjalmar reads the gift as a bribe and shreds the letter, then confronts Gina about whether or not Hedvig is his biological daughter. Gina refuses to answer unequivocally and, even to Gregers' horror, Hjalmar disavows her as his child and leaves the house: "Don't come near me, Hedvig! I can't bear seeing you," he cries as he starts for the door (196). Confused, Hedvig bursts into tears. She reasons, though, that since the wild duck was given to them as a present and she dearly loves it, it follows that Hjalmar could love her if she were a foundling and not really his biological child. Desperate for a remedy, Gregers asks her to sacrifice the wild duck to Hjalmar as proof of her love for her father: "What if you, in a sacrificing spirit, gave up the dearest thing you own and know in the whole world?" he asks (198). Thinking this might work, Hedvig agrees and says she'll ask Old Ekdal to shoot the wild duck for her. Convinced that his plan for salvation and redemption is back on schedule, Gregers departs and leaves Hedvig to receive comfort in her mother's arms. "That's the way it goes," Gina observes, "when these crazy people come around, summoning up their ideals" (198).

Hjalmar's firm decision to move permanently softens quickly at the beginning of Act 5, but not before he shoos Hedvig away from him again. He refers to her as an "intruder." Fighting back tears, Hedvig steels her resolve and softly says, "The wild duck," and takes the pistol down from the shelf and steals into the loft space, and closes the doors behind her (207). Hjalmar meanwhile complains to Gina about all the necessary preparations required to do before he can leave. He resents having to take his father with him as well as the entire attic menagerie: "The joys of life *I* have to renounce are higher than rabbits," he pontificates (208). Gina tells him that he could stay in the living room for a couple of days and Hjalmar re-introduces that idea a bit later as if it were his own. Gina brings him food and hot coffee and even adds fresh butter for his dry bread to coerce him further to stay. Finally, he spies the torn letter and deed of gift from Werle that he had discarded on the previous evening. Reasoning that it his father's money, as well as "the other person's," he pastes the letter back together as if to cancel his earlier dramatic gesture and pronouncement (209).

Gregers cannot hide his disappointment when he discovers that his friend has been eating and sleeping at such a pivotal moment. To save face, Hjalmar rationalizes that he rests only to build the strength necessary to leave his home forever. He admits, though, that Relling came up with the idea of the invention and that he only kept up the charade because he imagined that Hedvig believed in it. Now, he doesn't know what to believe and he associates the thought that she might not be his biological child with the darker thought that she might not ever have loved him: "She's managed to blot the sun right out of my life." Gregers assures him that he may yet get the proof of her love that he needs. "Hedvig's completely free of deceit," Gregers assures his friend (211). Hjalmar fears that he will lose Hedvig to the riches of Mrs. Sørby and Werle at any time. He's only a poor photographer, he laments dramatically, and wonders aloud if Hedvig has just been waiting for the right time to leave. Hjalmar simply cannot remove the doubt from his mind in the absence of tangible proof: "If I asked her then: Hedvig, are you willing to give up life for me?" (212).

A gunshot reports from the attic as if on cue and Gregers assures Hjalmar and Gina that Hedvig has made the sacrifice to prove her love. What they discover in the attic, however, is Hedvig's lifeless body, which they carry into the light of the studio. "The pistol must have gone off," is all Hjalmar can muster (214). Relling enters but can do nothing for the girl—she's already dead from a point-blank shot. Hjalmar beats his breast, clenches his fists, and cries dramatically to the heavens: "And I drove her from me like an animal! And she crept terrified into the loft and died out of love for me" (215). The defrocked Molvik, who came in with Relling, plays the part of a priest: "Praise be to God. Dust to dust, dust to dust—" (215), at which point Relling, not flattering his friend any more, shuts him down by stating that he is drunk and should be quiet. Gregers insists that Hedvig's death will release the greatness in Hjalmar and that the "grief of death" (216) will allow this glory to last a lifetime (216). Relling contends that Hjalmar will simply use her death to dramatize his own self-pity. "If you're right, and I'm wrong, then life isn't worth living," insists Gregers (216). Life is surely not what Gregers wants it to be, but his blind ambition to make it so results in the tragic death of a young girl.

Hedda Gabler (1890)

> "For once in my life I want to have power over a human being."

Plagued by fear of scandal, Hedda Gabler substitutes vicarious, aesthetic experience for sexual freedom and independence. She refuses to make a spectacle of her life. Ironically, one of the indelible images in the play is the description of her as a young woman with beautiful long hair, dressed all in black and riding upon General Gabler's horse while brandishing his pistols through the streets of town. As she grew older, however, she elected to play life safely and conservatively. Instead of running off with the brilliant but wild Eilert Løvborg, she married his staid colleague, George Tesman, a professor of cultural history. The play picks up upon their return to town after their six-month-honeymoon abroad. George spent beyond his means for the honeymoon and their new house with the prospect of receiving a full university professorship. Judge Brack, the local bigwig who also prepared the house in the Tesmans' absence, virtually assured Tesman that the official appointment was merely a formality. Judge Brack reports now, however, that Tesman will have to compete for the job with Eilert Løvborg who has just published a brilliant new book and returned to town. Worried that he might regress to his former wild ways, Thea Elvsted, Løvborg's new companion and a former classmate of Hedda's, confides that the shadow of another woman seems to haunt Eilert and she fears that the woman might also be in town. Hedda does not let on that she is the one with the hold over Løvborg. When Løvborg visits the Tesmans, he and Hedda resume their flirtatious pose in an almost exact re-creation of one they struck years earlier. After admitting that perhaps she did love him then, Hedda recants, but she cannot resist testing the power she once had over him. She challenges Løvborg to attend Judge Brack's party where she envisions that he will impress an audience with the brilliance of his new manuscript on the future of the human race and that she, and not Thea, will have been the muse who made it possible. Unfortunately,

Løvborg cannot control his impulses and he drinks excessively, loses his manuscript and becomes violent when he discovers the loss. Ultimately, the police arrest him and Judge Brack informs Hedda that no home in town will welcome him and that he has lost any chance of winning the university post.

George, it turns out, picked up the manuscript but didn't return it to Eilert. Instead, Hedda convinces her husband to give it to her. She doesn't give it to Eilert, either, but burns it after a fateful meeting with Eilert in which she finally realizes that she has lost her competition for him to her rival. Still unable to come to grips with her sexual attraction to Eilert, she plants the idea of suicide in his mind and gives him her father's pistol with the directive to die beautifully. If she cannot have him, no one shall, and his suicide will prove that he is too good to live in the world. This attempt to influence and wield power fails miserably as well. Eilert does manage to kill himself, but accidentally and grotesquely. Worse for Hedda, Judge Brack says that the police investigation will surely uncover the fact that Eilert shot himself with Hedda's pistol. Brack will remain quiet about what he knows, he intimates, if Hedda allows him visitation rights. He has always had his sights on Hedda and any opportunity that he might be able to exploit for his own sexual delight. Meanwhile, Tesman, who feels guilty about the business with the manuscript, now dedicates himself to publishing Eilert's book by putting together all of the accumulated notes. Mrs. Elvsted joins in this enterprise with renewed enthusiasm and Hedda observes that this new partnership completely excludes her. Alone and trapped, desperate to avoid falling under the power of anyone else, Hedda withdraws to play the piano in an inner room.

Løvborg's visit to the Tesman house in Act 2 prior to Judge Brack's bachelor party marks the crucial scene and first turning point in the play. Although George Tesman and Eilert Løvborg are both scholars working in the same field, they could not be more different. Tesman ruminates over the past with his laborious study of "domestic handicrafts of Brabant in the Middle Ages" (*Four Major Plays* 228), whereas Løvborg's current book is a history of civilization up to the present day, and his just-completed manuscript is a sequel and visionary tome that suggests "what lines of development" the future is likely to take (260). Despite his apparent academic superiority, Eilert assures Tesman that he only wants to make a fresh start and that he does not plan to publish the new volume until Tesman has received the coveted university appointment. "I only want to win in the eyes of the world," Eilert says (261). Tesman could care less about that and his mood quickly changes to one of jubilation. Hedda offers Brack, Tesman and Løvborg a celebratory parting cup of cold punch, but Eilert declines, just as he had an earlier invitation to read his manuscript at Brack's party.

In order to speak intimately, Hedda pulls out an album of pictures from her honeymoon to show Eilert while the two other men withdraw for conversation in an adjoining room. She admits that she doesn't love Tesman, but she insists that she's not going to have any affairs, either. Eilert presses to find out whether she ever loved him. She evades him by saying that they were "two true companions" who used to sit in this same room and talk intimately with an illustrated magazine between them as General Gabler sat nearby (264). The relationship broke off when Eilert initiated a sexual advance. Now, he wonders why she didn't shoot him, literally, and she admits that she was afraid of scandal back then and was too big a coward. She then makes a further confession: "That wasn't my worst cowardice—that night" (266). She didn't sleep with him and she regrets it, but she's not about to relent now, either.

The replay of the past in the present is a familiar Ibsen trope, whether it is the son returning in the form of the father in *Ghosts*, the visions of the white horse of Rosmersholm, or Hilda Wangel demanding her castles in the air in *The Master Builder*, but there is a clear difference in this play. Hedda as much as admits that Løvborg is the love of her life and laments that things ended between them years ago with love unrequited. And yet, after consciously articulating her past mistake, Hedda maintains that things have not changed and she repeats the same mistake again by rebuffing Løvborg. For his part, Løvborg is all in and would drop his alliance with Thea Elvsted for a chance to run away with Hedda Gabler. While Hedda is unwilling to make the same sacrifice in her life of social position and privilege and safety, she is also unwilling to let go of Løvborg completely and she refuses to lose him to a rival such as Thea Elvsted. Hedda transforms all of the sexual energy that exists between her and Løvborg into her competition with Thea in order to hold sway over him and vie as the propelling force of his genius into the world with his new manuscript. The triumph of Løvborg in the "eyes of the world" might have severe consequences for Tesman's career, but Hedda does not consider such possibilities for a second: she wants Løvborg to succeed and she wants to be the positive, if not manipulative, force that motivates the man. In the process, she turns Løvborg into an aesthetic object, a kind of Greek god, and she withdraws from intimate experience and direct contact with others to a vantage point of vicarious existence through his prospective exploits and accomplishments.

Rebuffed by Hedda and understandably hurt and angry, Løvborg attempts to make Hedda jealous by calling attention to Thea's appearance and calling her his true companion, leaving the sexual nature of the relationship a bit ambiguous. Hedda now takes the offensive and suggests that Løvborg, a violent alcoholic, should have a drink in order to show others that he can exert self-control. Hedda increases pressure on Eilert by letting on that Thea arrived earlier in the day worried sick over what Eilert might do. She tests Løvborg's manhood further by pointing out that the "disgusting judge" watches them (269). Now, Eilert, challenged by all, downs one drink and then another. Hedda stops him from further drinks by reminding him that he will read his manuscript at the party. Løvborg regains his calm and reassures Mrs. Elvsted that everyone will see that he's a completely reformed man. Thea begs him not to go, but Hedda remains confident in Eilert's resolve. She imagines that he will make a triumphant success at the party and will return later that night in time to escort Thea home. Intent on proving that she, not Thea, is the most influential force in Eilert's life, Hedda declares: "For once in my life," she says, "I want to have power over a human being" (272). She fancies that Eilert will return later that night with vines leaves in his hair, a romantic and idealized image, right out of Greek mythology, of the divine! Hedda remains confident about Løvborg's success even when he does not come back after night turns into the next morning. Thea voices her anxiety regarding Eilert's whereabouts, but Hedda, who slept soundly, repeats her ecstatic vision of Eilert as Dionysus, with vine leaves in his hair.

The scene described above reveals Hedda as highly manipulative, but is she effective? Is she powerful? Subsequent events show that nothing turns out the way Hedda plans and that she cannot accomplish anything she sets out to do. The scenes previous to the one above, starting at the very beginning of the play, also present Hedda as manipulative and seemingly powerful, but a closer examination reveals that she is more victim than victimizer and much more powerless than powerful, even though she at a glance appears to be quite the opposite. In the opening scene, for example, George's aunt, Aunt Julie, arrives early in the morning to greet the mistress of the house on the very day of her return from her honeymoon. Alone downstairs while the couple is still asleep, Aunt Julie discloses to the housekeeper that George has received his doctorate while abroad and should be now addressed with his new title. She further hints that he may soon have another title as well, and though she does not say "father," she certainly implies that Hedda is pregnant. Aunt Julie never expected her nephew to marry such a "catch" and the prospect of Hedda tied down with what Judge Brack will later call Hedda's "solemn responsibility" delights her. She kills Hedda with her very kindness.

George Tesman's actions, too, show that he is less in love with Hedda Gabler than the idea of her loving him. When he comes down to meet his aunt, he says little about his romantic getaway but instead lectures her about the joys of academic research. Aunt Julie cannot believe that Hedda is not pregnant after a six-month honeymoon, but George, oblivious to his aunt's insinuations, brags about the amount of research that he conducted at libraries and archives on his trip. He studied the entire time! When Julie asks him how he plans to make use of such a big house, George comments that the two extra bedrooms will make wonderful libraries for his expanding collections. She even asks whether or not he has any "expectations," but Tesman replies blankly that he has an expectation of receiving a professorship—something Aunt Julie already knows. He can't wait to get to work, he says, because now he has such a hospitable environment in which to bring his research to fruition. At Aunt Julie's prompting, he mentions Hedda as an afterthought as "the most beautiful part of it all!" (228).

Julie's presence in the house after having just met the newlyweds at the pier a few hours ago irritates Hedda upon her entrance and Julie infuriates Hedda further when she presents George with his old bedroom slippers that he had missed so much on his honeymoon. Hedda stops this unwanted intrusion by seemingly innocently commenting on the ugliness of the maid's hat lying on the chair knowing full well that the hat belongs to Aunt Julie. The business with the hat puts Hedda's mean streak and penchant for cruelty on display even as it hides George's insensitivity and Julie's play for dominance. Insulted by Hedda's blunt rudeness, Julie prepares to leave at once, but George stops her by commenting on Hedda's plump and buxom figure. Indeed, Hedda is described as wearing a "loose-fitting gown" as if to deny a full view of her figure. George's comments, which seem to confirm Hedda's pregnancy that George denied in the previous scene, draw Julie back in with her appraisal of Hedda. She takes Hedda's head in both of her hands, according to the stage directions, and promises to make herself prominent in the new household: "I won't let a day go by without looking in on you two," she vows (231). Julie, unlike Hedda, speaks politely, but the intent of her message to insert herself into the family and to uphold and defend her nephew against anything Hedda might try is very clear to Hedda. While Hedda seems to be more dynamic and charismatic than either George or Julie, the latter two, by either male prerogative or cagey demeanor, wield degrees of control about which Hedda can only dream.

The visit of Thea Elvsted to the Tesman household in Act 1 offers the most dramatic example of Hedda's illusion of power. Thea made the long trip from her rural home to look for Eilert Løvborg, the tutor of her stepchildren, who has left her home and been in town for a week. She worries about him and beseeches the Tesmans to look out for him, completely unaware that Hedda has any past relationship or connection with Eilert. Hedda attempts to exploit Thea's naiveté in order to gain more knowledge about Løvborg and his circumstances. She pins Thea down for a heart-to-heart talk even though the two were never friends (Hedda once tried to burn off Thea's hair when they were in school together) and Hedda doesn't even know Thea's first name (she calls her Thora). Hedda assumes that she is much stronger than Thea because Thea is clearly intimidated by her and afraid of her. But Thea's revelations shake Hedda to her very core. First, Thea admits that her husband does not know that she has left in search of Eilert. Next, Thea claims that she will never return to her husband and that she has left home for good. "But what do you think people will say about you, Thea?" Hedda asks. Thea doesn't care—she only did what she had to do to live. During their time together, Eilert gave up drinking. She rehabilitated him, and he talked to her about serious subjects and made "a real human being out of me." Ultimately, they began to share in his work like "true companions," as Hedda says. That was the same phrase that Eilert used to describe Hedda and him long ago. Thea worries that their relationship cannot last, not simply because of the threat of Eilert's return to his dissolute ways, but because of a "woman's shadow between Eilert Løvborg and me" (241). Eilert once confided to Thea that the woman threatened to shoot him with a pistol when they broke off their engagement but that he has never been able to forget her. Hedda convinces Thea that the woman in question must be a redheaded singer in town named Diana. Thea calms down, but these revelations shock Hedda. Thea had the courage to act boldly, Hedda did not, and the contrast between the two reveals the former as the more powerful and dynamic character.

In terms of power, though, no character rivals Judge Brack, the smiling villain who does not really seem so until the very end. His desire to gain power over Hedda and force her to sleep with him at his discretion and whim motivates all of his actions. As catalogued earlier, Aunt Julie allows Judge Brack to arrange the terms of the mortgage for George and Hedda's house, and also loans for furniture and carpets. It was Brack, too, who assured Tesman that the university post was all but certain and encouraged him to marry Hedda and spend money in advance of a formal offer. And it is Brack, too, who frightens Tesman with news that Løvborg might compete for the single university position. He suggests that the Tesmans spend more prudently in the near future until the university renders a final decision. And, finally, Judge Brack hosts the bachelor party at which both Tesman and Løvborg attend and it is at this event that Løvborg falls apart and fails miserably to meet Hedda's admittedly idealized standard of success. Brack arrives allegedly to pick up Tesman for the party, but he comes early via the garden entrance, the back entrance, in order to chat with Hedda in private. She enjoys his company because she can speak frankly with him and because she believes that he has no chance of ever wielding any power over her. Hedda confides that she is already bored with her marriage, that she doesn't love Tesman, and that she married him out of a kind of last-chance desperation. Brack makes it clear that he would like to sleep with her and suggests that a triangular relationship could be very satisfying. Hedda, although flirtatious with the judge, makes it clear that she will not expose herself to potential scandal.

All of the early scenes present Hedda as seemingly dominant and in control, but close examination shows that she is in a much weaker and more precarious position than any of her adversaries. On the one hand, George Tesman cannot believe his good luck that allowed him to marry Hedda Gabler, but on the other he seems to be far more preoccupied with his professional career and standing and the well-being of his two aunts than any concerns about his new wife's needs. Hedda remains an afterthought for him. Hedda frightens and intimidates Aunt Julie, but that does not stop the insinuations and threats from the old woman about the "joyful" prospects of a baby to come. Thea Elvsted naively believes that Hedda is her friend, despite what happened between them as classmates, but her decision to leave her husband in pursuit of Løvborg shocks Hedda to her core because it is an action that the seemingly more confident and outspoken and authoritative woman would never do. While Thea may mistake Hedda for her friend, Hedda makes a greater error by taking Judge Brack into her confidence and not perceiving him as a dangerous and real threat. She flirts with him and never considers the possibility that he is much more manipulative than she and that he can leverage his wealth and social influence to carry out his veiled dark purposes.

Given Hedda's dismal track record of influence over others, the third act brings home more news of failure regarding her latest effort to exert her will. Act 3 begins the morning after the bachelor party at Judge Brack's with Tesman's return home and his description of what happened during the bacchanal. Tesman heard Eilert read from his brilliant new manuscript, but, under the influence of alcohol, Eilert turned the evening into a kind of orgy and ruined any chance of success through his outrageous behavior, including a rambling and incoherent speech in praise of the woman, presumably Thea Elvsted, who inspired his work. Tesman confesses to Hedda that he wished that he had written such a masterpiece, and that he, unnoticed by all the others, saw Eilert accidentally drop his manuscript on the walk home. Tesman rationalizes his decision to pick it up but not return it to Eilert immediately because he feared that his friend was too drunk, but that he intends to return it to him as soon as his friend has a chance to sober up a bit and Tesman gets a little sleep. Hedda urges him not to give back the original and irreplaceable manuscript until she has a chance to read it. Tesman adamantly refuses his wife's request because he knows that Eilert will be beside himself if he realizes the loss. Despite his moral indignation at Hedda's suggestion, Tesman quickly forgets about the plight of his friend when Hedda distracts him with news of the imminent death of Rina, Aunt Julie's sister. An announcement of Brack's arrival further hastens Tesman's retreat to his other aunt's deathbed and Hedda promises to keep the manuscript safe until her husband returns.

Brack stops by, even before he's changed out of his evening clothes, in order to inform Hedda of Eilert's activities and to make certain that he won't be a future fixture in her home. He regards Eilert as a threat to his ideal triangle with the Tesmans and delights in the lurid account of what happened the previous night and the opportunity to destroy Hedda's idealized picture of Løvborg. He tells Hedda that Eilert spent the rest of the night at Mademoiselle Diana's parlor (the redheaded singer referenced by Thea at the beginning of the play) where he had been a favorite in past years. At her place, Løvborg became enraged because he thought someone there had robbed him of something valuable (his manuscript). Løvborg got in a row with a police officer who eventually arrested him and took him to the station house. Hedda cannot hide her disappointment with Eilert's performance (no vine leaves in his hair). Brack explains his motive to speak of Eilert's nocturnal exploits as a preemptive warning for Hedda to close her house to him as indeed all the decent homes will now be closed to him. Brack admits that he's willing to fight to keep his position in the house as the "one cock of the walk" (282). Hedda appraises him as a dangerous character in a "tight corner" and she adds that she is relieved that he has no hold over her at the present. Brack threatens her with a somewhat rhetorical question: "If I had, then who knows just what I might do?" (283). Hedda and Brack banter throughout the course of his prolonged exit via the back way of the garden. Hedda jokingly suggests that she might shoot Brack with one of her pistols, but she does not yet fully realize the dangerous extent of her vulnerability.

Løvborg bursts in and next insists upon talking to both Hedda and Thea at once. He tells Thea that it is time for them to separate and Hedda believes at first that she has won a final victory as Løvborg's muse and inspiration. Thea confronts him about what he's done with the manuscript and Løvborg lies and tells her that he shredded and tossed it into the fjord. Hedda starts to challenge him and say it isn't true, but she stops herself. Løvborg elaborates a self-dramatizing tale of death and destruction: "I've torn my own life to bits. So why not tear up my life's work as well—" (286). Devastated, Thea says that it is as if he'd killed a little child—her child. Once Thea leaves, Hedda, with her rival now seemingly out of the way, questions Løvborg whether or not the situation is so "irredeemable." Løvborg insists that Thea has broken his desire to live his wild life as in the old days and that he cannot return to his former dissolute ways. Hedda cannot fathom how such an innocuous-seeming person could hold such power over him, while she can exert no influence over him. She prods Løvborg to open up to her by calling him heartless for destroying the manuscript and he finally divulges the truth by way of analogy. The worst thing a father can do is not murder a child, he explains, but to lose it carelessly as if the child were unimportant and useless and of no value. Løvborg simply could not tell Thea that he lost his only copy of his manuscript. Hedda rationalizes that it is only a book in the end, but Eilert insists that Thea's "pure soul was in that book" (287). She asks him what he intends to do and he says, rather ambiguously, "Nothing. Just put an end to it all. The sooner the better." Moving to him, Hedda implants the idea in Eilert's mind of a beautiful suicide and gives him one of her pistols as a "souvenir." "You should have used it then," he says, referring to the time when she pointed it at him long ago. "Here! Use it now," she directs him (288). After he leaves she retrieves the manuscript and leafs through a few pages. Then, she sits near the stove, opens its door and begins tossing sheets of the manuscript inside: "Now I'm burning your child, Thea! You, with your curly hair! Your child and Eilert Løvborg's. Now I'm burning—I'm burning the child" (288). Hedda's final snatch at victory over Thea and over Eilert is an act of violence and vengeance as well as self-destruction. If she is unable to have him, no one, especially Thea Elvsted will either. At the same time, Hedda feels that if she were to have a child, it should be with Løvborg and not her husband. As she burns the manuscript, she performs a ritualized abortion.

Act 4 culminates with the failure of Hedda's project and then her own act of escape or defiance. Confident at the outset that Løvborg will carry out her directions, Hedda tries to cover up the tracks of what she has done. Appalled initially, George changes his attitude when Hedda tells him that she burned Eilert's manuscript in order to save his career. That she could show her devotion to him in this way flatters him and causes him to drop immediately all of his protest. Overtaken with the idea that Hedda has "a love that burns" for him, George attributes Hedda's wild actions to an affliction suffered by young married wives (293). Hedda almost tells him that she is pregnant, before stopping and telling him to talk to Aunt Julie about it. Almost beside himself with joy, he cannot contain his excitement about this news and wants to tell the maid and anyone else as soon as possible (292). Before running out to spread the news, Tesman's thoughts return to Eilert and he says that he feels bad about the situation. His hypocrisy strikes Hedda as absurd, as well as the ease with which she can salve his conscience, but Mrs. Elvsted soon arrives having heard rumors that something has happened to Eilert. Judge Brack enters next and confirms that Løvborg has died.

Hedda blurts that she is sure that Løvborg shot himself. Brack regards her suspiciously but verifies that indeed he appears to have committed suicide. He evades the question of where he died but does say that he was shot in the chest. Hedda questions whether or not he was shot in the temple, but concludes to herself that the chest is just as good. Hedda appalls the gathering with her claim that there is "beauty in all this," but she explains: "Eilert Løvborg's settled accounts with himself. He's had the courage to do what—what had to be done" (296). Others dispute this claim, Mrs. Elvsted calling the suicide a product of "delirium," Tesman that of "despair." Mrs. Elvsted says that his addled state of mind must have led him to tear up his manuscript, a statement that surprises Brack and stirs Tesman's guilt. Mrs. Elvsted wonders aloud whether Eilert's manuscript could be pieced back together and Tesman picks up on her hope immediately. Thea says that she kept all his notes that she used for dictation. Together, now, Thea and Tesman move into the inner room and sit down to work collaboratively right away.

Hedda continues to wax poetically about the beauty of Eilert's death and Brack senses that Eilert meant a great deal to her. He then proceeds to inform her about what really happened regarding the circumstances of Løvborg's death. Police found him shot in Mademoiselle Diana's boudoir—he went there again raving about something stolen—a lost child. Brack thought it must have been his manuscript but admits he might be mistaken since Mrs. Elvsted just said that Eilert tore it up himself. He didn't shoot himself in the chest, either, but in the bowels. Revolted by this news, Hedda accepts the failure of her mission. Finally, the pistol Eilert used Brack recognized as Hedda's and the police, he says, will trace it to the owner. An investigation could lead to scandal, Brack asserts, but nothing will happen so long as he remains quiet. Hedda realizes now that Brack holds power and that she is no longer free. Gloating, Brack replies: "One usually manages to adjust to the inevitable" (302). Hedda checks with Tesman and Thea and finds them deep in their reconstruction project already. She notes that Thea has taken her place beside her husband just as she previously took her place next to Eilert Løvborg. Tesman says that he will be very busy in the foreseeable future and that Judge Brack will have to keep Hedda's company. Hedda goes into the inner room to rest, but she very soon begins to play the piano. Tesman bids her not to play and Hedda pokes her head in to say, apologetically, "From now on I'll be quiet" (303). Mrs. Elvsted plans to move in with Aunt Julie in order for she and Tesman to be able to work all the time over there. Judge Brack plans to have Hedda all to himself. "We'll have great times here together, the two of us!" he exclaims (303). On cue, a shot rings out from the inner room that startles Judge Brack: "But good God! People don't *do* such things!" (304). Ironically, Hedda shoots herself through the temple, an act of beauty, as she imagined Løvborg might have done, a desperate act of defiance and resignation designed to escape the tyranny of living under Judge Brack's thumb.

Trapped within the straitlaced and misogynistic and paternal society in the late 19th century, Hedda Gabler nevertheless lacks the necessary courage to disregard the decorum and social customs of the day. That Hedda refuses to follow the dictates of her heart makes for her personal tragedy. That she has a second chance to change her mind and amend her path, but adamantly refuses again to do so is doubly tragic and provides a moral lesson. She cannot make the world up as she likes. Hedda withdraws to an inner room and her eventual offstage suicide thwarts any view of cheap spectacle. Ultimately, though, the gesture does have "a kind of beauty in it" with its steadfast discretion, insistence upon integrity and lack of any accompanying explanation.

Why? Seen in this light, Hedda triumphs over Judge Brack, but also over a theatrical audience that more than likely wants to bring her down from her father's high horse and make her face what she has done. Her disdain for the crowd, as well as her fear of it, whets and sustains her theatrical legacy.

The Master Builder (1892)

> "The young—don't you see, they're retribution—the spearhead of change—as if they came marching under some new flag."

Master Builder Solness fears that Ragnar, a draftsman under his employ, will usurp his stature and surpass his career. He does not tell the young man that he has the talent and promise to develop an independent career for fear that he will launch a capable rival. Instead, he does everything in his power to keep the young man in the dark about his potential to make it on his own. Solness even flirts with Ragnar's fiancé as a means of manipulation and domination, as well as an opportunity for self-exaltation. Fearful of the young man, Solness lets in a young woman from his past, Hilda Wangel, who has traveled some distance to meet him after an absence of almost 20 years. She, not Ragnar, catalyzes Master Solness' destruction. When she was a girl she witnessed the builder cut the ribbon at a ceremony for one of his glorious churches and climb the tower on the building to place a wreath on its highest point. He kissed her, she says, and promised one day to build her a castle in the air. Now, Hilda claims, she has returned to collect on her promise, but she discovers that Solness is not the man he had seemed to be years ago. She considers his petty behavior toward Ragnar, Ragnar's father and Ragnar's fiancé as beneath him, and encourages him to build monumental works and towering achievements that dwarf common homes for ordinary people. Hilda prompts Solness to unleash his inner troll and satisfy his ego needs without simultaneously feeding his guilty conscience. Freed from herd mentality, Solness surprises his wife and apprentice architects at the end by scaling the tower of his newest home and hanging the wreath himself. He had been afraid to make a climb for years, and Ragnar and his contemporaries gather to mock his latest failure. Now, with Hilda proudly looking up from below, Solness stands alone above the fray and shouts to God and the firmament. Suddenly, though, he loses his balance. Master Builder Solness, an artist in the twilight of his career, suspends his dizzy conscience to reclaim his greatness, but ultimately falls to his death in pursuit of the impossible and the unattainable.

The correlation between the fate of Solness and the career of playwright Ibsen is inescapable. Similarly, Ibsen details the final days of another artist, sculptor Arnold Rubek, and his relationship with his female model, in his very last play, *When We Dead Reawaken* (1899). But it is even more remarkable to note how Ibsen critiques and revaluates his dramatic technique in this play quite differently than in any previous effort, beginning with the fact that the female character, Hilda Wangel, reprises her appearance from a previous Ibsen play, *The Lady from the Sea*, a work that also happens to be one of the most satisfying in fulfilling an essentially comic structure, and one that also almost parodies the trope of the dying artist. *The Master Builder*, too, is a strange kind of comedy that undermines the idealism that often surrounds the artist. The play announces its theme as "youth versus age" in the very beginning as the central focus of the play. Ibsen, as he is wont to do, alters and widens this perspective in the unfolding scenes that follow, but returns to it at the end with the inevitable conclusion that comes with such a battle. Solness fights against nature and what is natural—out with the old, in with the new—and loses. So the ruthless comic structure offsets the potential pathos of the aging artist. Within that comic structure, too, Ibsen blows up his favorite device of the "buried secret." Textual evidence verifies in this play that the secret from the past did not and could not have caused the event that shaped the future and distorted the past for Solness. This is important, too, because the action of the play, unlike any other Ibsen play, takes place in Solness' head. If Ibsen's plays explore the limits of the ego and the will, this play goes about as far as Ibsen's technique could show about making the inner processes of the human mind and psyche visible on a stage to a theatrical audience. Hilda Wangel arrives from another Ibsen play in order to function as a screen for Solness to project all his thoughts and feelings. This play lacks the drive of the previous three plays, but the idea of the play is the finest of all and Ibsen takes his exploration of the human will as far as he can take it in the final stage of his playwriting career.

Like the opening of *The Wild Duck*, the first scenes of *The Master Builder* skew the perspective of the main action. Old Knut Brovik, a former architect and now an assistant to Solness, submits his last request to his boss. Before he dies, he wants to see if his son, Ragnar, a draftsman for Solness, has what it takes to be an independent builder and also mentions that he'd like to see Ragnar marry Kaja, the bookkeeper. Solness claims that there is nothing that he can do to help Ragnar, since he simply cannot make up commissions. Brovik counters with a proposal for Ragnar to take the commission from a couple that Solness just dismissed out of hand. Brovik argues that there is plenty of room for more than one builder, but Solness, concerned that Ragnar's new ideas might actually surpass his own, refuses to give up the commission that he said he did not want. Trapped in a corner, Solness does not relent and breaks the old man's heart: "I'm made the way I am!" he exclaims, "I can't change myself over" (314). Sadly, Brovik agrees and slinks away. Solness' refusal to bend and give any ground to youth establishes him as a potentially tragic character, but it also puts him in an unfavorable and unsympathetic light even as it posits his inevitable defeat. How will he win against nature and the decay of the flesh?

Perhaps to compensate for what he knows to be an unfavorable position against the natural order of things, Solness reaffirms his power over Kaja in the next scene. He keeps Kaja from leaving with the Broviks with the pretense of needing to dictate a letter. Privately, he makes sure that she remains devoted to him by inquiring whether or not she is behind the push for Ragnar's independence. With regard to marriage, she tells Solness that she did care for Ragnar at one time—until she met Solness. Now, she says she'll never care for anyone else and wonders if it were possible to continue with Solness in his office even if Ragnar were to leave on his own. Solness, however, flirts with Kaja only as a means to keep Ragnar close because he considers the young man as a potential rival. Just as Solness pushed Ragnar's father out of the way years ago, Solness fears that the son will live to usurp Solness' position. Mrs. Solness (Aline) intervenes and watches the scene with distrust as though she's familiar with her husband's habits with young women. She views Kaja circumspectly as she reports that Dr. Herdal has arrived to see her and would also like to say hello to Solness as well. Solness asks Kaja to bring him Ragnar's drawings to look over and she doesn't suspect that he wants mostly to see whether Ragnar can provide any competition for him. In order to continue his affair with Kaja, Solness convinces her that Ragnar must keep his job.

In the third scene, Dr. Herdal examines Solness and plays the part of his confessor. The "doctor" role is almost a cliché for such a task, but Ibsen develops this expository scene with a dramatic twist at the end. To placate Dr. Herdal, Solness begins a "strange story" that chronicles the root and growth of his relationship with Kaja (320). One day he hatched the idea of hiring her in order to keep Ragnar in the office as well. He said nothing of it, but merely wished for this to transpire with every fiber of his being. Lo and behold, Kaja came to see him the next day and acted as if it were a *fait accompli* and she had already been hired. Once she started working, she began to drift away from Ragnar and toward Solness as if he had some magnetic power. He never explained his real motive for hiring Kaja to Aline because he actually enjoys the "beneficial self-torment" of allowing her to think ill of him. He likens it to a small payment on a "boundless, incalculable debt" (322). It actually eases Solness' burden of guilt for his wife to think ill of him about something that he has not done, when she is completely unaware of the thing he has done to ruin her life. Against Herdal's protestations, Solness insists that he may very well be mad or at least close to madness. He recalls the event that led to the start of his career: the fire that destroyed his first house. Herdal calls it a stroke of luck, but Solness counters that it was his wife's family home that burned. Herdal remembers, too, the terrible event that followed the fire—the death of his two children (although he doesn't refer to the children explicitly here). Still, Herdal sees the event as the spark that ignited Solness' successful career: "But you yourself—*you* rose from those ashes. You began as a poor boy from the country—and now you stand the top man in your field. Ah, yes, Mr. Solness, you've surely had luck on your side" (323). His luck turned into Aline's misfortune. This amazing luck, too, threatens to paralyze Solness with fear as he waits for his luck to change. As if on cue, a knock at the door interrupts the dialogue.

Hilda Wangel enters, not Ragnar Brovik, a pretty young woman in her early twenties dressed in a hiking outfit with sailor blouse and sailor hat, and voices surprise that Solness does not recognize her. Finally it dawns on Solness that he has met her years ago, when she was just a little girl, when he went up and built a tower on the old church up in Lysanger. Hilda confirms that it was ten years ago to the very day that they met. On his way to his other house calls, Dr. Herdal jokes with Solness that youth really did knock at the door this time. Solness laughs, too, thinking that he has dodged another bullet. In fact, though, Hilda Wangel poses a much more grave danger to Solness than Ragnar ever could. Just as Solness has not seen Hilda since she was a very little girl, a theatrical audience has not seen Hilda since she appeared as a supporting character in *The Lady from the Sea* (1888). In that play, Hilda enjoyed a flirtatious and vicarious relationship with a terminally ill young sculptor who was naively unaware of his fate. And, while the drama as a whole critiqued the artist's idealism and outmoded way of thinking, particularly with respect to his sexist views on women and marriage, Hilda stoked her own vivid imagination with idealistic visions of the dying artist. To her sister, Hilda describes the pleasure of watching this romantic spectacle as if she were in the front row of a theatrical event:

> To watch him and to get him to say it isn't serious and that he's going to travel abroad and be an artist. He really believes every bit of it, and it fills him with such a joy. And yet it's all going to come to nothing, absolutely nothing. Because he won't live long enough. When I think of it, it seems so thrilling [*Complete Plays* 61].

Filled with romantic visions of artists and death and dying, Hilda arrives at Solness' door to claim what she says he promised her years ago. She describes the day when Master Builder Solness climbed up the scaffolding surrounding the tower of the church he had built, straight up into the sky, and hung a gigantic wreath on the weather vane. Hilda was one of the schoolchildren dressed in white gathered to watch the ceremony below. Solness now recalls one particular child who screamed so loudly and waved her flag so frenetically that indeed he became dizzy and almost fell. That little "devil,"

Hilda admits, was her, and Solness agrees that it must have been. Hilda recalls that she never experienced anything as exceptional as this event in her entire life. Hilda remembers him singing from on high as well, although Solness assures her that he's never sung a note in his life. Hilda claims that he told her that one day she could be his princess. Solness would return in ten years, according to Hilda's story, and carry her off like a troll to some foreign land where he would buy her a kingdom. He bent her back, according to her, and kissed her many times.

Solness adamantly denies that he ever did such a thing. At first, he says she must have dreamed the event. Then he changes tack and says that it must have been his own thoughts that created, willed and desired the very things that Hilda describes. Finally, though, seeing that Hilda is unmoved, Solness confesses that everything happened just as Hilda said it did, though it is not clear that things really did happen that way. Now, he wants to know, what happened between them after that event. Hilda reminds him, however, that it is now exactly ten years to the day since he made his promise to her. Solness can't believe that she seriously believed that he would return and make good on what was probably a bit of a joke at the time. Hilda assures him that she did not think of it as a joke, that she truly expected him to carry her off "like a troll" (333). Solness wonders aloud if she is playing with him, whether she really means what she says and he asks her if she knew that he was married and she says that she certainly did. Nevertheless, she's come to demand her kingdom! Solness confesses that he doesn't build large towers above churches any more, only "homes for human beings" (334). Hilda asks whether he could build even a small tower over a modest home and Solness says that that is exactly what he has wanted to do, but that the public won't tolerate it. He is building a new home now, however, and it has such a tower that is very high. Solness now seems glad that Hilda has come and he sees her as the answer to his search that has been ongoing for many years. He's alone, he tells her, and he's grown afraid of the new and the young. Hilda suggests that instead of trying to block them, he should "open your door to the young" and welcome change. He can't possibly do that, he explains: "The young—don't you see, they're retribution—the spearhead of change—as if they came marching under some new flag" (336).

An enormous burden of guilt holds Solness back from building anything new. The opening scene of Act 2, the following morning, features dialogue between Solness and his wife, Aline, in which he tries to assure her that things will get much better when they move into their new house. He concedes that the fire that burned their former home to the ground was a "terrible blow for you," but Aline emphasizes that Solness can never build a new home to replace what she lost (340). She does not blame him for the disaster; mere bad luck, she believes, caused the fire. Solness, on the other hand, feels responsible for what happened and that he must atone for it. Aline also suffers from guilt. Her children, it turns out, did not die in the flames. She cannot forgive herself for what happened after the fire when she became weak and sick and her babies took ill from her and subsequently died. She blames herself for not being strong enough and Solness begs her not to think about it any more. The future holds no promise of any change, she asserts: "It can never be different. Just as empty—just as barren—there as here" (341). When Solness asks why, then, they decided to build a new house, Aline treats the question as rhetorical and suggests that Solness look introspectively for the answer. In return, he accuses her of hidden meanings and silent reproaches and even harboring thoughts about his sanity. He's not mad, he then says, but he does suffer, he admits, from an incalculable debt to his wife. When she asks him to explain, Solness still proves somewhat elusive: "I've never done anything against you—not that I've ever known. And yet—there's this sense of some enormous guilt hanging over me, crushing me down." Without hearing the full story, Aline agrees now that her husband must be very ill to imagine such things. "I suppose so—something like that," Solness replies, before his mood lifts with Hilda's entrance: "But it's brightening up" (342). Hilda, young and fresh and vibrant in the morning light, does not truck with guilt.

Dialogue between Hilda and Solness dominates the rest of the act. Solness concludes, at one point that he must have willed Hilda to come to him. Indeed, she functions less as an independent character than a blank canvas upon which Solness projects his inner thoughts and feelings. His belief in his own special powers to will Hilda to him, not unlike how he earlier spoke of Kaja, gets to the heart of the buried secret in this play and how it functions in a unique way in concert with Solness' brand of magical thinking. Hilda's rebellion against traditional morality appeals to Solness because she gives voice to thoughts about such things as duty and ambition that Solness has never felt free to express. He explains to her how the tragic fire launched his career as a builder. The price of success, however, was his wife's happiness and his two infant sons' lives. His awful good luck has caused him to give up any hope of future happiness. Hilda interjects that the fire could not possibly have been Solness' fault, but he stops her by saying that that is precisely the riddle of the whole tragic situation. He is both innocent and guilty—because he wanted the fire and believes that he willed it to happen. Hilda responds to him as if he were mentally ill. The buried secret in the past, the cracked chimney that Solness detected in his home and hoped would start a fire, was definitely not the cause of the eventual fire that engulfed the home. Still, Solness feels guilty about his dark thoughts. Hilda wishes his conscience were more "robust" so that he could pursue what he wanted in the world (356). Solness comes alive with the recognition that he and Hilda possess similar "trolls" that threaten to lead them astray. Emboldened by Hilda, Solness finally agrees to write a complimentary word on Ragnar's drawings and he summons Kaja to dismiss her from his employ. Aline, who witnesses these decisions, reasons that her husband must merely have replaced Kaja with Hilda, but Solness shocks her with his vow to climb the tower on his new house to hang the ceremonial wreath. Alone again with Hilda, Solness promises to give her the kingdom that she has demanded from the beginning and which he promised her ten years ago.

Just as the second act began with a scene between Solness and Aline in which they gave voice to their guilty feelings, a parallel scene between Hilda and Aline opens the third and final act with an admission that changes the course of the drama. Sitting on the veranda with a view of the scaffolding surrounding the new house, Hilda asks Aline whether she is happy about moving in to the new house and, while she admits that she *should* be happy because her husband would like her to be happy, she is not. Mrs. Solness subjugates her own desires and will to an idea of "duty" that enslaves her. Both she and her husband shut down their egos in efforts to atone for what they think they might have done in the past. Hilda assumes that Aline still suffers from the deaths of her two children. Surprisingly, Aline asserts that the deaths of her two boys were acts of Providence for which she should be grateful. What disturbs her the most on a daily basis, she confesses, are the dolls, surrogate children, that she lost in the fire. Just as Solness feels guilty about his role in the fire and even feels that his thoughts or powers caused the blaze, Aline feels guilty about her attachment to the inanimate dolls, relics from her own childhood, that burned up and can never be replaced and about which no one even thinks to ask. Faced with the loss of her real children, there is simply no proper or accepted venue to mourn the loss of the dolls. Yet, in a very real way, the emotional attachment to the childhood dolls constituted a significant part of Aline's identity and it was as though she shriveled up and burned along with the house belongings. Relieved to be able to tell someone about this loss, she is also glad that Hilda does not laugh at her.

Solness surmises upon entering that his wife must have been brooding to Hilda about the dead twins. Hilda informs him that she has now decided to go away before her affair with Solness escalates. She could take the place of a stranger, but now that she has gotten to know Mrs. Solness she cannot injure her. Against Solness' protestations, Hilda, in a remarkable reversal of her previous stance, advises him to do his proper duty by his wife. It's too late for that, Solness replies, because the devils have had their way with him and led him to Hilda. His awful good luck has ruined him again and robbed him of the joy of life! He tells Hilda that his career is over that he has no new plans to build anything at this point. Hilda assesses the situation in which they find themselves as "senseless," but Solness maintains that the obstacle to his happiness is someone whom he has no right to leave and that it is his duty to remain faithful in marriage to his wife (370). In order to pursue his object of desire Solness would need a "robust conscience" (371). Solness promised Hilda a kingdom once, and every kingdom has a castle—and that's what Solness must build for her. They joke and tease one another as they imagine the ideal castle for Princess Hilda: tall on every side with an enormous tower, "free on every side." Solness promises to climb up and join Hilda in the tower. Hilda elaborates that they will work together to build beautiful things in the future. The most beautiful thing in the world is a "castle in the air," she says, and they are easy to construct: "Especially for builders who have a—dizzy conscience" (372). The imaginary is the only realm in which Solness can succeed while his feet remain firmly on the ground.

He vows to build Hilda's castles in the air if she will go with him hand in hand. She demands that he climb the tower in order to prove his devotion to her: "Then let me see you high and free, up there!" she cries. He's afraid to do it but Hilda urges him to attempt the "impossible" (380). Ragnar and all the witnesses who attend the ceremony for the new house doubt that Solness has the courage or the inclination to ascend the tower. When an onlooker spots a figure on the climb, the assembled group assumes that it is the foreman. To their collective horror and great astonishment, they soon realize that it is Solness on the scaffold and they mark his progress with dread and anticipation as the figure rises in the distant offstage space. After reaching the top and placing the wreath and waving his hat, all things that he said he would do, the crowd watches in horror as he loses his balance and begins to fall. Hilda, "as if petrified," speaks: "*My* master builder" (383). After reports filter through that he is dead—that he fell on the quarry rocks and that his head has been crushed, Ragnar says that, in the end, Solness couldn't make the climb. But Hilda has the last word: "But he went straight, straight to the top. And I heard harps in the air" (384). She remains transfixed in "dazed triumph" upon the tower from which Solness fell.

The graphic description of Solness' crushed head, akin to the particulars of Eilert Løvborg's suicide in *Hedda Gabler*, undercuts the highly romanticized vision of the tragic hero that Hilda's uplifted face tries to reflect. The spectacle of Solness' rise up the tower and subsequent fall thrills her and a theatrical audience gets to see her reaction to the offstage event. In fact, her position as a spectator recalls the views of Hilda Wangel from *The Lady from the Sea* in which she excitedly spoke of watching the death of Lyngstrand, the young and terminally ill artist, with romantic pleasure. When asked by her sister about the root of such pleasure, Hilda claimed that it was enjoyable to watch as a spectacle because nothing would come of it. Lyngstrand's pose as an artist amounted only to so much playacting, and Hilda responded to it as an interested audience member attending an entertaining play. The fact that it was not real, that it had no basis in reality, that Lyngstrand would never do any of the things that he said he was going to do, allowed Hilda to imagine circumstances as if she were attending a play. Correspondingly, Solness voices frustration near the end of the play to Hilda that everything that he has done has amounted to very little and does not count for much. He uses the same kind of language to describe his career's work that Hilda uses to appraise Lyngstrand's accomplishments in the earlier play: "Nothing really built. And nothing sacrificed for the chance to build, either. Nothing, nothing—it all comes to nothing" (379). Solness cannot build "castles in the air" and his pursuit of that objective, stoked by Hilda's encouragement, ends predictably with his death that might seem tragic—an heroic attempt to transcend human limitations—if it were not the inevitable and necessary consequence of his vastly inflated ego.

The death of Solness actually fulfills the comic structure in which old age gives way for youth and, just so, young Ragnar emerges as the hero of the play. The meanness and smallness and pettiness of Solness toward Ragnar, who only begs for a good word or two that he can bring back to his dying father's bedside appalls even Hilda. That Solness could refuse to make a dying man proud, happy and content is almost despicable to her and she labels his actions as "hard," "wicked," and "cruel" (353). Despite the fact that Solness ultimately relents under pressure from Hilda and writes a few kind notes on Ragnar's drawings, the son later reports that his father suffered a stroke and did not receive the pages in time. Solness encourages him to stay home with his family, but Ragnar insists upon attending the house ceremony and he is intent, along with all the other apprentices, to humiliate Solness when he fails to climb the tower. Ragnar, like Aline in an earlier scene, views Hilda as the replacement for Kaja in Solness' life and warns Hilda that Solness will take possession of her mind just as he did Kaja's. Hilda realizes that her desires come dangerously close to those of Kaja's, but she blunts the attack by informing him that Solness only kept Kaja close as a means to keep Ragnar. This thought pleases Ragnar and he enjoys the thought that the great master builder might actually fear him. He regrets that Solness kept him down for so many years and made him doubt his own talents and now gathers with many other young architects and builders to watch and gloat over Solness' public failure. Even Ragnar, though, is impressed that Hilda witnessed Solness climb a high tower once. Hilda proudly says that he is going to do it today, but Ragnar doubts that it will ever happen again. Solness' ascent up the tower amazes Ragnar because the younger man knows how much fear that his mentor must have overcome in order to make the attempt. He quickly negates the entire experience as soon as he realizes that Solness has died in a catastrophic fall: "How horrible this is. And so, after all—he really couldn't do it" (384). Those are his final words in the play, the voice of a realist perhaps, but one who briefly had hopes, even after all that he had suffered at the expense of Solness, that the master builder would actually succeed. The death of Solness frees Ragnar to emerge as the new master builder. Youth wins, as it always and inevitably must against old age. It remains very much an open question as to what and how much Ragnar has learned from the experience of Master Builder Solness' rise and fall.

PART 2

Chekhov
Life in the Subjunctive Mood

Konstantin Stanislavsky, the great Russian actor, director and teacher, began research in earnest on what would become his system of acting in 1906, only two years after Chekhov's death, with the intent to unlock the creative imagination through conscious techniques. Based upon his experiences on the stage, Stanislavsky had become increasingly aware of the variability of one performance from another in the same production due to differing degrees of inspiration on any given occasion. How could he offset the dulling effects of repetition from one performance to the next, he wondered, without drawing upon the actor's need for a creative surge of heroic insight and energy when the curtain rose? He reasoned that a series of mental techniques and physical exercises that related to the circumstances of a specific role could help the actor to establish a fundamental standard of performance that could tolerate the natural variance of a repeated theatrical performance. At the same time, he concluded that reliance upon certain principles and techniques could actually liberate the actor in performance and spark creativity, imagination and natural ability to flourish.

One of the core techniques of Stanislavsky's approach to achieving truth and believability on stage is something called the "magic if," whereby the actor recognizes and accounts for the circumstances of the fictional situation, but yet pretends that they are true. In his autobiography, *My Life in Art*, Stanislavsky gives voice to the actor's credo: "All these properties, make-ups, costumes, the scenery, the publicness of the performance, are lies. I know they are lies, I know I do not need any of them. But *if* they were true, then I would do this and this, and I would behave in this manner and this way towards this and this event" (466). In this manner, according to Stanislavsky, the actor recognizes the reality or truthfulness of the performance dynamic and simultaneously commits to the fiction of the dramatic situation. "What would I do," the actor asks, "if I were this character in these given circumstances?" This fundamental question begins the process of character interpretation: "From the moment of the appearance of *if* the actor passes from the plane of actual reality into the plane of another life, created and imagined by himself. Believing in this life, the actor can begin to create" (466). Stanislavsky (1863–1938) published his theories of acting at the end of his career and then posthumously in a series of books beginning with *An Actor Prepares* (1936), and followed by *Building a Character* (1949) and *Creating a Role* (1961). In the third chapter of the first book, "Action," Stanislavsky, masquerading as the Director Tortsov, again emphasizes the importance of the "magic if" to the actor: "*if* acts as a lever to lift us out of the world of actuality into the realm of imagination" (*Actor Prepares* 43). Previously in the same chapter, he makes a bold statement regarding the desire to escape the mundane trappings of everyday life: "Every person who is really an artist desires to create inside of himself another, deeper, more interesting life than the one that actually surrounds him" (41). While he talks specifically about artists and the artistic impulse, this statement has a much more narrow application and a much deeper impact when related to the works and worldview of Anton Chekhov.

Despite having previously acted in and directed all four of Chekhov's major plays at the Moscow Art Theatre, including *The Seagull* (1898), *Uncle Vanya* (1899), *Three Sisters* (1901) and *The Cherry Orchard* (1904), Stanislavsky failed to notice any connection or similarity between his acting theories regarding the "magic if," and similar subjunctive statements espoused by Chekhovian characters in all of the plays.[18] Chekhov, ironically enough, often did not agree with Stanislavsky's interpretation of the plays. In fact, Stanislavsky frequently assumed the wrong roles for himself in Chekhov's plays, and consistently misread them as far as the playwright was concerned. And Stanislavsky treated Chekhov's plays far more realistically than the playwright had conceived them.[19] While the productions were notably heavy in atmospheric mood, including cricket chirps, Stanislavsky paid little attention to the prevailing grammatical mood that dominates each play. The subjunctive mood expresses a condition that is doubtful or contrary to fact. In Chekhov, the subjunctive comes in to play most when characters employ Stanislavsky's "magic if" as a means of escape from the facts of the boring circumstances in which they find themselves.

If I could only be or do this, the Chekhovian character reasons, I would be content. But, in a twist, the subjunctive mood necessarily defers attainment of desire. In *Three Sisters*, for example, the Prozorovs depend upon not going to Moscow in order to talk about their future happiness when they will go to Moscow. As long as they do not actually go, then they can say that they would be happy if they did. And, of course, in that play, when they encounter Colonel Vershinin, the Lovesick Major from their childhood, their disappointment stems from the fact that the reality of him now, not the fantasy of him as they remember from years ago, forces them to think by extension of Moscow as a real place, too, as a place that has changed over time and is not just a locale of idealized dreams, an abstract concept in which to place all one's hopes and dreams for the future. Moscow, in the aging face of Vershinin, loses its romantic luster (*Plays* 264–268).[20] The "magic if" for the characters allows them also to think of themselves as dramatic characters—as Hamlet, as the Man in the Iron Mask, as a Schopenhauer or a Dostoevsky, as a tragic heroine from Pushkin, or a doomed tragic figure in a romantic novel—and thus fantasize about an existence that has no basis in reality.

Contemporary critic Vladimir Kataev, whose book *If Only We Could Know! An Interpretation of Chekhov* invokes the subjunctive by quoting the curtain line of *Three Sisters*, highlights the unrealized aspirations and yearnings of all the characters in *The Cherry Orchard*: "[They] have their hopes and dreams, great and small, comic or moving, realizable or obviously impracticable. Chekhov points out unceasingly that these hopes and dreams are formulated and expressed in an identical way: the frequency with which the *subjunctive mood* (if only...) occurs in the characters' monologues and dialogues is extremely high" (277–278). The subjunctive mood in Chekhov creates an alternative and hypothetical world and existence in which characters imagine life without any consequences. Konstantin is a brilliant writer in love with Nina; Vanya is a great thinker and scholar; likewise, Andrei Prozorov is a brilliant professor at the University of Moscow in *Three Sisters* and Masha, Olga and Irina all live happily there, having moved from their home in the provinces to the big city. Of course, as Chekhov might say, this is all nonsense. None of these dreams comes true, but the power of the subjunctive mood breathes life into the lives of the characters just as surely as the "magic if" sparks the creative imagination of the actor on stage.

Just as Stanislavsky asserts that actors long to create a more interesting life on stage than the one that surrounds them in ordinary life, so, too, Chekhovian characters dramatize their lives and adopt artistic and literary models as their ideals for living. *The Seagull*, Chekhov's play about art and artists, is a natural venue to see this principle at work. Indeed, Masha reveals herself as aspiring to a dramatic life with her first entrance and the very beginning of the play when she announces that she is "in mourning for my life" (111). Masha poses as a dramatic character and parrots melodramatic lines that sound comically overblown and inauthentic. The writer Trigorin later observes, she "takes snuff, drinks ... always wears black" (132). In this way, Chekhov dramatizes exponentially by creating a dramatic character that aspires to become a dramatic character. Old Sorin, a lifetime minor bureaucrat, explains his habit of drinking sherry and smoking cigars as his desire to live. He needs to add something to his ordinary routine, he says, in order to give him the sense that he is alive, though Dr. Dorn warns that when he does such things, "you are no longer the real you" (128). Even the artistic characters, though, resort to theatrical behavior in order to express themselves fully. When Trigorin threatens to run away with Nina, the actress Arkadina stops him with a tearful, passionate monologue that resembles the dialogue from the melodramas in which she frequently stars. Trigorin, for his part, woos Nina with a speech that appears to eschew fame and celebrity—he claims he would be happy if he were able to do nothing but fish in the nearby lake—but this self-effacing speech is exactly the means to seduce a naïve and provincial young girl. Nina, too, in her final appearance, makes a long speech in which she claims to have discovered the meaning of life, but the allusions to Konstantin's little play as well as to Pushkin suggest that she struggles to convince herself fully that she has found her purpose.

Nina clings to a dramatic model of behavior in this final scene, the stoic heroine, and prompts critic Richard Gilman to see her as the redemptive figure for suffering and the one who will live "bravely and with honor." Gilman elaborates in *Chekhov's Plays: An Opening into Eternity*:

> Something essential has been saved out of the entire human substance of the play, the principle of relief from fatality that governs all comedy is now in place, so that the imaginative balance is toward what remains, not what has been lost. Konstantin is the cautionary figure in this dramatic positioning of selves and self-questioning, as Nina is its force of redemptive acceptance [99].

Gilman believes in the sincerity of what Nina says and claims that she has matured and that "she has learned what it means to be an artist" (94). Perhaps, but Chekhov undercuts idealism with irony and positions Nina as a self-dramatizing, self-sacrificing victim on the altar of art. Nina raves madly about her desperate situation and repeatedly likens herself to a seagull and the art for which she suffers in reality amounts to performing in front of men who leer at her in backwater outposts such as Yelets. Despite her self-delusions, Nina recalls images of childhood and the rural environment around a beautiful lake that she left behind to pursue a career as an actress. She hints at what she missed, but she does not return to that innocent world.

With its focus on art and artists, *The Seagull* is easily the most theatrical of Chekhov's plays, but characters in all his plays display theatrical behavior as a means of adding significance to otherwise mundane lives. Dr. Astrov in *Uncle Vanya* plays the part of matinee idol and Yelena, the old professor's young wife, functions as a kind of temptress. Even a supporting character such as Telegin, nicknamed Waffles because of his acne, plays the stock part of a jilted and forsaken lover. In *Three Sisters*, Solyony imitates the poet Lermontov, and Tuzenbach retires from the military and changes clothes in order to fashion a new look as a private citizen. Chekhov's last play, *The Cherry*

Orchard, presents the most dramatic characters of all his plays. The maid Dunyasha plays the part of a coquette; Yepikhodov presents as an unlucky and ill-fated buffoon; the footman Yasha pretends to be a worldly man of taste and sophistication; the eternal student Trofimov holds to his lofty ideals as a defense against growing up; Carlotta performs magic tricks and presents herself as a woman of mystery; Gayev bumbles his way through conversations by miming billiard shots; the old retainer Firs performs senility and invokes the virtues of the distant past as a defense against meaningful interactions in the present. Madame Ranyevskaya, the most theatricalized of all, sweeps into rooms and brandishes telegrams from her Parisian lover that beg her to return, and then casually discards them as if she did not care. All the characters, then, demonstrate dramatic behavior and aspire to theatrical models that heighten experience. They do what Dr. Dorn accuses Sorin of in *The Seagull*: "You smoke a cigar or take a drink of vodka, and you're no longer Pyotr Nikolayevich—you're Pyotr Nikolayevich plus something else, something that gives you a new identity, and you start thinking and behaving as if you were another individual entirely" (127–128).

In terms of action, reliance upon the subjunctive mood negates the need to do anything. The "magic if" for Chekhov creates a drama of stasis in which time becomes the subject of each play. Particularly in his last two plays, *Three Sisters* and *The Cherry Orchard*, whether it has been ten years since father died or the impending auction of the estate on August 23, time ticks inexorably. Why don't the characters do anything to better their lives or forestall unfortunate or unwanted events? Richard Gilman sees perceptively in Chekhov a similarity to Samuel Beckett: "all of Beckett's characters and nearly all of Chekhov's are reduced to the essential tasks of getting through the days and nights, making their way, with what is left to them, through time" (*Chekhov's Plays* 80). There is "Nothing to be done," as Estragon says in the opening line of *Waiting for Godot* (7). Later, in his essay on *Three Sisters*, Gilman emphasizes the daily struggle of characters to get through the days of their lives:

> Time passes or stretches out, time surrounds, and things are lost in it, continuously, without fail. Nothing is salvaged except as traces in the spirit and through the valor of the art. For the play's beauty lies in the recognition it gives, the enactment, of deprivation and diminishment as our condition, the essence of what we go through and, in struggle and doubtfulness, either come to terms with or evade [*Chekhov's Plays* 194].

While the dramatic spectacle in Chekhov produces laughter with recognition that characters lack self-knowledge, it is impossible to laugh at them without also admiring their struggle and their heroic attempts to withstand and endure the vicissitudes of fate and fortune. Unlike Ibsen's characters that pursue a goal as a dog might dive after a wild duck that has sunk to the bottom of a lake, Chekhovian characters avoid doing what they say they want to do. To pursue a goal is to progress consciously in time toward the inevitability of death. The subjunctive mood, on the other hand, provides an escape and an inspiration, similar to the one that an actor might have on stage, for a life of creative imagination that refuses to embrace the rhythmic repetitiveness of everyday life.

Chekhov's radical new drama substitutes the subjunctive "magic if" for indicative realities. Konstantin, the young writer in *The Seagull*, seems to speak for Chekhov when he makes an impassioned declaration regarding the state of the art: "What we need are new forms! We need new forms, and if we can't have them, then we're better off with no theater at all" (114). He goes on to explain his ideals for a new kind of theater: "We have to show life not the way it is, or the way it should be, but the way it is in dreams!" (116). Interestingly and perhaps not coincidentally, Stanislavsky, discussing his work in *My Life in Art* that led to his new system of acting, expressed his thoughts in a manner very similar to that of Konstantin in the play: "It was necessary to picture not life itself as it takes place in reality, but as we vaguely feel it in our dreams, our visions, our moments of spiritual uplift" (434). Stanislavsky identified with Konstantin and treated the character in *The Seagull* as if he were the very voice of the playwright. Stanislavsky's interpretation of all Chekhov's works agrees entirely with the aesthetic that Konstantin espouses in Chekhov's first success. About Chekhov, the Russian theater legend says:

> Read him in the kitchen of life, and you will find nothing in him but the simple plot, mosquitoes, crickets, boredom, gray little people. But take him where art soars, and you will feel in the everyday plots of his plays the eternal longings of man for happiness, his striving upwards, the true aroma of Russian poetry, in no smaller measure than it is felt in Turgenev. There you will understand the talented work of Treplev [Konstantin], and in his rules of the theatre you will recognize a great deal that is important for the art at all times, something like what Hamlet says in his scene with the actors [*My Life* 347].

Chekhov tinges his portrayal of Konstantin with much more ironic complexity than Stanislavsky admits. While Konstantin and Stanislavsky valorize the search for a new plane of existence, Chekhov is not nearly as rhapsodic about the future, say, as are his characters. Chekhov satirizes the creative effort of Konstantin and pokes holes in that righteous, youthful character's folly. At the same time, Konstantin's little play mocks Chekhov's dramaturgy of indolent life on the Russian estate. At most, one can say that both the playwright and character agree that something is wrong with the contemporary theater and the problems that Konstantin articulates are the very ones that Chekhov, as well as Ibsen and Strindberg, try to solve with their unique contributions to modern drama. It is tempting to champion, as Stanislavsky does, Konstantin's idealistic vision for a new kind of theatrical experience, but Chekhov shows that while Konstantin may be right about what is wrong with the contemporary theater, he does not have the talent or ability to fix it.

Complicated feelings toward his actress-mother temper Konstantin's critique of the contemporary theater. His comments come prior to the performance of his new play and he both wants to impress her and to compete with her and prove his own artistic mettle. But, even more than her artistic approval, he wants her love and he is never able to get that in the full measure that he desires. Having said that, what Konstantin says about the contemporary theater in the late 19th century is accurate and demonstrates the need for a new kind of drama. With respect to the type of commercial plays in which his mother stars, Konstantin explicitly mentions two titles, *Camille* and *The Fumes of Life*. *La Dame aux Camélias* by Alexandre Dumas, *fils*, from his novel, first produced in 1852, has featured many famous actresses in its international history, including Eleonora Duse, Sarah Bernhardt, Helena Modjeska, and Greta Garbo in the American film. More recently, Charles Ludlam played the role in drag beginning in 1973 and many times later at his Ridiculous Theatrical Company. *The Fumes of Life* by Bóleslav Markevich (1822–1884), a reworking of his own novel, *The Abyss*, is largely unknown today and Chekhov might have referenced it for personal reasons. Translator Paul Schmidt added this quote from Chekhov regarding Markevich's play in the notes to *The Seagull*: "Chekhov hated this kind of writing and promised his editor to write a parody of it" (161). Donald Rayfield's biography of Chekhov includes another delicious note that reveals Chekhov's feelings for his fellow Russian writer, who, of course, was famous long before Chekhov. In June 1884 Markevich was living in a comfortable dacha near where Chekhov lived at the time. Chekhov told his editor, Nikolai Leikin, in August: "This Kammerjunker has angina and will probably give you material for an obituary." Markevich died in November and the owners of the estate offered the Chekhovs his dacha (106).

In his critique of his mother's kind of theater, the commercial theater, Konstantin decries, first of all, its banality of appearances, and then its simplicity of meanings:

> The curtain goes up, the lights come on, you're in a room with three walls, and there they are, these servants of art, and all they do is show us how people eat, drink, make love, walk, and wear clothes! And then they try to draw some kind of moral, some nice *easy* little moral, something you wouldn't mind having around the house. You go, they give you the same stuff over and over and over ... and it makes me sick! I want to run away from it all, the way Maupassant ran away from the Eiffel Tower, he thought it was so ugly and vulgar [*Plays* 114].

The onstage behavior that Konstantin finds so offensive could at first glance be applied to Chekhov's plays as well. The playwright expressed his artistic credo in an oft-quoted statement: "Let the things that happen on stage be just as complex and yet just as simple as they are in life. For instance, people are having a meal, just having a meal, but at the same time their happiness is being created, or their lives are being smashed up" (Brustein 154). Of course, Chekhov differentiates himself from other writers, including those to whom Konstantin refers, by making the meals, conversations, love affairs, etc., the foundational rhythm of life that the drama interrupts. The characters on stage behave as regular folk even though they aspire to attain the status of dramatic characters in other works of literature. This is the exact opposite of the kind of characters that Konstantin criticizes: dramatic characters who try to pass themselves off as regular people in the name of great art, all the time showing themselves off to be some kind of superior people. In plays such as *Camille*, dramatic actors attempt to pass themselves off as everyday people even as they wield all the artificial tricks of the theater. Chekhov presents everyday people who aspire to be dramatic characters or at least worthy of being the subject of dramas.

Camille offers beautiful costumes worn by beautiful people, a romantic plot, dramatic acting scenes, themes of undying love and self-sacrifice, and a whiff of moral turpitude mixed with sexual licentiousness, as well as accompanying hypocrisy, and provides an excellent example for what ails the theater according to Konstantin. The easy little moral at the play's center is summed up best by Marguerite's own statement: "And so, whatever she may do, the woman, once she has fallen can never rise again. God may forgive her, perhaps, the world never" (Dumas fils 140–141). The courtesan with the honest heart of gold has been ill due to the hazards of her lifestyle and displays the telltale cough of tuberculosis from the beginning of the drama. Young and dashing Armand pays her a visit and shortly thereafter declares that he has always loved her and she finally admits to loving him in return. Just at the moment when it appears their mutual happiness will be assured, Armand's father arrives to beg Marguerite to forsake her lover, his son, in order to remove the stain on the Duval family name that prevents Armand's sister from marrying into proper society. Marguerite sends her lover away and he only comes back at the very end when he has found out why she did what she did. Unfortunately, he is too late. Marguerite's heart remains strong but her consumptive lungs collapse and so does she into her lover's embrace as the curtain falls.

The drama, as countless productions have proven, makes for exciting and affective theatrical production by exploiting the twists and turns of its plot for great effect. Yet, in direct proportion to the undeniable theatricality of it all, the play offers no substantive critique of contemporary life. The completely conventional morality of the play, for example, sentences Marguerite to die practically before the play begins. There is no hint, really, at any other alternative choice. In the hands of another playwright, the theme of undying, passionate love might be investigated and critiqued as being something other than unquestionably positive and desirable. Armand claims that he has loved Marguerite since he first saw her years ago, but he has never spoken to her until the time of the play. He loves her, perhaps, but he does not know her. And, to whet his appetite for love, he has followed Marguerite for years and virtually stalked her: "If I were to tell you that I have passed whole nights beneath your windows and that for two months I have treasured a glove that you dropped..." he explains to her (121). Love for Armand crosses the border, perhaps, into obsession, but the real texture of his emotional feelings for her are never developed beyond the flatness of his declaration. Marguerite may be a courtesan and doomed to an early death for atonement of her sins, but within the fiction of the drama both she and Armand are "good" people in possession of fully undiluted virtues. The action skillfully manipulates the feelings of an audience, perhaps, but it certainly doesn't provoke an audience to think about the obsessive nature of love and the strange beliefs of a society that would impose the death penalty upon Marguerite for, in her polite words, loving too much. Good, effective, and theatrical scenes substitute for a critique or a questioning of modern society and its inhabitants.

Konstantin's play in *The Seagull* revolts against every aspect of the kind of theater represented in *Camille*. Instead of dialogue, he presents a monologue; instead of painted scenery, interior rooms, and lavish costumes, Konstantin puts a single actor on a bare stage with unadorned nature as the only backdrop; instead of intrigue drama and contemporary events, he focuses on the future: "make us dream of what this place will be two hundred thousand years from now!" (118). As such, the little play that opens the first of four major plays for Chekhov seems to parody the playwright's work as well with its dramatization of future life on the planet. In all the Chekhovian plays there is endless talk, or "philosophizing," about what life will be like in the future, especially in *Three Sisters* and the speeches by Vershinin and Tuzenbach. Here, though, Chekhov, through the experimental writings of his character, Konstantin, actually dramatizes what the future will look like to great comic effect. The role of the "World Soul" portrayed by Konstantin's girlfriend, Nina, must stand alone onstage and narrate about the current state of the universe:

> For more than a thousand centuries the earth has been lifeless, no single living creature yet remains.... And the weary moon in heaven lights her lamp in vain. The cranes in the meadows awake no more; their cries are silent; the flight of beetles in the linden woods is stilled. All is cold, cold, cold. All is empty, empty, empty. All is terror, terror, terror [118].

It is not surprising that the audience, led by Konstantin's mother, Arkadina, quickly grows restless and cracks enough jokes about the play to infuriate Konstantin and prematurely bring down the curtain. Who could take this stuff seriously? Yet, as wobbly and amateurish as Konstantin's initial dramatic effort seems to be, it does possess a kind of hypnotic and natural beauty, also, that haunts *The Seagull*. While Konstantin's dramatic text may be poor, his creation of a space for the event shows talent and imagination and he is confident about the merits of his new kind of drama. Before the play begins, he extols the virtues of his new kind of theater to his Uncle Sorin: "Now, this is what I call a theater! A curtain, two wings, right and left, and then nothing. No set. Empty space! The curtain opens, all you see is the lake and the far horizon. And the curtain will open at exactly eight-thirty, just as the moon rises" (113).

Predictably, Arkadina takes offense and labels her son's effort as "Symbolist raving" and denigrates his new form of art as "just old-fashioned nastiness" (120). The fact that he did not write a traditional play of the sort that she usually performs strikes her as a personal attack. The fact that she links it with the Symbolist movement of the 1890s reveals her genuine fear of the new age in modern drama that threatens to displace her. Given the inherent symbolism of Chekhov's title, too, *The Seagull*, Arkadina's attack also puts Chekhov's own aesthetic in conversation in the play, yet the playwright cleverly mocks the symbolism and drains the title of possible meanings. The over-determined bird in Chekhov's play appears as a metaphor, a literary allusion (to both Ibsen and Pushkin), as a material object (the dead bird that Konstantin presents to Nina in Act 2 that, somewhat hilariously, remains onstage for the rest of the act), and finally, as a stuffed and mounted taxidermy specimen in Act 4 two years later. The ubiquitous bird loses meaning through its various presentations and many forms.

Despite Arkadina's outburst, Konstantin's play receives positive reactions as well from the assembled guests. His rival, the writer Trigorin, his mother's lover, admits that he didn't understand the play at all but that he felt that the scenery was beautiful. Of course, he says this after his introduction to Nina and he considers the young ingénue as part of the scenery! Dr Dorn is the most appreciative of Konstantin's work and he goes out of his way to compliment the young man and to encourage him to keep writing. As a middle-aged medical doctor, Dorn figures to be the man of reason in the play and indeed he seems to spout a lot of common sense throughout the play. He admires Konstantin's work and puts all artists upon a kind of pedestal. In his advice to the young writer, he tells Konstantin that everything he writes must have "a clear, concise central idea" (124). This sounds good enough, but his evaluation is nothing more than the tendentiousness of contemporary critics of the time who maintained that art needed to advance a single message for maximum effect.

Interestingly, the most telling criticism of Konstantin's play from a Chekhovian perspective comes from Nina. She protests the lack of action in Konstantin's play (a frequent attack against Chekhov as well) and suggests that it would be better served with a love story in it. All of Chekhov's plays are filled with love stories. He once described *The Seagull* as having "a ton of love" in it. Aborted or failed love plots fill all of Chekhov's plays. Nina also complains that it is difficult to act in Konstantin's play because there are no "ordinary" people in it (116). Konstantin rails against the artificiality and heightened theatricality of his mother's theater in which the actors, the "high priestesses of art," flaunt their talents, but Nina observes that Konstantin's play has no human beings at all, and that the "World Soul" struts and frets upon an empty stage. In Arkadina's traditional and commercial theater, as well as her angry son's theater of the future, the drama does not relate to ordinary human behavior and events. Although Konstantin makes valid protests against the contemporary theater and possesses a vision for a new kind, he does not have the talent to execute such a dream. That talent, refreshingly, belongs to his creator, Chekhov! Chekhov's innovation is to present ordinary people on stage who aspire to dramatic significance by modeling after literary characters or literary tropes and themes or an imaginative life that they cannot possibly realize. Their pathological tilt away from the routines of daily living causes them to miss what is often most important and life sustaining.

Ivanov (1889), Chekhov's early full-length play, provides an excellent example of the struggle of an ordinary man who wishes he were extraordinary. Chekhov describes his protagonist elegantly and succinctly in a letter to his friend and editor Alexi Suvorin in December 1888: "Ivanov is a nobleman who has been to the university and is in no way remarkable" (Karlinsky 76). The titular hero is an attractive man of 35 saddled with huge debts and a sick and dying wife of five years whom he no longer loves. He dallies with a much younger woman whose parents have money and to whom he owes money, and, finally, a year after his wife, Anna, dies, he plans to marry Sasha. However, on the day of the ceremony he tries to call the marriage off, and, after an argument with the righteous Dr. Lvov, who challenges him to a duel, he retrieves his revolver, runs out of the house, and shoots himself out-of-view to end the drama.

In his youth, Ivanov used his talents and energies and capabilities to work tirelessly and to promote any number of good causes and reforms. But none of those efforts has produced satisfying results that can sustain him. Now, he is tired and bored with everything. There is no new cause for him in which to believe. He tries to explain via a metaphor in Act 3 the circumstances in which he now finds himself: "You know, I used to have a hired man, Semyon—you remember him. And once—it was harvest time, he wanted to show off for the girls, show how strong he was, and he tried to shoulder two bales of rye. Well, he tore a muscle or something inside, and he died soon after. And I feel as if I've torn something inside too" (*Plays* 88). In his personal life, too, he claims that he once loved his wife passionately and that he swore to love her forever, but that five years have passed and now he loves her no longer. Ivanov fancies himself as a "superfluous man" in the

Russian literary tradition of Turgenev: "I'm intelligent, I'm in the prime of life, and I could die of shame when I realize that I'm turning into some kind of Hamlet, a completely superfluous man. It fills me with shame! It torments my pride, it weighs me down, and I suffer..." (77). The self-dramatizing that Ivanov indulges in belies the fact that he is not who he thinks he is—the subject of literary art! He is not a great man; he certainly is no Hamlet. Ivanov cannot reconcile himself to the fact that he is not the man he aspired to be in his earlier days.

When he confronts Sasha in Act 4 and attempts to break off their marriage at the last moment, he returns to literary analogy and Shakespearean tragedy to make his point: "It's time to be sensible. I've been playing Hamlet, you've been playing Ophelia, and it's time for us both to stop" (102). Ivanov realizes at the end that although he's been "playing" Hamlet, he is not Hamlet. The intolerable difference between "playing" and "being" provides ample motive for his suicide. The desire to model life after the lives of dramatic characters in plays and novels leads to bitter disappointment and failure when the narrative of a lived life doesn't compare favorably to the plot developments of an entertaining play or novel. Ivanov holds himself in contempt for what he's become, and after all the frenetic activity of youth has ceased, he cannot recognize his face in the mirror. Ivanov is a good man and compared to many of the people of his community, he's much better than most. But he is not the person he once thought he was or would be and life has not turned out the way he thought it would.

Ivanov makes little use of the subjunctive case per se, but the idea of the subjunctive proves instructive for an appreciation of the play. The subsequent famous plays, however, make explicit use of the subjunctive with respect to the clash between ordinary and extraordinary lives as well as life as it is and life as characters wish it to be. At the end of the pivotal third act of Chekhov's final play, *The Cherry Orchard* (1903), Lopakhin reproaches Liubov Andreyevna for losing the estate and then concludes: "Oh, if only we could change things, if only life were different, this unhappy, messy life..." (373). To anyone who would listen, which, actually, was no one, Lopakhin warned from the beginning of the play of the impending auction of the estate on August 23. That moment passes at the climax of the play without the inhabitants doing anything to prevent a buyer from purchasing the family home. The eventual and inevitable buyer, Lopakhin, marvels at his good fortune, but quickly reverses himself and mourns the fate that now deprives him of his dreams.

If things were different, Lopakhin, who loves Madame Ranyevskaya and has ever since he was a little boy, might marry her and save the estate for all of them. But class and social barriers make him a completely unacceptable choice for her, and indeed she never thinks of such a union as a solution to her financial problems and future happiness. If her only son had not drowned on the estate years ago, the event that prompted her to leave in the first place, perhaps she would want to return and to settle in her childhood home. As it is, the place and past haunt her with painful memories and it is significant that the initial scene in Act 1 and the final act is the room that served as her son's nursery. If Madame Ranyevskaya were not bent on a pathological self-destruction in her romantic pursuit of her lover in Paris, then perhaps she could find a more appropriate match with someone who truly loved her and did not wish to exploit her. If she were not obsessed with a self-dramatization of her own unhappy life she could make wise decisions regarding the future of the cherry orchard and her family estate. Things, though, are not different. They are, as the common vernacular puts it, what they are. Madame Ranyevskaya returns to Paris at the end and Lopakhin will cut down the cherry orchard, subdivide the property and build summerhouses along the river to lure tourists and vacationers. Ah, the future!

The young writer Konstantin in Chekhov's first great success, *The Seagull* (1895), quotes from *Hamlet* just as Ivanov did and postures as a tragic hero. At the beginning of the play, Konstantin espouses all sorts of theories about the modern theater, but his own play, a Symbolist sort of rant, is not very good. A couple of years later, Konstantin is a published writer but not entirely successful. He writes under a pseudonym as the elder writer Trigorin observes, and remains a mystery "just like the Man in the Iron Mask"(152). The young writer, in contrast to the veteran, however, has already run out of things to say. He tries to blame his inability to write on Nina for abandoning him and running off with Trigorin instead of him. Earlier in the play he cries to his mother: "If you only knew! I've got nothing, nothing left! She doesn't love me, and I can't write anymore.... All my hopes are gone" (141). At the end, he tries one last time to make Nina responsible for his inability to write and begs her to stay with him or let him go with her. "Ever since you left," he claims, "since I saw my first story in print, my life has been unbearable. My youth got snatched away, and I feel as if I've lived ninety years already" (158). Protestations of a broken heart aside, Konstantin crumbles because he cannot escape his mother's early label of him as a pathetic amateur. He kills himself because he cannot reconcile the mediocre present state of things and situation in which he finds himself with the past version of himself bent on new forms and changing the world through modern art.

Uncle Vanya in the play that bears his name (1896) is another unremarkable man who aspires to greatness. He has worked his whole life on a rural farm and sent the profits to support his brother-in-law who was a university professor in Moscow. He worshipped Serebriakov as a beacon of culture and civilization. Unfortunately, after the Professor retires, Vanya realizes that none of Serebriakov's published books will transcend the life of the author.

Now, Vanya feels cheated and views the Professor as a fake and he blames him for ruining his life, even though Vanya sent him money for years in an unfailingly generous and consistent manner. After all these years, Vanya knows it is too late for him to make a mark himself and he laments giving up his own life for the sake of somebody whom he doesn't think now is as talented as him. If the Professor had written transcendent works on the life and times of Russia in the 19th century, then, according to Vanya's thinking, life would have been worth the sacrifices he made on the Professor's behalf. Vanya simply cannot tolerate the dullness of everyday life as he experiences it now without the heightened mission of supporting great scholarly works that will make an impact on human relations for years to come. Life duped him and wasted his talents in the service of a fraud. Vanya clings to this narrative and never considers that he should have tried to accomplish something for himself.

Finally, the choral ending of *Three Sisters* (1900) in which Masha, Irina and Olga huddle together, sounds a refrain from the scene in *The Seagull* in which Konstantin shares his pain with his mother: "If only you knew," he says to her. Here, the Prozorov girls listen to the band playing as the military regiment marches out of town forever. They contemplate a return to normalcy and the boredom of everyday life that threatens to stretch on and on for days without end. "The music sounds so happy," Olga observes, "so joyful, it almost seems as if a minute more, and we'd know why we live, why we suffer. If only we knew. If only we knew!" (319). The line, from which Kataev draws the title of his book, suggests that if the girls could see into the future that subsequent generations of people lived peacefully and happily after they themselves had died, then they would have felt that life would have been worth it and that they had sacrificed their own happiness for the betterment of humanity. The focus upon a future that cannot be seen or even comprehended, however, distracts them from the present situation. The Prozorovs listen intently as the military band marches into the distance, but they scarcely notice that their brother's wife has displaced them from their own home.

Self-dramatization at the expense of self-knowledge or awareness comes at a steep price. To be sure, the gap between who characters aspire to be and who they really are creates the space for comic recognition. Characters at odds with themselves invite laughter and their focus on the future and prospects that are little more than pipe dreams almost covers, but not entirely, the poignancy and point of the Chekhov's plays. It is one thing to observe the individual divorced from the self, but the more profound problem surfaces with the realization that those same comic Chekhovian characters are divorced from all others as well. For all the love talk in the plays, for all the talk in them, period, the characters exist in a kind of existential vacuum. All the so-called "philosophizing" about the past and future could be labeled more accurately as "bullshitting." There is no important information in any of those long speeches. Popular opinion may claim that nothing happens in Chekhov, but, from the standpoint of the characters, though, they work extremely hard to insure that nothing happens! They do not use language to establish and strengthen the bonds of intimacy with others. Rather, they talk in order to avoid the possibility of intimacy. They talk in order to avoid the introspection that comes in the quiet space of silence. Seen this way, the Chekhovian play is a blank page that characters try desperately to fill as a strategy to avoid confrontation with themselves and others.

From this perspective, Chekhov reacts against the Ibsenian model of direct action. Ibsen's protagonists assert their wills against the world in pursuit of a singular objective. The plays routinely demonstrate the limits of the will as characters misinterpret events based on faulty data or false information. Such characters often discover that the world is not as it appears. Chekhovian characters avoid such mistakes by reinventing themselves as actors in the play of their lives. By putting life circumstances in the conditional mood, the subjunctive, they do what actors do in creating believable performances on stage and at the same time they eliminate any chance that something will actually happen due to their roles in an elaborate fiction. Thus, they skirt the pitfalls of the Ibsenian hero, but they also fail to do whatever it is that they say that they want. In pursuit of what could or would be if things were different, characters frequently fail to see and miss the significance of what remains or what is there, or just, what is. They think, too often, that happiness lies somewhere else, in the future, perhaps, far off, and that it is unattainable for them in the present. What separates Chekhov's four great plays from the early *Ivanov* are moments, however brief, that show what the characters most desperately want and need but fail to cherish or sustain for any length of time.

What is left after all the empty moments fade away? Not much, maybe, except everything that is truly important. Again and again, Chekhov shows characters that pay attention to the wrong things and miss what is most important by always looking for happiness in the wrong places. At the end of *The Cherry Orchard*, adversaries Trofimov and Lopakhin meet to say goodbye. Trofimov, the eternal student, is the voice of freedom and speaks incessantly about the future and the freedom of mankind. Lopakhin, conversely, is the man of business, whose plan to save the estate is to destroy it and build a commercial enterprise. Another vision of the future! And, yet, amidst their philosophical and political clash about the nature of things and the meaning of life, the two shake hands as friends and Trofimov takes time to comment upon Lopakhin's sensitive hands and how they appear to be the hands of an artist. He goes on to say that such sensitivity is not just in his hands, but that Lopakhin is that way on the inside, too. It is a simple and startling observation, generous, and reveals that two men, who disagree about almost everything, can have a point of contact and share insight and brotherly love and affection. Lopakhin possesses many different qualities, not just a single attribute, but the tumult of the final scene of departure threatens to bury this insightful exchange. In direct counterpoint to the preceding exchange, the final scene calls out the vast discrepancy between what characters say and what they do. Ironically enough, after all the talk about the whereabouts of the old servant Firs and assurances that he has been taken care of, everyone forgets him in the end and locks him alone in the house.

Rifling through the pages of his manuscripts in Act 4 of *The Seagull*, Konstantin arrives at an epiphany regarding his artistic career: "The more I write, the more I think it's not a matter of old forms and new forms: what's important is to write without thinking about forms at all. Just write and pour out whatever's in your heart" (156). Ironically, at the end, Konstantin echoes the words of his established literary and romantic adversary, Trigorin, from the very beginning of the play. In response to Arkadina's outburst against Konstantin's play in Act 1, Trigorin says, simply: "Everyone writes the way he wants ... the way he *can*" (120). While both men talk specifically about the art and craft of writing, their words valorize the Chekhovian point of view with respect to the importance of truthfulness, honor and integrity of the individual. Even more significantly, both writers stress the importance of getting on with what one does on a daily, rhythmic basis. The writer ... writes. The true writer, each suggests, is one who writes without thought to fame or critical attention that the work might engender but only according and in tune with the sensibility and unique aesthetic of the individual author. By extension, then, what is true for the exalted artist is true for the ordinary person as well. In fact, the ethos expressed by two such different artists as Konstantin and Trigorin indicates the writers' involvement in the daily routines as much as any others. Other characters might see the artist as above the trivialities of everyday life, but Konstantin and Trigorin attest to the fact that the best writers immerse themselves in the daily processes and routines of everyday living. The rewards of an artist's life, or the life of an owner of a small, rural estate, come from quiet living in harmony with the ticking vicissitudes of nature and the natural world—the beauty of the environment, certainly, but the beauty of nurturing one's own soul as well. Chekhov dramatizes the existential vacuum that results from looking outside the self and thinking that the secret to happiness can be found by achieving fame or moving to Moscow or getting another job or, indeed, by becoming another person. It is not easy to live within the confines of one's own realm, but such an inauspicious and humble existence might bring contentment and even happiness that results from self-knowledge and patterns of movement that coordinate harmoniously with the repetitive rhythms of everyday living.

The Seagull (1895)

> "If you only knew! I've got nothing, nothing left! She doesn't love me, and I can't write anymore.... All my hopes are gone..."

Konstantin Gavrilovich tries to impress his actress-mother by writing a play with his girlfriend, Nina, as star upon a makeshift stage outdoors on the family estate. Oddly, while his mother is a famous commercial star, the play he presents is very strange and avant-garde, with no real people in it. Not surprisingly, his mother, Arkadina, makes jokes at the little play's expense and the entire performance literally goes up in sulphuric smoke. Konstantin runs away in anger, followed only by another neighbor, Masha, who pines for him everlastingly despite her own marriage to a local schoolteacher. In the days that follow, Konstantin keeps mostly to himself and stays away from the house. Nina, on the other hand, who wants to be an actress, gravitates to Arkadina and to her boyfriend, Trigorin, a famous writer. Trigorin indulges a seemingly harmless flirtation with the young and impressionable girl and Konstantin challenges the older man to a duel and even makes a furtive suicide attempt. In the climax at the end of Act 3, Nina confides to Trigorin that her mind is made up to start a stage career and that she will go to Moscow. Thrilled, Trigorin kisses her and tells her where to stay in the city where he might next contact her.

Two years pass in the interval between the third and fourth acts. The inevitable happened, as Konstantin explains in the beginning of Act 4, during that time period. Nina's affair with Trigorin did not last and she had a baby by him who subsequently died. Her acting career was not successful, either, and reports have surfaced that she may be a bit crazy. For his part, Konstantin has become a moderately successful, published author, though even this limited success has not transformed him and his life in the ways in which he had formerly dreamed. Instead of the tyro of years earlier, he now seems to side sympathetically with Trigorin in terms of the purpose of art: to write what and how one wants and as simply as one can. Arkadina and Trigorin have just returned to the country after a two-year absence. Nina, too, has been spotted on the estate, and she now steals a visit with Konstantin when he enters his private study. She wonders aloud about what might have been had she not met Trigorin, whom she says she still loves passionately. She tells the tragic love story of her life, but says that she has found her calling as an actress performing in the rural provinces. Konstantin begs her to stay but she exits to make her next scheduled appearance on tour. Alone, he cannot face the aimless drift of his own life and quietly shreds his manuscripts one-by-one and then withdraws and shoots himself. Konstantin competed for his mother's love by becoming a writer, but he ultimately commits suicide when he discovers that he has nothing to say.

None of the above sounds like the makings for comedy, but the opening lines establish a comic rhythm that adheres to classic joke structure. In *Directing Plays: A Working Professional's Method*, Stuart Vaughan outlines the five parts of the joke as he learned and inherited them from the vaudeville theater: the plant; the pause; the point; the amplifier; and the bridge (253–255). "Why do you always wear black?" Medvedenko the schoolteacher asks his wife at the start of the play (*Plays* 111). "I'm in mourning," Masha responds, completing the plant, then pauses for the twist before making her point, "for my life." She amplifies the point, perhaps with a dramatic gesture, by adding, "I'm not happy." Medvedenko's failure to understand her leads to his next question and comparisons between his life and hers provide a bridge to the next routine of questions. This brief exchange establishes a pattern that recurs throughout the dialogue that remains continually disconnected and out of sync. Absurdly, both characters in this scene compete to see which one has things the worst, but neither can see past his or her personal situation. Chekhov thoroughly theatricalizes both characters. Masha wears black, takes snuff and clearly performs her tragic situation to the hilt and for maximum effect. Medvedenko plays the part of the unrequited lover whom Masha rejects because of his poverty. Masha makes it clear, though, that she would not love him even if he were not poor. His whining and complaining and constant talk of money disturbs her refined sensibilities and sensitivities for the tragic life: "All you ever do is talk and talk about money. You think there's nothing worse than being poor, but I think it's a thousand times better to go around in rags and beg on the street than.... Oh, you wouldn't understand" (112). Worked up to a dramatic pitch, Masha cannot finish her dramatic comparison, perhaps because she realizes the absurdity of her claim and also because she knows that her partner cannot comprehend what she's saying because he's consumed with his own personal drama. The elaborate self-dramatizations are all the more pointed because they play in front of a makeshift stage in a beautiful lake setting. Indeed, all the characters act as if they were in a play, and the comedy plays in the gap between the dramatic aspirations and realities of each character.

The flight of the seagull through five acts further traces the comic spirit of the play. The Moscow Art Theatre famously selected the seagull as a symbol for the company and adorned the front curtain of its theater with an image of the bird, even though the bird in Chekhov's play is a strange symbol that appears to offer profound meaning, but that even the characters confess not to understand. Early in Act 1, Nina, the star and only actor in Konstantin's play, arrives out-of-breath from her house across the lake, having escaped from her parents' watch in order to perform: "My father and my stepmother don't like my coming over here. They say you're all a bunch of bohemians. They're afraid I'll want to be an actress. But it's the lake that attracts me, as if I were a seagull" (115). A provincial girl with stern parents, Nina yearns to be famous and become an actress in the city. Her identification with the seagull is a poetic reach and her following line to her boyfriend seems worthy of the popular stage in its own right: "My heart's overflowing with you," she says, a bit of an odd construction when a simple "I love you" might do better. The exchange that follows seems more odd than the previous utterance. Immediately after they kiss, Nina pulls away to ask, "What kind of tree is that?" How invested can she be in her boyfriend when she comments on the background as a means to divert attention and avoid intimacy? What's more, she then asks, innocently but ridiculously, "Why's it so dark?" (116). Impatiently, Konstantin exclaims, "Because it's almost night! Things get dark at night!" Konstantin plays the part of the romantic hero and proclaims his undying love for her and begs to stand in her garden all night and stare up at her bedroom window. This pledge is not unlike the actions of Marguerite's lover in *Camille*, Armand, who fell in love with her by watching her for two years: "Ever since the day when I first saw you, beautiful, and proud. From that day I have watched you from a distance and in silence" (Dumas fils 119). Konstantin's play may rebel against popular melodrama and traditional stagey stuff, but he resorts to cheap clichés himself when he feels the need to announce his love and devotion to Nina.

Later, in Act 2, when Konstantin senses that Nina no longer loves him, he makes a symbolic gesture that further alienates her by presenting her with a dead seagull that he shot and which he lays at her feet. He vows that someday he will shoot himself in the same way. Nina does not understand him, but he claims that everything is painfully obvious: she didn't like his play; she thinks he's a mediocre talent; she thinks that he is a failure just like all the others do. He continues to confound Nina with strange allusions: "When you're cold to me like this, I can't believe it; it scares me: it's like I woke up one morning and the lake had disappeared right into the ground!" (131). Worse yet, he senses that she likes Trigorin. When he spies his rival in the distance, he mocks him as "the real talent" and hails him as entering just like Hamlet, even reading a book ("Words, words, words"). He practically throws Nina into Trigorin's lap. Earlier, he had played the role of Hamlet to his mother's Gertrude; now, he cedes the starring role to his romantic rival and vacates the scene.

The company she keeps with such a famous man fills Nina with wide-eyed admiration and adulation. Envious, too, she believes that Trigorin leads a "beautiful life" unlike ordinary people (132). This stops him and prompts his discourse on why he's a little crazy with his obsession for writing. He talks at length about his life as a writer: "Every word you and I are saying right now, every sentence, I capture and lock up in the back of my brain. Because someday I can use them!" (133). The writer's life is not glamorous to him and fame holds no meaning for him. He simply writes and writes and writes. Nina asks him if the "process of creation" gives him even a few moments of "sublime happiness" (133–134). The act of writing is enjoyable, Trigorin allows, but he loses interest and turns to the next project the moment a work is published, knowing that what he has done is wrong. Aware that he is talented, Trigorin's also aware of what Konstantin said earlier with respect to Turgenev and Tolstoy: that Trigorin falls short in such comparisons. Humorously, Trigorin offers his own epitaph for his tombstone: "Here lies Trigorin. He was a good writer, but Turgenev was better" (134). That such a blunt assessment does not diminish his discipline or compulsion to write surely renders him the most tragic, if not most sympathetic, character in the play.

Trigorin's serious talk about the life of the writer completely seduces Nina. She doesn't understand a word of what he says, she thinks he's only being too modest and humble, and she continues to validate him as a great artist. Trigorin goes on and on in part because he likes the response he gets from her, but her conclusion makes clear that she has not heard anything he has said on the subject: "If I could have that [fame], I'd put up with rejection, poverty, disappointment; I'd be willing to live in a garret and starve; maybe I wouldn't even like myself … just as long as I was famous! Really, spectacularly famous!" (134). Finally, Trigorin spies the dead seagull, the large bird that has been visible throughout the scene, comments upon its beauty and then proceeds to jot a few phrases in his notebook, a new idea, he says, for a short story: "The shore of a lake, and a young girl who's spent her whole life beside it, a girl like you…. She loves the lake the way a seagull does, and she's happy and free as a seagull. Then a man comes along, sees her, and ruins her life because he has nothing better to do. Destroys her like this seagull here" (135). Trigorin displays his artistry with this little description that might serve equally as a fable for Chekhov's play. Arkadina interrupts to announce that she and Trigorin will stay a bit longer at the estate and, intoxicated by the sudden turn of events, Nina's curtain line seals her fate: "My dream!" (135).

Two years later, all of Nina's dreams have been destroyed. When she peeks in to say goodbye to Konstantin in Act 4, she is much thinner than before and no longer a romantic and idealistic young girl. She has traipsed around the property for a week, gathering the nerve to see Konstantin, whom she feels she has wronged. She came to see the little theater where she had performed two years ago and she cried when she saw it. She appraises their situation: "You're a writer, and I'm an actress. We've both been sucked into the whirlpool. And that was such a happy life, back then. We were still children. I'd wake up in the morning and start singing. I was in love with you, I was in love with fame.... And now?" (157). Now she must catch a train to Yelets to perform the winter season repertory for men who leer. Clearly, though, Nina rewrites the life she led in the past, because she couldn't wait to escape from it. She wasn't particularly happy and she certainly wasn't in love with Konstantin. Konstantin replies to her in the high-blown rhetoric of the cheap plays in which his mother stars:

> Nina, I cursed you, I hated you, I tore up your letters and photographs, but I realized every minute that my soul was tied to yours forever. I can't *not* love you, Nina, I just can't. Ever since you left, since I saw my first story in print, my life has been unbearable. My youth got snatched away, and I feel as if I've lived ninety years already. I call your name, I kiss the ground you walked on, everywhere I turn I see your face ... I'm cold as an empty cave, and everything I write is dead [158].

He begs her to stay or to allow him to go with her, an abrupt about face from his earlier, clinical descriptions of her. Just as Trigorin once did, Konstantin now thinks Nina might hold the key to unlock his writing again; or, alternatively, that her love might save him from having to face his writing again.

Sounds from the adjoining room alert Nina to the fact that Trigorin is also in the house. Nina claims that she still loves him completely, though she knows her love is the subject of a short story. She recalls again how happy she and Konstantin were as children and then recites the opening of Konstantin's play again, and then, without another word, hugs Konstantin and leaves. Just before that, though, Nina says that over time she has grown up and believes in the theater now as an art form and feels that she has become a real actress. She has learned what the answer is because she has suffered, but now she is strong, and she tells Konstantin what she has discovered: "the main thing isn't being famous, it's not the sound of applause, it's not what I dreamed it was. All it is is the strength to keep going, no matter what happens. You have to keep on believing. I believe, and it helps. And now when I think about my vocation, I'm not afraid of life" (159) Konstantin confesses that he doesn't know where he is going and that he doesn't know what his work is for or who needs it.

Critic Richard Gilman interprets Nina's talk on art and acting as a heroic vision of fate and human suffering. In *The Making of Modern Drama*, Gilman exalts Nina as the voice of the playwright who delivers the moral message of the play: "She is the first of Chekhov's heroines of existential sobriety, whose education is in discovering how to submit to limits and in learning about what cannot be, and her story is played out under the symbolic form of the seagull: free, vulnerable, an emblem of besieged destiny" (135). In his later book on Chekhov, Gilman continues to praise the maturity of Nina as she recognizes her passionate love for Trigorin: "yet without allowing this to at all weaken her resolve to forge her own life as an artist or in any way diminish her determination to endure" (*Chekhov's Plays* 94). Gilman's praise of Nina approaches the same romantic heights that Chekhov takes pains to undercut. Three times in the final scene, Nina says: "I'm the seagull," a faint recollection of her first appearance in the play when she said that she was drawn to the lake as a seagull, but also an homage to Trigorin's idea for a short story in which a man comes along and destroys a beautiful bird for no good reason. Yet, each time Nina also negates her statement ("No, that's not it") as if she were struggling with her thoughts. She wipes her brow and claims she is tired and hungry. She is clearly not well. She may be, as Konstantin alluded in an earlier scene, mentally ill. Her persistence in her acting career, too, despite the tawdry descriptions, has elements of romanticism with its inflated view of art's values and importance and her role as a suffering artist willing to die for her craft.

Prior to Konstantin's offstage suicide, the focus shifts back to Arkadina and Trigorin and others who have been playing lotto. Shamrayev, the foreman on the estate, presents Trigorin with the stuffed and mounted seagull, which Trigorin had previously requested two years previously, about which he now recollects absolutely nothing. The seagull, in its final appearance in the play, mounted ceremoniously on a stick, means nothing to him and is not a symbol of anything to him, just grist for his writerly mill. Konstantin had been highly critical of the professional writer throughout the play and comments about how easy the process must be for Trigorin: "Trigorin has his technique all worked out; it's easy for him." Now, Konstantin begins to appreciate the vast difference between the two of them and how much better his rival is at his craft. He makes a profound realization: "The more I write, the more I think it's not a matter of old forms and new forms: what's important is to write without thinking about forms at all. Just write and pour out whatever's in your heart" (156). Sadly, there is nothing left in Konstantin's heart at the end of the play. He destroys all of his manuscripts in silence and then makes his final exit.

In the end, though, Konstantin is more right than wrong with his critique of the contemporary theater and it would be a mistake to dismiss him as an abject failure. Early in Act 1, prior to the performance of his play, he accurately describes the commercial theater in which his mother stars and against which he rebels:

> She *loves* the Theater, she thinks she's serving the cause of humanity, she thinks she's a high priestess of Art, but what I think is, that kind of theater is tired, it's all worn out. It's so restrictive! The curtain goes up, the lights come on, you're in a room with three walls, and there they are, these servants of art, and all they do is show us how people eat, drink, make love, walk, and wear clothes! And then they try to draw some kind of moral, some nice *easy* little moral, something you wouldn't mind having around the house. You go, they give you the same stuff over and over and over ... and it makes me sick! [114].

On the one hand, it is clear that the young man responds in large part the way he does to cover his own pain and hurt feelings from his mother's neglect and he holds the theater at large responsible for his broken relationship. On the other hand, though, the critique blasts the middlebrow sensibilities and values of the contemporary, commercial theater that remain vital even today. Even more piquant, however, is the critique salient against this Chekhovian play, *The Seagull,* in which Konstantin appears as a character. Chekhov seems to level an attack through the young writer against his own brand of theater in which not much happens, but even more so against the behavior of characters in the play. Konstantin can't stand the histrionics of acting on the commercial stage; Chekhov presents characters in his play, including Konstantin, who behave as if they were characters in a play. Against this fake reality and mere surface of appearances, Konstantin gives voice to his artistic credo: "We have to show life not the way it is, or the way it should be, but the way it is in dreams!" (116).

That goal sounds idealistic, if not profound, and it proves to be extremely difficult to stage in material terms. Nina, the young actress charged with embodying the "World Soul" in the play, points out that it is hard to act in the play because there are no living people in it. She reveals her provincial attitudes about theater and art when she tells her playwright boyfriend that a play ought to have a love story in it, but nevertheless she articulates the acting challenge of the anti-realistic theater and a snippet from the play is enough to reveal a comic parody of what Konstantin takes very seriously. He introduces his play with narration about what life will be like in 200,000 years and his little play of the future deteriorates quickly: "All is cold, cold, cold. All is empty, empty, empty. All is terror, terror, terror" (118). Nina, as the World Soul, has very little to do and no one to address. There is nothing for her to do on stage except to recite her lines. The audience grows restless early, particularly Arkadina, who asks, "Is this supposed to be symbolic?" (119). The special effects don't work very well and Arkadina pokes fun at the smell of sulphur that presages the appearance of two red eyes in the distance as the Demon. Outraged by her comments and what he perceives as her attempt to steal the show and direct all the attention upon herself, Konstantin angrily brings down the curtain: "I'm very sorry. I forgot that only the chosen few can write plays—or act in them. I tried to break into the charmed circle, and see what happens! I ... I just..." and exits the stage and runs away (120).

Dr. Dorn expresses the range of ambivalence that surrounds the reception of Konstantin's avant-garde effort. He philosophizes to himself that he apprehends the play as something new and different. He tries his best to encourage the young man to write more and to praise his efforts and after Konstantin hugs him desperately and appreciatively Dorn feels impelled to say even more what's on his mind regarding the arts: "Every work of art has to express some great idea. True beauty is always a serious matter" (124). These statements are little more than clichés and are standard critical practices of the time. Konstantin just wants the compliments, but Dorn looks to say something even more profound: "But if I could experience, just for a moment, the excitement that must come with artistic creation..." Not unlike the young Nina, Dorn places artists as ideal figures apart from ordinary existence as it is lived by women and men. Konstantin hears none of it, comically; he simply wants to know where Nina went.

Set against the backdrop of the lake, the little stage captures, frames, and thereby magnifies the beauty of nature. Konstantin consciously discards the tenets of the conventional theater, including the stagehouse with its capacity to present painted illusions, in favor of the trees, lake and moon on the family estate: "Now, this is what I call a theater! A curtain, two wings, right and left, and then nothing. No set. Empty space! The curtain opens, all you see is the lake and the far horizon. And the curtain will open at exactly eight-thirty, just as the moon rises" (113). The beauty of this natural scene is what Nina recollects in the final act, and despite her criticisms of Konstantin's play at the time, she goes out of her way to revisit the lake theater before going further on her theatrical journey to Yelets. The kind of theater that Nina performs in, a far cry even from the traditional theater that Konstantin criticizes, has no relation at all to nature and natural beauty. Elapsed time erases the memory of the little play and the makeshift stage remains as something of an abandoned and decrepit relic of naïve youth. Medvedenko comments on the terrible weather in Act 4 and suggests that the little stage that was constructed for Konstantin's play be taken down. "It's bare and ugly, and the curtain keeps flapping in the wind. It's like a skeleton. Whenever I go past it at night, I think I hear someone crying" (146). The person crying is probably Nina, but no one knows for certain.

Just as the makeshift stage stands for a moment of forgotten and forlorn beauty, a single moment of quiet affection that crops up quickly and disappears abruptly carries the weight of the entire play. Toward the end of the third act, Konstantin finds himself alone with his mother and he asks her to change the bandage on his head. In an unseen moment in the time interval between Acts 2 and 3, Konstantin made a suicide attempt that resulted in a misfire that only slightly wounded him. In a manner typical of Chekhov, Arkadina makes a joke about Konstantin's bandage looking like a turban and that a delivery boy commented that he looked like a foreigner. Arkadina's joke, however, is just an icebreaker for her to connect with her son in the only sign of love and affection between them that happens during the entire play. She kisses his head and re-wraps a bandage around his head, during which time Konstantin kisses her hand and recalls a time long ago when his mother was acting in the State Theater and attended to one of the tenants and her children who had been badly beaten in a fight. Konstantin prolongs the moment by connecting the past with the present: "The last few days, I've loved you the way I did when I was little. Totally, tenderly. You're all I've got" (140). The moment breaks when Konstantin states that Trigorin has come between them. He doesn't, interestingly enough, say that Trigorin has taken Nina from him, but that he has taken his mother from him. Konstantin deliberately provokes his mother by calling Trigorin first a coward and then a second-rate writer. And, in between, he suggests further that Trigorin is making a fool of Arkadina by spending time and talking with Nina. Arkadina takes the bait and begins to insult her son: "People with no talent but lots of pretensions, all they know how to do is attack anyone with *real* talent" (141). Hurt where he is vulnerable, Konstantin lashes back and trades insults about his mother's commercial work in "cheap, second-rate plays!" A succession of vicious verbal blows from Arkadina ends up with a knockout punch that reduces Konstantin to tears. In succession, she calls him a "Symbolist," a third-rate writer from Kiev, a member of the middle class, a "sponge," an "amateur," and finally a "nobody." Their violent exchange reduces both of them to tears before a final embrace and the son's exclamation: "If you only knew! I've got nothing, nothing left! She doesn't love me, and I can't write anymore.... All my hopes are gone..." (141). They make up and Arkadina urges her son to talk to Trigorin and say that he's not mad anymore but Konstantin cannot do it. With Trigorin's return to the room, Konstantin retreats. "The doctor can fix the bandage" is his sad exit line (142). For all the talk of love and art in the play, Konstantin wants simply for his mother to dress his wound and minister to his needs. She can do it, beautifully, effortlessly, but only for a few moments, after which they both lash out at the other. It should be the most natural thing in the world for a mother to tend to her son and for each to express his and her heartfelt love. But time and again, Chekhov shows these moments of real connection, of real beauty, as fleeting and elusive. Ego and affectation get in the way. But, more than that, characters indulge theatrical behavior and the "magic if" to dodge the very happiness that they say they seek.

Uncle Vanya (1896)

> "If I'd had a normal life, I could have been another Schopenhauer, another Dostoevsky!"

Professor Alexander Serebriakov retires with his young second wife, Yelena, to the family farm run by his daughter from his first marriage, Sonya, and her uncle, Ivan Petrovich (Uncle Vanya). Vanya now realizes that the professor is not the academic luminary that he had assumed and that, quite to the contrary, he has already faded into obscurity. After Vanya and Sonya financially supported Serebriakov for years in the belief that he was conducting important research that would achieve lasting fame and also benefit all of humanity, Vanya now feels that all of their efforts were for nothing. Worse, he feels that he sacrificed his own potentially brilliant career as a productive thinker by slaving for a man whom he now regards as a phony. To make matters still worse, Vanya loves the beautiful Yelena, whom he regrets not marrying years ago. She, however, is an enchanting siren who has attracted the local doctor, Astrov, to call almost every day and who almost indulges in an affair with him. Sadly, Sonya is madly in love with Astrov from afar, but he in no way feels the same way about her. Matters come to a head when Serebriakov proposes the sale of the farm to support his future lifestyle in the city. Enraged by the professor's audacious thoughtlessness and insensitivity, Vanya chases him throughout the house with a pistol aiming to shoot him, but repeatedly (and comically) misses. In the aftermath of this outburst, Serebriakov and Yelena decide to leave and the rural routine returns to normal as both Sonya and her uncle settle down to manage the farm and its accounts. Ironically, Sonya's closing lamentation on the repetitive nature of things belies the quotidian joy and pleasure that she and her uncle experience in the daily routine of life on the farm.

The titular hero leads the way in looking elsewhere for happiness by focusing on the past as the source for present discontent. Vanya is jealous of Serebriakov on two counts. First, he has to deal with the fact that the professor had a long and distinguished academic career but that he did not. Vanya has never done anything and now he fears that he will never do anything: "I can't sleep nights, I'm so depressed, I'm so angry—all that time wasted, when I could have been doing everything I can't do now because I'm too old!" (*Plays* 214). Secondly, he regards Serebriakov as a fraud:

> Here's a man who for the last twenty-five years has been lecturing and writing about art, and he knows nothing whatsoever about art! For twenty-five years he's been regurgitating other people's ideas about realism, naturalism, all that bullshit. And now he's retired, and it turns out he's a complete fraud! He has no reputation whatsoever! For the last twenty-five years, all he's been doing is keeping some better man out of a job. And look at him: he walks around like he'd just stepped off Mount Olympus! [212].

Vanya, according to this narrative, was the better man whose career Serebriakov suppressed. The old man's success with women, first with Vanya's sister, who idealized the professor, and now Yelena, further antagonizes and infuriates Vanya. Again, in his own mind, Vanya believes that Serebriakov stole Yelena away from him, but that he can somehow win her back by professing his ardent love. "Just let me talk to you, tell you how much I love you—that's all I need, that's enough to make me completely happy," he says to her in an otherwise casual moment (218). Completely unmoved by his protestations, Yelena begs him to be quiet. Later, Vanya makes another play for Yelena as a relief from dwelling on his own miserable past and succession of missed opportunities: "I haunt this house like a lost soul; it makes me crazy, the thought that I've thrown away my life and I'll never get it back. My past is gone, wasted on stupidity, and the present is so pointless it's grotesque. And that's it, that's my life, and that's my love, and what can I do about it? My feeling for you is hopeless, like a ray of sunlight falling into a black hole. I'm dying" (222). Naturally, he's a little drunk and out of control and maudlin on account of the lateness of the evening and the amount of alcohol that he has consumed. Yelena asks him why he's drinking like this, when he never used to do so: "So I can feel for a few minutes like I have a real life..." he retorts (223). Vanya's melodramatic tone and enthusiasm for the part of the rejected lover is appropriate for the purely fictional relationship he has constructed with Yelena.

She leaves him alone to ponder how he first met her and question why he didn't marry her ten years ago when she was only 17 and he was 37. In a revealing monologue, Vanya imagines how he would comfort her during the present thunderstorm. He realizes, finally, that this is pointless fantasy and switches subjects to what he diagnoses as the root cause for his hopeless situation. He and Sonya worked tirelessly on the behalf of the professor and supported his research. "I lived and breathed for him! Everything he wrote was a work of genius to me," Vanya recalls (223). Now, however, faced with the professor's retirement he realizes that all those efforts were a waste of time. "It turns out he's a complete unknown, the stuff he wrote is all academic drivel, hot air! And I'm a fool! I see it all now—I've been made a complete fool!" (223–224). He did it to himself because he wanted to—because he wasn't able to be a "brilliant personality" himself. Just as Vanya's romance with Yelena is a product of his imagination, so, too, is the notion of Vanya as a leading intellectual. Although Vanya wonders what might have been if things had been different, there is no reason to suggest that the twin scenarios of marriage to Yelena or a university professorship could ever actually happen.

Vanya's diatribe climaxes at the end of Act 3 with his outrageous claim: "My life is ruined! I had talent, I was smart, I had energy.... If I'd had a normal life, I could have been another Schopenhauer, another Dostoevsky!" (243). No textual evidence substantiates this statement. Vanya might have been a famous Russian novelist or German philosopher—or not. Who can really say what might have been? But it certainly does not follow logically that a "normal life," whatever that may entail, would lead to such an extraordinary outcome. But Vanya never even attempted to lead a life of the mind on his own. He claims that he gave up his life for the professor's, but Serebriakov never asked him to do this and is completely unaware of the extent of Vanya's sacrifice. Vanya, rather, chose to do what he did and only now regrets his decision with the present knowledge that time affords. He exits through the center door saying that he knows now what he must do and vows that the professor will remember him for a long time.

Befuddled by Vanya's reaction to his plan of selling the farm, Serebriakov announces that he cannot live under the same roof as Vanya and says that Vanya should move into the barn or the neighboring village—an odd and self-centered request given that Vanya has been living in the house for years, the house is really partly his, and that Serebriakov is the visitor. For her part, Yelena wants to pack immediately and leave with her husband as soon as possible. Sonya, from her knees and almost in tears, begs her father to understand that she and her uncle have saved money for years and done without themselves in order to send extra funds to help Serebriakov advance his academic career. Yelena urges her husband to talk to Vanya and the professor agrees and goes in search of his brother-in-law to see what he can salvage. A shot fires from offstage and Yelena screams. The professor runs back into the living room in terror: "Stop him! Stop him! He's out of his mind!" (244). Yelena struggles with Vanya over the gun in the doorway, but Vanya successfully wrenches it away from her and follows the professor into the room and fires the pistol a second time. "Missed! I missed again!" he exclaims, throwing down the gun and falling into a chair. "What am I doing? Oh, what am I doing?" he asks as the climactic act ends.

The attempted murder plays as comedy because no one gets hurt, but also because the gesture manifests Vanya's misdirected thinking about the cause of his unhappiness. He blames the professor for ruining his life but the professor is oblivious to having done anything to him. Serebriakov feels entitled to the good life, yes, but he never questioned that Vanya was doing something that he would one day regret. The professor is an old fool, perhaps, but he serves as the scapegoat for Vanya's inability to take responsibility for his own talent, dreams, health and ultimate happiness. Ironically, the professor wants to sell the farm that Vanya seems to hate and his plan calls Vanya's bluff about its value to him. Vanya postures that running the farm has prevented him from living his life as he wanted. It is all about Sonya's inheritance, he tells himself, but he is her partner and he has loved the estate as much as Sonya. Vanya would be completely adrift if he were to leave the farm for good. He has adapted his entire life to its rhythms and he does not want to change. The professor's plan exposes Vanya's lie to himself about his choices and his wants and desires. He simply does not know how to live with the truth.

As much as Vanya ruminates over his past, his sidekick and drinking companion, Dr. Astrov, ponders the future as an escape from the tedium of daily living. "How long have we known each other?" asks the doctor to Marina, the old Serebriakov family nurse, in a shameless bit of opening exposition in the first scene that out Ibsens Ibsen. At least 11 years, she reports, two years, maybe more, before Sonya's mother, Vanya's sister, died. During that time, Astrov says, he has grown old because he's never taken a day off for needed rest. He's also bored. "Life is boring, it's stupid, it stinks ... it really gets to you after a while" (209). He has no feelings anymore, and no capacity to love anyone (except Marina!) because of what he has repetitively seen and experienced—the impoverished conditions in which most people live and the hopelessness of treating them. He recalls how miserable he felt when a patient died on his operating table before he could attempt to save him. He doesn't see a bright future in any of this. "What are people going to say about all this a hundred years from now?" he questions (210). God will admire the effort, Marina assures him.

Later in the first act a medical emergency at a nearby factory requires the doctor's attention. By way of goodbye, he invites Yelena and Sonya to visit his place sometime to see his nursery and the state forest next to his land. Sonya expresses her feelings for the doctor by expounding on Astrov's preservationist hobby as a way to "recognize beauty" (216). Vanya remains unconvinced, but Astrov passionately questions the wisdom of needlessly destroying natural resources and physical beauty.

> You have to be a barbarian to burn all that beauty in your stove, to destroy something that can never be replaced. We were born with the ability to reason and the power to create and be fruitful, but until now all we've done is destroy whatever we see. The forests are disappearing one by one, the rivers are polluted, wildlife is becoming extinct, the climate is changing for the worse, every day the planet gets poorer and uglier. It's a disaster! [217].

His attention to nature and the forests gives him a sense of accomplishment that his profession as a doctor deprives: "...every time I drive by a stand of trees that I persuaded the owners to spare, or hear the breeze at night in young trees I planted myself, I realize that I *can* do something about the climate, and if a thousand years from now people are a little happier, then it's partly because of me" (217).

Drunkenness brings out "what might have been" in Dr. Astrov as well as Vanya in their shared scene in Act 2. Alcohol allows him to forget the world as it is and to perform surgeries perfectly (in his mind) and feel that he is at peace with the world and not a freak. Regarding his ecological pursuits, he brags: "I'm convinced I am the bearer of blessing for humanity—enormous blessings for humanity!" (225). When Sonya enters the room, however, he bows out sheepishly to retrieve his tie.

Sonya complains to Vanya that she cannot do all the work on the farm without his help. She cannot understand why he drinks all the time and acts like a teenager with the doctor. "When you don't have a real life, you make do with dreams," her uncle answers. When he goes to bed, Sonya calls out Astrov and asks him not to imbibe with her uncle anymore because it is bad for him. Before he leaves, too, Astrov philosophizes to her about life and human nature. While he loves life in general, he hates the life people actually lead and can't stand his own personal life as well. "I can't see any light in the distance," he says. Sonya calls him a sensitive person, "a beautiful human being," and begs him not to destroy himself as he so eloquently describes other people destroying the natural beauty of the world so wantonly (227). In his personal narrative, Astrov describes his keen aesthetic sense as all that remains for him: "It's too late for me, my life is over, I'm old, I'm all worked out, I've gotten vulgar, my feelings are gone, don't think I could have a relationship with another human being, I can't love anybody anymore. The only thing that still moves me is beauty" (228). Sonya disguises her next question in the guise of a theoretical question about what Astrov would do if someone loved him. In response, he says he could not love anyone, then says goodbye again and leaves quickly. Alone, Sonya holds out some hope just because he didn't say "no" exactly. She wishes she were better looking: "Oh, why aren't I beautiful? It's awful, just awful, being so plain, and I am, I'm ugly, I know I am, I know I am!" (228). If she were beautiful, her line of thinking suggests, she wouldn't have any trouble getting Astrov to return her love.

Although Sonya would make an excellent wife, Astrov gravitates to the physical beauty of Yelena, although he envisions nothing serious coming of the relationship. In a scene reminiscent of the flirtation between Trigorin and Nina in *The Seagull*, Astrov woos Yelena with his charts of ecological degradation. He shows the land and the flora and fauna on three different maps as it existed 50 years ago, 25 years ago, and as it exists at the present time. His comparative analysis reveals a steady loss of natural resources to the point that Astrov predicts total destruction of the environment in another ten or 15 years. As the doctor becomes increasingly passionate about his subject, Yelena withdraws and hardly listens. Slowly, silently, she draws him out to reveal his interest in her instead of Sonya. At the same time, whereas Sonya is a marriageable woman, Yelena is a beautiful distraction whom Astrov pursues to indulge an idle, casual, brief sexual adventure. Yelena knows, Astrov says, exactly why he has been coming out every day to visit the farm and whom he wants to see. Yelena pretends not to know what he is talking about, but Astrov insists that she must agree to meet him somewhere to commence an affair. Worked up into a passion, he grabs her and says: "We have to do it—you can't get away from me now!" (238). Amidst staunch protests, Yelena finally relents and kisses him and rests her head for a moment against his chest, before pulling away abruptly with a change of intention and a loud "No!" (238). Just prior to that, Vanya returns in the doorway with a bouquet of roses. Astrov continues to push her for a rendezvous time and place, but Yelena, spying Vanya at last, breaks free and moves away in a highly embarrassed state. Sweaty and agitated, too, Vanya tries to tell them that everything is all right and not to worry. Astrov covers the moment by talking about the weather as he rolls up his charts and exits quickly. Yelena approaches Vanya and tells him that he must arrange immediately for her and the professor to leave the farm. After Vanya tells her that he saw and heard everything, she repeats with emphasis that they must leave today!

One might think that the professor would be the lone contented person in the household, but that is simply not the case. He has had a fulfilling life, he admits, but now even in his old age he wants more of the same. He fears that he repulses his young wife: "You're young, you're beautiful, you've got your health, you want to live, and I'm an old man with one foot in the grave" (219). For Serebriakov, life in the country is a kind of grave and he misses the vibrant cultural activity of a major city. He has come to the family farm after retirement only out of necessity—financial and physical. He feels entitled to live in the manner in which he has become accustomed and resents the fact that everyone resents him. "I sit here in this graveyard, surrounded by stupid people saying stupid things. But I'm still alive! I still want to be famous and successful, I want all the excitement I used to feel! This place—it's like a prison" (220). He wears everybody out with his incessant demands. The professor expects everyone to care for his gout and rheumatism and provide an answer for his trouble breathing. He complains that Sonya has given him the wrong pills. Only the aged Marina can help him and she treats him as if he were a little child in a rush of attention that pleases the professor greatly.

At the start of the third act, Serebriakov requests everyone to gather later at 1:00 in the afternoon in the living room for an important announcement. At the end of the act at the appointed time, he begins his speech: "I have summoned you, ladies and gentlemen, to tell you that an inspector general is on his way to pay us a visit" (240). The professor surely meant his literary allusion as a comic introduction to his text, but the set-up puts the audience, in the living room and in the theater at large, on notice that something momentous, and probably unpleasant, is about to happen. In a long-winded speech that indicates his nervousness about its contents, Serebriakov tells them that he is an old man who needs to consider the interests and future of his family (which means only himself and Yelena). He has come to the conclusion that they cannot continue to stay in the country because they are simply not country people. On the other hand, he does not make enough money now for them to live in the city. What to do? He proposes to sell the property and put the proceeds into managed funds that would make living possible and even allow them to buy a vacation home in Finland. Vanya immediately turns apoplectic; he simply cannot believe his ears and demands that the professor repeat his plan. The proposal does not give any inkling of where Vanya or Sonya or Mrs. Voinitsky will go after the sale of the home. Furthermore, Vanya points out, the farm was a gift to Sonya as her inheritance from Vanya's father. Sonya inherited the property when her mother died. And the property never could have been purchased, Vanya claims, if he had not given up his share of the inheritance. After Vanya's violent outburst, things settle down back to a more normal routine in the final act. The professor withdraws his proposal to sell the farm and decides to return to the city with his wife. He and Vanya make up, embrace, and Vanya assures the professor that he and Sonya will continue to support Serebriakov with proceeds from the farm: "We'll send you exactly what we used to, the very same amount. Everything will be the way it was before" (250). The professor can't resist making a small speech before he leaves—his one piece of advice is that they should all work and do "something useful."

The planned departure of Serebriakov and Yelena promises restitution of order and a normal routine on the farm. Still, Vanya despairs and denies that he took a bottle of morphine from the doctor's bag, and still regrets that he shot at the professor twice and missed both times! "I'll never forgive myself," he declares (246). The fact that he has not been arrested leads Vanya to think that others think he's crazy. Who is crazier, he thinks aloud: the no talent who pretends to be a professor or the young woman who marries the no talent and then carries on an affair in front of everybody (he witnessed Yelena kissing Astrov)? Astrov asserts that Vanya is not crazy: "you're just the comic relief around here" and he refuses to address seriously Vanya's complaints (246–247). He is a freak like him and thus completely normal. Vanya protests and voices his life's lament one more time: "All I want is a different life! I want to wake up some morning, some bright, quiet morning, and find that the past has vanished like smoke. (*Cries*) All I want is a new life. Tell me how to find one ... where should I look...?" (247). The doctor assures him that it is completely hopeless: "But you and me ... the only thing we have to look forward to is a little peace and quiet when we're finally in our graves." After such nihilistic philosophizing, the doctor persists in asking about the missing morphine. Sonya enters and joins the doctor with a plea to give it back. She empathizes with Vanya's state of mind, but she will not consider or condone suicide: "I'm just as unhappy as you are, but I won't give in to despair. I have to accept things the way they are. I have to go on living until I die. You've got to do the same" (248). Vanya finally relents, and then adds that he must now occupy himself with work full time.

By way of goodbye, Astrov half-heartedly pursues his affair with Yelena. He tells her that she leads a useless life and that she's bound to succumb to the temptations of an affair at some point, so why not do it now with him in the country where such an affair can be staged as in Turgenev! Yelena wants to shake hands and part as friends. Astrov describes her and her husband in a way that defines the dramatic action of the play: "You and your husband show up here one day, we're all busy working away at our little jobs, we get things done, and all of a sudden we have to drop everything and spend all our time taking care of you and your husband's gout." He observes the fact that he has abandoned his practice and his property since her arrival. "Wherever you and your husband go, you destroy whatever you find, don't you?" he asks (249). Aware that he could never survive an affair with Yelena, Astrov comments on the irony of their meeting and mutual attraction: "We got to know each other so well, and now all of a sudden we'll never see each other again. That's the way it goes, I guess." With no one around, he asks to kiss her. She agrees. Then, she embraces him "violently," before announcing immediately: "Time to go." "Then go! The carriage is here; just get in it and go!" Astrov exclaims (250).

Nothing changes. The end marks a return to the beginning. Everything is the same, as though the professor and his wife were never there. A feeling or mood of resignation, if not deep sadness sets in and persists through to the end of the play. Yet, in a strange way, all of the characters get almost exactly what they truly want or need—they simply cannot recognize or distinguish between what they say they want and what they actually need. At the start of Act 4, Telegin comments on the dramatic events that he has recently witnessed: "It was a scene worthy of an old master" (245). Just as Serebriakov introduced his big announcement in the previous act with an allusion to Gogol, Telegin notes the recent gunplay of Vanya as a theatrical gesture, but also the courtship of Yelena by Astrov that caught the attention of everyone. Marina, the old nurse of the family, looks forward to the return of the normal and traditional routine on the farm: "Maybe now we can go back and live the way we always did. Breakfast at eight, dinner at one, a little supper in the evening—do things right, lead a good Christian life again. (*Sighs*) I haven't had a decent dish of dumplings in months" (245). It is not just the peripheral and supporting characters who pine for the way things used to be, but the main characters as well, Vanya no less. Near the beginning of the play he complains about the chaos of a broken routine. He enters for the first time in Act 1, all rumpled after a nap, upset about what has happened since the arrival of the professor and his young wife: "I don't sleep right, lunch and dinner I eat too much, I drink too much ... not a very healthy way to live" (210). He used to work all the time; now, he does not. Marina adds: "Before they came, we had dinner in the middle of the day like normal people; now we have to wait till after six." Despite what he says later in the play, Vanya likes his work on the farm and thrives in the repetitive order of his daily regimen.

Act 4 takes place in Vanya's room, which also doubles as the office for the estate. Among various things in the room, one curious object deserves special attention: "A large map of Africa hangs on the wall, clearly of no use to anybody" (245). If this were an Ibsen play, the map would play a vital role in the unfolding events of the action. The Ibsen economy of stagecraft would require full use of every scenic detail and property. The heavy curtains in the first act of *Hedda Gabler*, for example, suggest Hedda's closed-in life and her restlessness to escape from it. Judge Brack enters from the rear in the third act in order to demonstrate his easy access to Hedda; the photo album of her honeymoon that Hedda shares with Løvborg replays their scenario from the past in which they huddled together in the presence of her father. Here, though, in the Chekhov play, the map does not seem to serve any direct or obvious purpose. Why is it there? In the final moments of the play, just prior to his final exit, Astrov refers to the map and comments: "It must be hot in Africa right now. Really hot" (252). Vanya agrees, but no more is said on the subject. The doctor drinks his glass of vodka and quickly departs. Of course, such a banal comment might be the awkward cover for an emotional farewell in which neither party, Astrov or Vanya, knows quite what to say to the other. But the map's odd presence in the background might just represent a place of escape and novel refuge, just as the professor and Yelena depart for Harkov and eventually other cities in search of a home that is hospitable, habitable and exciting. Far removed from the rural life on a country estate in Russia, the foreign and exotic continent of Africa exists as a fantasy for a better life somewhere else. The fact that Vanya, Astrov, the professor and Yelena all think that they would be happier in another time, another life, another place creates a vacuum in the present in which the subtle beauty of nature passes unnoticed.

After all the visitors leave, Sonya and Vanya and the rest of the rural dwellers finally return to their tasks: Sonya refills the inkwell, lights the lamps and leafs through ledgers; Vanya shuffles papers at his desk; Marina darns stockings; Mrs. Voinitsky reads a book; Telegin tunes his guitar. Outside, the horses and carriages pull away from the house. Vanya confesses his unhappiness to Sonya and she delivers a long final speech on the present state of despair and hardship that will turn into rest in the afterlife in which "all our earthly woes will vanish in a flood of compassion that overwhelms the world!" (253). Her rhapsody on the future after life on earth has ended, however, belies the calm and rhythmic beauty of the present quiet and orderly domestic scene. In an earlier exchange with Yelena, Astrov said how much he enjoyed the silent company of Sonya and Vanya:

> Whenever I get completely fed up with things, I head over here and spend a couple of hours fooling around with these [his ecological charts] ... Vanya and Sonya sit there doing the accounts; I sit in my corner drawing away. I feel relaxed and at home, and there's always a cricket chirping somewhere. But it's a pleasure I don't allow myself too often ... maybe once a month [235].

The very end of the play dramatizes what Astrov described as both beautiful and desirable in the first act. A return to silence, order and calm is exactly what the characters have longed for throughout the play. Now, all is quiet. Sonya's paean to work decries the repetitive dullness of their everyday lives, without notice that such activities also give daily life its meanings and joys. The rhapsodic conclusion dramatizes the ironic disconnect between voices of despair and the rhythmic beauty of nature from which those same voices emanate.

Three Sisters (1900)

> "I feel happy. It's almost as if I were seeing these trees for the first time in my life; they all seem to be looking at me and waiting for something. What beautiful trees they are! ... This tree is dead, but it still moves in the wind with the others. I feel like that; if I die, I mean, I'll still be part of life somehow..."

On the anniversary of their father's death, the Prozorov sisters remember their former home in Moscow and declare their fervent desire to return there soon. Moscow soon comes calling to their provincial town with the arrival of a military garrison and specifically in the form of Lt. Colonel Vershinin, who remembers the girls when they were very small. Unfortunately, the young and dashing "lovesick major" whom they remember stands before them as a much older and much less dashing middle-aged man, a physical reminder that the Moscow of their dreams might also be romantically idealized. Soon Masha, who is married to the local schoolteacher, and Vershinin begin to carry on a hopeless love affair and Irina, the youngest, dallies with a young officer named Tuzenbach. The third sister, Olga, a schoolteacher resigned to remaining single, swears, however, that she would have loved her husband had she ever married. Brother Andrey, the last sibling, also dreams of the city and life there as a distinguished professor at Moscow University. At odds with this dream, though, is his marriage to a provincial girl, Natasha, who seems bent on settling down in the local town. Her social climbing and maternal fecundity mark the progression of time in the play. She pursues a clandestine affair with the provincial big-wig politician name Protopopov (unseen in the play) and also delivers two children, Bobik and Sophie (also unseen), in successive acts of the play as she literally takes over the house and displaces both Olga and Irina from their rooms in the family home, leaving the sisters on the outside looking in by the final act. Andrey abandons all his former dreams and, fatter and slower than at the beginning, merely pushes the baby stroller by play's end. The military garrison breaks camp and Vershinin and Masha say goodbye for the last time. Irina's half-hearted marriage plans go awry, too, when her betrothed dies in a pointless duel. After the last soldiers depart, the three sisters huddle once again to lament the passing of time and the lack of certainty in an unsure world.

In the previous play, *Uncle Vanya*, the rhythmic beauty and quiet cadence of the closing offsets Sonya's depressive monologue on the toil of everyday life in order to show, ironically, how the rural inhabitants miss what's most important and life sustaining in the world about them. Critic Northrop Frye claimed in his theory of genres that the ending of *Three Sisters* came as close to "pure irony" as the stage could get (285). The opening scene of the play, however, provides an even more compelling example of Chekhov's ironic stage and the comparison between it and the ending of *Uncle Vanya* demonstrates Chekhov's brilliant dramaturgy. The stage design in *Three Sisters* designates a big living room separated by columns from a dining room upstage that allows for simultaneous scenes to occur between the sisters downstage and the military officers upstage. Downstage in the living room, color of dress differentiates the Prozorovs: Olga in dark blue, Irina in white, and Masha in black. Olga provides necessary exposition in her opening monologue, noting that their father died exactly one year ago on May 5th, the same day as Irina's birthday. They were sad then and the weather was bad, but now they feel happy and it is a beautiful spring day. Olga recalls that their father, a general, got his brigade command 11 years ago and they left Moscow then to come to where they are now in a rural town. Olga says she woke up with a feeling that she wanted to go back home to Moscow. Later, she says that there is only one thing that keeps her going, and her younger sister, Irina, completes the sentence, enthusiastically, "Going back to Moscow, as soon as we can" (*Plays* 260). The conversation of the military officers upstage in the dining room, however, interrupts and undercuts such rhapsodic optimism. Oblivious to what the Prozorovs are saying, the soldiers' timely interjections render the force of the sisters' speech moot. While the characters are unaware of the commentary, the theatrical audience sees the separate scenes as one and hears the men upstage negate what the women say downstage. For instance, after Olga announces that she wants to go back home to Moscow, Chebutykin, a military doctor, responds, "The hell you say!" Tuzenbach amplifies the doctor by adding, "You're right, it's all a lot of nonsense." The men do not respond to Olga in any naturalistic sense; they are, in fact, in a separate room. But the audience perceives the men's remarks as responding to what Olga has said. This identical pattern repeats two more times in the same scene. After Olga repeats the Moscow refrain, the stage directions indicate that both Chebutykin and Tuzenbach laugh. At the end of the scene, after Olga imagines that if she had been someone else she would have gotten married and loved her husband, Tuzenbach interjects: "Nothing you say makes any sense! I can't take it anymore" (260). The two separate scenes next become one when the officers move downstage to greet the sisters.

After the very first scene of the play, then, it is clear that the sisters will never go to Moscow and the subsequent repetitions of that stated desire only further drain the possibility of such an action. The stage directions for Irina's final line at the end of Act 2 indicate that she is "Alone, longing," as she exclaims: "I want to go to Moscow! Moscow! Moscow!" (292). After a year and a half since the events of Act 1, Irina is no closer to Moscow than she was at the beginning of the play. The arrival and departure of the military garrison bookends the action of the play within a two-and-a-half year interval during which the repeated invocations of Moscow actually insure the fact that the sisters will never leave for the city. By the end of Act 3, Irina sounds more desperate in her appeal to Olga: "I beg you, please! There's no place in the world like Moscow! Let's go, Olga! Please!"(305). Moscow, in the collective imagination of the Prozorovs, including Andrey, is not really in the world. It is an abstraction, an escape, a place where they are not. Masha slips into the subjunctive to express her idea of happiness to Vershinin: "I think if I lived in Moscow I wouldn't care what the weather was" (285). She can only say that, Vershinin points out, because she is not there. He elaborates his point by recalling a story he read about how a prisoner noticed birds from his cell window that he had never bothered to see previously in his life of freedom. Masha's idealization of Moscow, Vershinin claims, is analogous to the prisoner's birds: "once you're actually living in Moscow you won't notice it anymore either. We're never happy, we can never be happy. We only *want* to be happy" (285). As if to confirm such nihilism, a message arrives for him from his daughter that says his wife has taken pills again and that he must leave immediately.

Vershinin masks his unhappy and nagging domestic situation by endlessly philosophizing about the future, an even greater abstraction than Moscow. On the one hand, he maintains that nothing in this life is important or makes any difference to future generations: "No one will remember us. That's fate; there's nothing you can do about it. Things that seem important to us, serious and significant things … the time will come when they'll all be forgotten—or they won't seem so important anymore" (267). On the other hand, he also waxes poetically about the future in the same act. Referring to the education and cultural sophistication of the Prozorov family, he argues that they might be paving the way for a better life in the future. Over time, he says, there will be more and more people like them: "In two or three hundred years, life on earth will be unimaginably beautiful, astonishing. Man needs a life like that, and if we don't have it yet we must wait for it, dream of it, prepare for it, and that's the reason we must be able to see and know more than our fathers and grandfathers" (269). In a later discussion in the following act, Vershinin again argues that the future will be much better than present times and that they are all working for that glorious day right now even though they will never experience the fruits of such labor: "In two or three hundred years ... well, in a thousand, maybe—the number of years isn't so important—a new and a happier life will begin. Of course, we'll never see it, but we are working toward it right now. We work for it, we suffer for it, we create it, in fact. And that's the whole point of our existence. That's what happiness is, I think" (282). Moments later, he reiterates his views: "Our task is only to work and work; happiness is reserved for our descendants. (*Pause*) It's not for me. It's for my distant descendants." In this fashion, Vershinin seems to explain or justify his own unhappy situation without having to take any actions to change or fix it.

He sticks to this script all the way to the end of the play. As he prepares to leave town with the brigade he stops at the Prozorovs to say goodbye to Masha, with whom he's fallen in love, for the last time. Waiting for her, he awkwardly fills the silence with more chatter about the future: "Life isn't easy. Sometimes it must seem stupid and hopeless, but we have to remember that it is getting constantly brighter and better, and I don't think the time is far off when it will be completely bright" (315). So much of this endless and repetitive talk of the future is not so much philosophizing, as it is cover to avoid silence or, even more, honest communication. Here, at the near end, Vershinin reveals that all his talk merely defends against the piercing silence of perceived accusations: why did you leave me? How much do you love me? When will you come back? Will you ever come back? He and Masha barely exchange any words in their final embrace and Masha begins to sob "violently" (316). In "Writing for the Theatre," playwright Harold Pinter posits a psychological axiom: "The more acute the experience the less articulate its expression" (11). The emotional connection between Vershinin and Masha produces no sound at all. Olga finally intervenes in order to peel Masha from him. Here, at the end, the scene reveals the repetition of speeches about the future as a rhetorical device to quell silence, ward off awkwardness and avoid emotional catharsis. The final parting of Masha and Vershinin prompts an emotional break from previous deliberate obfuscations. For a brief moment the defenses between them go down.

In the preceding scene in Act 4, Andrey, too, addresses the future as a beacon of hope against his dark present of broken and unrealized dreams. He laments the passing of time and asks what happened to his life: "We barely begin to live, and all of a sudden we're old and boring and lazy and useless and unhappy" (313). He generalizes about people and the human condition but he is talking specifically about his own life, choices and predicament. For example, he says that wives cheat on husbands and that the husbands pretend that they don't know about it, but this predicament describes exactly his own situation. He comforts himself with thoughts of the future that remain non-specific and completely abstract: "The present is awful, but when I think of the future, I feel better; in the distance a light begins to break, I can see freedom; my children and I will be free from laziness, from drinking too much, eating too much every Sunday, from too many naps after dinner, from living like insects…" (314). Thinking of his sisters, Andrey calls out to them and begins to cry. Alone and candid, Andrey grasps at the future in the distance as if it were a rung on a ladder for him to climb to safety. He has become a passive spectator viewing his own life as it passes by in a rush of time that he has no way to stop or change in direction. He focuses on the future because he cannot deal with everyday life and thoughts of a happy future in the distance that he will never see allow him to neglect the ramifications and consequences of his own decisions. As if to emphasize that point by way of stark contrast, Natasha interrupts his reverie by yelling at him from inside the house to stop talking for fear of waking little Sophie. Completely whipped, Andrey promises to be quiet and enters his house.

Irina's idea of work joins "Moscow" and the "future" as the third major abstract concept that characters employ to offset encounters with the here and now. Prior to Vershinin voicing virtually the same thing, Irina shares her belief that the whole point of life is to work: "The reason we're unhappy and think life is so awful is because we don't know what it means to work. We come from families who thought they never had to work…" (317). It does not matter what job one pursues, she says, but the work itself gives meaning to life: "How wonderful it must be to get up at dawn and pave streets, or be a shepherd, or a schoolteacher who teaches children, or work on a railroad. My lord, not even a man, a horse or something, as long as you work—anything's better than waking up at noon and having breakfast in bed and then taking two hours to dress. What an awful life that is! I want to work the way I want cold drinks in hot weather" (261–262). Of course, Irina has never held a job. In fact, as her other sisters remark, she has never worked a day in her life. Tuzenbach, who is in love with Irina, chimes in with his own ideas about the nobility of work. He says this to impress Irina and to defend attacks against her and to demonstrate his like-mindedness with her. He couches the idea of work in political-revolutionary terms in which the idle aristocrats must give way to the united workers of the world: "And now the time has come, there's a storm gathering, a wild, elemental storm, it's coming, it's almost over our heads! And it will clean out our society, get rid of laziness and indifference, and this prejudice against working and this lousy rotten boredom. I intend to work, and in twenty-five or thirty years we will all work! All of us!" (262). Tuzenbach, too, looks to a future that precludes his participation and he eulogizes the need for work without ever having to commit his own back to it.

Irina, to be sure, does go to work and her series of jobs in the subsequent acts help to mark further the passage of time. In Act 2, she returns home worn out after a long day at the telegraph office. She reports an incident at work in which she rudely treated one of the clients and decides that she is ill suited for this type of employment. Irina longs for some poetry in her work and this job was not what she had in mind when she declared that she had a powerful desire to work. By Act 3, she's sick of work altogether and hates her new job at the municipal building. She's now 24 years old and working all the time: "my brain has shriveled up." She, too, with the realization that she might never leave and return to Moscow, is in an existential crisis: "There's no satisfaction in any of it, and the time passes and you realize you'll never have the beautiful life you dreamed of; you just keep digging yourself deeper and deeper into a hole.... I'm in despair, I am really in despair! And I don't understand why I'm still alive. I should have killed myself long ago" (301). As she weeps, Olga advises her to marry Tuzenbach even though he is not very good looking. Irina admits that she's dreamed of the man she would meet and fall in love with in Moscow, but that it is all "a lot of nonsense" (302). This is the same word, "nonsense," that the soldiers use to contradict Olga and Irina's opening salvo in praise of Moscow. In Act 4, Irina finally announces that she will marry Tuzenbach on the following day and that they will leave immediately to begin their new life together in which she will teach school and he will work in a brick factory.

While Irina's skipping from one job to the next does not accomplish much, Natasha's gross materialism drives the action as she takes over the Prozorov household. Among Chekhov's four great plays, she comes the closest to being an actual villain. She arrives as an outsider, Andrey's girlfriend, at the end of the first act. He loves her, he says, because she is so "ordinary," a reaction no doubt to the over-refined education that he believes has set him apart from everyone else in town (275). In an act of self-destruction, however, he proposes marriage and he kisses her to close the act. The next act resumes after a few months have passed and much has changed already. Andrey sits with his book while Natasha moves about and frets whether their baby boy, little Bobik, suffers from a draught. She declares that it would be much better for Bobik if he had a warmer room and points out that Irina's room gets sun all day long and suggests that Irina should vacate her room and move in with Olga for the good of the child. Andrey avoids conflict with her; in fact, he avoids speaking to her altogether. In Act 3, Natasha quarrels with Olga and suggests that she move down to the basement to avoid further conflicts. Her ulterior motive, however, is to provide another bedroom for her new addition, little Sophie. By the final act, Natasha rules the family completely and Masha refuses to enter her own home. Natasha announces that she will move Andrey and his screeching violin to Irina's former room. With Irina scheduled to leave the next day, Natasha declares that more changes in the household are imminent: she plans to cut down all the old trees around the house first thing. Before leaving to admonish one of the maids about a fork that has been left outside, she imparts fashion advice to Irina, an ironic switch from the opening scene in which the Prozorov girls criticized Natasha for her poor taste in clothes.

There's nothing subtle about Natasha and her quest to procure everything that she thinks her family needs. At the same time, her aggressive and progressive moves on the family home remain in the background. In the foreground, the inert family members, who seem incapable and unwilling to make any definitive action that could change their lot, watch time pass by and their lives slip away. In particular the love affairs between Masha and Vershinin as well as that between Irina and Tuzenbach stand out as notable failures in which all parties seem to accept defeat from the outset! Each couple adds a theatrical quality to its interactions in order to protect against real pain that comes from an honest investment of emotions. The characters "play" at love as if they were actors in a play in order to retire safely when the scene they make ends. It would be a mistake to say that these casual affairs result from characters' boredom and their restlessness at having nothing better to do. They convince themselves that nothing matters and nothing makes any difference as a way to guard against inevitable disappointments that are only inevitable because of their actions. Two scenes, one from the second act, and one from late in the final act, demonstrate similar patterns that pertain to both couples.

Masha and Vershinin demonstrate their sensitivity, finesse, kindness and gentleness to each other by identifying deficiencies in their wedded relationships. Masha used to think that her husband, a schoolteacher, was intelligent; now she knows that he is not. Vershinin loves his two daughters but he can't stand their mother/his wife and complains about constant arguments with her. At the same time, however, neither Masha nor Vershinin plans to abandon his or her spouse. Establishing their unhappiness is a prerequisite for them to license a hopeless romance that has no future. Vershinin lapses into a theatrical vocabulary as he woos Masha: "You're a strange, wonderful woman. Strange and wonderful. I can see your eyes shining in the dark." Hilariously, Masha then moves to another chair and says, "There's more light over here." Vershinin escalates his love talk, calling her a strange wonderful woman again with more emphasis and punctuation, an outburst that causes Masha to laugh: "When you talk to me that way it makes me laugh somehow—even though it terrifies me. Don't say it again, please ... (*Half to herself*) No, go on, say it; what difference does it make?" (280). Masha realizes that she plays a scene worthy of 19th-century drama, perhaps a play she's even seen, but still decides to go along with it, partly because the scripted dialogue has a stagey quality divorced from real feelings and emotions. They play at love in order to protect themselves emotionally from its demands. With the entrance of Tuzenbach and Irina into the room, Masha immediately stops Vershinin from his grandiose lovemaking and they straighten up to act as though nothing has happened between them. In the end, though, as the previous description of their goodbye scene in Act 4 shows, genuine emotions penetrate the playacting and create a moment of raw tenderness. Both partners indulged an impossible affair that, in the end, came to fruition and devastated them entirely.

No such emotional fireworks take place between Irina and Tuzenbach. He adores Irina; she does not love him. The suppressed dialogue and intimacy of their last scene together in Act 4, in which so much is left unsaid, presents silent anguish that is painful to witness. They observe Masha's husband, Kulygin, walking through the garden and calling after his wife and Tuzenbach comments that he is probably the only man in town who wants the brigade to leave town. A pause gives space for Irina to tell Tuzenbach how much he means to her but she doesn't seize the opportunity. He begs leave of her for a little while, and although Irina is aware that something dangerous may be in the works, she cannot will herself to embrace the gravity of the situation. Tuzenbach tells her that he's loved her for five years, and notes that they are about to get out of this town together but that the only problem is that Irina does not love him. She'll marry him, she says, and be faithful to him, but she does not love him. Visibly upset, Tuzenbach presses Irina to say something intimate that will give this moment some higher meaning before he faces Solyony. Stretched to the breaking point, Irina begs him to stop. Tuzenbach obliges: "I feel happy. It's almost as if I were seeing these trees for the first time in my life; they all seem to be looking at me and waiting for something. What beautiful trees they are! ... This tree is dead, but it still moves in the wind with the others. I feel like that; if I die, I mean, I'll still be part of life somehow..." (313). He heeds the call for him and starts away, insisting, finally, that Irina not go with him. He makes a false exit, then stops to turn back and calls her by name. Once he has her attention, however, he cannot summon the words that are most on his mind. The stage directions indicate that he doesn't know what to say. His last lines read: "I didn't have any coffee this morning. Ask them to fix me some, will you?" (313). He covers the awkwardness and disappointment with a simple request and then leaves quickly. What he wanted to say, what he wanted to hear, remains unsaid and unheard. The scene that he envisioned in his mind, unlike the dramatic love forays of Masha and Vershinin, does not play with Irina. He dies shortly thereafter in a pointless duel.

An earlier scene with Olga provides a welcome counterpoint to the intimate evasions of Masha and Irina. Act 3 takes place at 2:00 a.m. during the midst of a terrible fire that consumes much of the town. Fire trucks rumble down the streets under a red sky outside the house. Exhausted, Olga nevertheless continues to pull clothes from a closet and pile them into the arms of her 80-year-old nurse, Anfisa, to deliver to the newly homeless and indigent population. Her opening monologue displays her generosity, but Anfisa, also exhausted, begs Olga not to send her away and claims that she is an old woman doing the best that she possibly can to serve the family. Olga does not understand what motivates this outcry and instructs the old nurse to sit and rest. Natasha, to be sure, voices the same platitudes of generosity as Olga, but she does not have the same kind spirit behind her words as the Prozorov sister. Of her civic duties, Natasha says matter-of-factly: "We should help out the poor anyway; that's one of your responsibilities if you're rich" (294). Natasha's only real concern, however, is with the health of her own family. She flies into a rage when she catches Anfisa at rest on the job: "She doesn't do a thing! She's a peasant, she should be living on a farm!" Indignant, Olga claims that her own sensibilities are too refined to tolerate Natasha's rude behavior which only further underscores her inability or unwillingness to stand up to Natasha's will. Olga defends Anfisa as a lifetime family servant of over 30 years, but Natasha has no truck with such sentimentality. The old woman simply fails to provide any meaningful labor.

The following scene is one of the most remarkable in the play in which the doctor, Chebutykin, drunkenly bemoans the death of a patient under his care the previous week. He thinks that he is alone in the room and the alcohol that he has imbibed provides the filter for him to speak freely in a rambling monologue that reveals his inner despair that has not been evident until this point. He laments the fact that he doesn't know anything and cannot remember any knowledge from his youthful days. This is one of the most honest and emotional scenes in the play in which helplessness in the face of life's unforgiving events overcomes a character. Similar to Astrov from *Uncle Vanya*, Chebutykin claims that his head and his heart are empty as a result of being around death and dying habitually. His capacity for empathy has completely dried up and left him feeling impotent and worthless, driven to drink, and drained of desire to exist any longer. After other characters gather to discuss the impact of the fire and Vershinin mentions the rumor that he's heard regarding the possible transfer of the brigade to Poland or even the Chinese border, Irina pipes up: "And we're leaving too!" (297). Punctually, on cue, Chebutykin smashes a clock to pieces and literally stops time to negate the force of Irina's vow.

A march sounds at the end of Act 4 to signify the brigade's withdrawal from town. Masha and Olga prepare to leave as well when Chebutykin enters and whispers something to Olga, after which he concludes: "Anyway, what difference does it make?" (318). Chebutykin announces that the baron has been killed in a duel. As the sisters cluster, he repeats: "What difference does it make?" Masha laments that they must start their lives all over again. Irina emphasizes the ritual of work and the routine of everyday living: "It's autumn; winter will come, the snow will fall, and I will go on working and working" (318). Olga finishes the threnody in praise of future generations who will look back with gratitude upon those who worked and suffered and paved the way for their peaceful and happy lives. Hearing the military band play, she concludes: "The music sounds so happy, so joyful, it almost seems as if a minute more, and we'd know why we live, why we suffer. If only we knew. If only we knew!" (319). As the music fades into the distance, Kulygin enters with Masha's hat and coat, Andrey wheels the baby carriage, and Chebutykin sings softly and reads his newspaper, before issuing his refrain: "What difference does it make? What difference does it make?" Juxtaposed to those lines, Olga repeats, "If only we knew! If only we knew!" The aesthetic beauty of the last moments with the sounds of the distant band, the repetition of lines, repetition of stage picture with the three sisters together again as they were in Act 1, repetition of iconic gestures from a multitude of characters seduce an audience into accepting what is said as reasonable and even somehow inevitable. The sisters suggest with their pitiful use of the subjunctive at the end that they would live differently, choose differently, if they knew how things (life?) would turn out in the end. That desire is understandable, but ridiculous and thoroughly unacceptable. Who can know how life turns out, when the real story of anyone's life remains a retrospective whose narrative trajectory only death ultimately determines? And until the end, the slope of that line, with its highs and lows, traces an unpredictable arabesque pattern in time and space. Unwilling to make that journey, in the face of uncertainty, with doubts about the future, and all sorts of fears about how things might turn out, the three sisters do nothing. They do not move.

What difference does it make? What does it matter if a baron dies, if a heart breaks, if a faithful employee wears out-of-service in her old age, if the town burns down, if no one cares about education, if decency and generosity are meaningless tokens? What does it matter? Isn't it all "nonsense"? Of course not, the repetition of these things throughout the play signifies their importance. The more characters might insist that nothing matters; the more the audience can see that things do matter. Relationships matter and make the difference between happiness and unhappiness. The encampment of the brigade in the Prozorovs hometown could have changed all of their lives. Time passes, and at the end of the play, the military brigade passes them by on the way out of town. What difference does it make? It could have made a world of difference and changed lives. But even if more opportunities to pursue their happiness do arrive, the action of this play suggests that the Prozorovs will not see them or take advantage of them or take any action to shake free of a crippling lethargy that leaves them puzzlingly inert and desperately sad, even as they force smiles and recite tired paeans to the future.

The Cherry Orchard (1903)

> "Oh, if only we could change things, if only life were different, this unhappy, messy life…"

Liubov Andreyevna Ranyevskaya leaves her lover in Paris, after he cheats on her and spends all of her money, and returns to her estate in rural Russia. She's glad to be home, she says, but she's haunted by the memory of her little boy who drowned there years ago. His tutor, who greets her at the house, reminds her of the past from which she has tried to run away. The caretaker of the estate, Lopakhin, son of a peasant and former serf, advises Andreyevna that the estate is up for auction due to delinquent mortgage payments. He, however, has come up with a plan to save the estate: cut down the old cherry orchard and subdivide the estate into many separate lots and build summer houses for rich people to rent. That would produce enough income, according to his calculations, to keep the household running. Unfortunately, Andreyevna and members of her family do not accept this logical, workable plan and they do nothing to prepare for the auction on 22 August except borrow a tiny amount of money from an aunt in Yaroslavl, an amount insufficient even to pay the taxes. Still, Gayev, Andreyevna's brother, attends the auction with the intent of purchasing the estate. On this day, Andreyevna, a terrible spendthrift, hosts a ball in anticipation of the auction's outcome. Gayev comes home tired, empty-handed and surprisingly speechless. The buyer, it turns out, is none other than Lopakhin, the poor boy who has become rich, and who boasts, drunkenly, that he now owns the estate upon which his forbears were slaves. Lopakhin turns the aristocrats out, but they want to go anyway. Madame Ranyevskaya, in particular, has received countless telegrams from her old lover in Paris begging her to return and now she feels she has waited long enough. Her treatment of the old family servant, Firs, explicitly manifests her indifference to the family home. She makes a lot of noise concerning the welfare and whereabouts of her old faithful retainer, but when she actually leaves she forgets about him entirely and leaves the old man behind in an empty house as the axes strike the cherry trees in the distance.

Arrivals and departures frame the action similar to all the previous Chekhovian dramas. Madame Ranyevskaya and her entourage sweep into the house in the early morning hours with excited frenzy: "I love this country, really I do, I adore it. I started to cry every time I looked out the train windows" (*Plays* 339). Lopakhin prepares to leave, but endeavors to reveal his plan to save the estate from auction before he goes. He tells Liubov how different she is from the rest of her family because she always treated him differently—as a person he means: "my God, my father slaved for your father and grandfather, my whole family worked for yours; but you, you treated me different" (340). Wound up, he almost tells her that he loves her, but she and the others do not listen and are "just not in the mood!" Instead, Liubov focuses on taking in her new surroundings amidst the excitement from the trip. Lopakhin persists, however, and informs the group that the estate can be saved provided that they clear out the cherry orchard and subdivide the land into lots for vacation homes. All the old buildings, including the main house must go. The income from this venture will allow them to more than pay off their debts. Lopakhin's simple business plan falls on deaf and uncomprehending ears. Andreyevna will not even think of it: "Our cherry orchard is a landmark! It's famous for miles around!" (341). Lopakhin points out that it is big, but unprofitable. Cherries are simply not a commercial crop anymore. Firs recalls that they used to be sent off by the wagonload to Moscow—but that was also when there was a cheap labor force to perform the necessary manual labor. Lopakhin insists that summer homes for the newly rich will bring in profits as the old cherry trees once did. Meanwhile, Varya brings Liubov a pair of telegrams that she had stored in the old bookcase. Andreyevna announces: "They're from Paris." Without opening either one, she tears them up and concludes, theatrically, "I'm through with Paris" (342). She may not be interested in saving her family home, but she does want to arouse the jealousy of her lover in Paris and demonstrate to her onlookers that she has no further need of that man. Also distracted by Lopakhin's proposal and looking for a way out, Gayev now delivers his homage to the bookcase: "For a hundred years now you have borne the shining ideals of goodness and justice, a hundred years have not dimmed your silent summons to useful labor" (342). It is the same sort of vague, abstract praise that Vershinin used to describe the future in *Three Sisters*, an elaborate evasion of what cannot be dealt with in the present moment: the prospect of change, doing business with Lopakhin, and an embrace of the future.

The first act takes place "in a room they still call the nursery" (333). Liubov remembers that she slept there as a child, but it is also where her dead son slept. Her daughter, Anya, recounts that her father died six years ago and that her little brother, Grisha, drowned only one month later. She explains: "And Mama couldn't face it, that's why she went away, just went away and never looked back" (338). Returning to the site of her private tragedy and grief, Liubov continues to mourn the loss of her son. She lapses into the subjunctive as she gazes out the window at the white orchard and reflects upon its beauty and the way it used to look when she and Varya and Gayev were much younger: "If only I could shake off this weight I've been carrying so long. If only I could forget my past!" Andreyevna exclaims (344). Her dramatic despair changes quickly, however, as she plays a joke upon Gayev and Varya by pretending to see her dead mother in a white dress. She "laughs delightedly" at her prank, a rapid shift that indicates that she enjoys her performance of despair. Her high degree of self-absorption leads her to make thoughtless, even tactless remarks directed at others, such as her first entrance when she tells her own adopted daughter, Varya, that she still looks like a nun (335), or when she greets Firs, her old family retainer a bit later after a long absence: "I'm so glad you're still alive" (339). But, when others are present she can quickly turn on emotional and theatrical fireworks, as when she notices the appearance of Trofimov, Grisha's former tutor, in the room. Once again, she begins to weep and wail: "My little boy drowned, lost forever.... Why? What for? My dear boy, why?" (345). She shifts quickly from this lament to note Trofimov's disheveled appearance as a kind of permanent graduate student. Commenting on his sister's behavior, Gayev allows that she is "lovely," but that she is also a bit of a "loose woman" (347). His frank remarks suggest another reason for her long absence from her native home other than grief for her dead son: She followed a series of romantic liaisons to various European countries.

Lopakhin presses his plan to cut down the cherry orchard in the second act, but neither Gayev nor his sister listens to what he says: "I tell you every day what you should do! Every day I come out here and say the same thing. The cherry orchard and the rest of the land has to be subdivided and developed for leisure homes, and it has to be done right away. The auction date is getting closer!" (353). Liubov and Gayev refuse to listen to him, in part, because, as Liubov says, the idea of building leisure homes for the new middle class is "all so hopelessly vulgar." But this excuse is really a rouge to cover the fact that no one actually cares enough to protect the cherry orchard—no one even wants to stay on the estate! Varya wants to travel and perhaps join a convent; Andreyevna wants to go back to her lover in Paris; Gayev says he wants to get a job; Anya, under the thrall of Trofimov, feels a moral need to move away from the estate that once exploited the labor of slaves. Lopakhin repeats the news of the impending sale and even supplies the name of the prospective buyer, but all they can say is that the old lady from Yaroslavl is supposed to send money, 10,000 or 15,000, even though it is evident that 100,000 or 200,000 is required. Lopakhin cannot understand why they do not heed his warnings: "Somebody tells you flat out your land is about to be sold, you don't even seem to understand!" (353). They understand perfectly well; they simply choose not to do anything to save the orchard.

After Lopakhin's protest subsides, Andreyevna confides her worries: "I keep waiting for something to happen. It's as if the house were about to fall down around our ears or something…" (353). She feels that God has punished her myriad of sins: (1) spending all her money; (2) falling in love with another man, during which time her son drowned in the river; (3) running away to France with her lover and buying a villa in Menton; and (4) facing abandonment after that same lover ran off with another woman. She wanted to return to her childhood home to recuperate from a series of losses. She concludes: "Don't punish me again!" and she pulls out another telegram from Paris and says that her lover is now sorry and wants her back (354). Once again, she tears up the telegram, but this gesture positioned as the climactic moment, the final revelation, suggests its importance to her. She ends by inquiring about the music that she hears in the distance. Delighted by the news that it is the famous local orchestra, she suggests that they have them over on an evening when they throw a party. Offhandedly, she advises Lopakhin to stop attending the theater in order to concentrate upon his "own reality" (355). She tells him that he leads a boring life and that he ought to get married, and that he should marry Varya.

Trofimov, the radical student, views Lopakhin as a capitalistic stumbling block in the way of human progress toward dignity and happiness and says that it is time to get to work: "Things that seem impossible to us nowadays, the day will come when they're not a problem at all, only we have to work toward that day" (357). Trofimov emphasizes that the search for the truth must be joined by action, not just talk, a rhetorical aspect of his speech that differentiates it, say, from that of Vershinin's in *Three Sisters*. (And yet, as events play out, Trofimov's ideology wears thin through repetition to reveal itself as an artful dodge of the truth and intimate relationships.)

Gayev announces sunset and delivers a poem in honor of the event that provokes comments to cease and desist. Out of the sustained silence that follows, the stage directions read: "Suddenly a distant sound seems to fall from the sky, a sad sound, like a harp string breaking. It dies away" (358). It is interpreted variously by the listeners as "an echo from a mine shaft"; "some kind of bird … like a heron"; "an owl." Firs recollects hearing the same thing when the serfs gained freedom in 1861.

The strange sound elicits disparate and conflicting interpretations from the characters on stage, but literary critics have also seized on this phenomenal moment to make their own wild statements.[21] Maurice Valency, perhaps seizing on Trofimov's vision of the future and the need to work, explicitly ties this event to his master theme of Chekhov as the "voice of twilight Russia" and finds in it the title of his book. David Magarshack roots the sound in the real world and insists that the sound was what Chekhov remembered as a boy when he would spend his summer months at a little hamlet in the Don basin (180). Harvey Pitcher takes a phenomenological approach rather than a biographical one to the scene: "Chekhov is widening the emotional horizons by presenting on the stage the mysterious emotional relationship that exists between men and the world of nature, and between men and the realm of sound" (183). Similarly, J. L. Styan surmises: "As music might, it introduces an aural symbol of time; it traps in our heads time past and time passing. Yet it also signifies the break with the past. To do all this, it must, like the artifice of the theatre itself, seem to stop time" (288). Like Valency, Styan makes the moment important by assigning symbolic value to it.

The search for an interpretation of the sound creates the same stir and uneasiness in the characters as the search for meaning in Chekhov's plays creates for his interpreters. Characters want to make things significant and they inspire a host of critics to do the same thing. Such heightening, however, obfuscates the difficult task of dealing with the here and now of what lies before and in front of each character. The moment calls attention away from what is happening on the stage and invites the characters to speculate about things that cannot be conclusively determined. The scene enacts what happens in all the plays, in terms of characters seeking meaning and significance far outside themselves and drawing disparate conclusions based on ideas and theories. If we only knew what that was, they might say, we would not be so frightened of the things in this world. But they do not know and they cannot know everything and what remains unknown and mysterious creates tension that drives them away. At the same time, though, they enjoy interpreting that which cannot be known as a means of diverting focus and attention elsewhere, anywhere but what lies before them. The phenomenal moment is not a symbol so much as a demonstration of the lengths to which Chekhovian characters will go to avoid dealing with each other. They look past each other and point to some other time and place, the future, when things will be better, but they do nothing to ensure or promote a better future by advancing relationships in the here and now of the present. The scene elegantly and dramatically shows how the characters miss chances to connect with each other and seize upon a mysterious event, the "breaking string," to fill the silence of the broken dialogue.

The pace approaches that of farce in Act 3 as Liubov decides to host a ball on the auction night of 22 August. An archway separates the downstage sitting room from the ballroom upstage and the possibility of simultaneous action in the two spaces replicates that of the first act. The adjacent, offstage billiard room produces sounds of the game. As dancers enter two by two to the beat of the famous Jewish band from the previous act Liubov anxiously awaits the return of her brother and news of the auction results. She momentarily regrets her decision to host a party at such a time, then counters in a refrain reminiscent of *Three Sisters*: "Oh, well ... what difference does it make?" (363). Varya tries to comfort her by saying that Gayev probably bought the estate with the money sent from Anya's rich godmother in

Yaroslavl, but everyone knows that the sum she sent is insufficient. Even Liubov admits that the 15,000 won't even cover the interest payment. Still, she dramatizes: "My fate … my entire life…. It's all being decided today" (364). Trofimov responds plainly and again echoes the recurring line from *Three Sisters*: "Whether they sell it or not, does it make any difference, really? You can't go back to the past. Everything here came to an end a long time ago. Try to calm down. You can't go on deceiving yourself; at least once in your life you have to look the truth straight in the eye" (366). Liubov counters that it's easy for Trofimov to see life so clearly because he hasn't really lived or experienced anything yet. He may be a better person than her, but he wasn't born on the estate and he did not grow up there. This is the only home that she has ever known: "I love this house! Without the cherry orchard my life makes no sense, and if you have to sell it, you might as well sell me with it" (366). After she embraces Trofimov and kisses him, she reminds him that her son drowned on this estate. She takes out a handkerchief to wipe away her tears and a telegram falls to the floor.

Liubov explains yet again that the telegram is from her lover in Paris and that she receives one from him everyday that implores her to come back. She supposes that she should go back to take care of him because he's sick. Here, she admits her real desires and implicitly explains why she has done nothing to save the orchard despite her dramatic protestations to the contrary. Her admission strikes Trofimov as offensive and Liubov then claims righteously that she loves this man and that she cannot live without him. Trofimov, upset, points out that her lover has been using her and robbing her blind and that everyone except her can see this. "He doesn't care a thing for you—you're the only person who doesn't seem to understand that! He's rotten!" (367). Andreyevna launches a counter attack and says Trofimov knows nothing of love, that he is probably still a virgin, and that he is "all wet" as Firs likes to say. He's simply never committed to love, she says. "At your age," she says, "you ought to be sleeping with someone!" (367). Incensed, Trofimov storms out of the room, but returns almost immediately to announce, almost hysterically, "All is over between us!" While Liubov sees through the idealism of Trofimov as a mask for interpersonal insecurity and fear of intimacy, Trofimov sees through Liubov's theatrical display of grief over the orchard and challenges her romantic attachment to her French lover. Each sees the other quite objectively, but fails to achieve any insight into one's own motives. It is a rare moment when honest emotions and interpretations clash, but after Trofimov storms out again Anya reports that he fell headfirst down the stairs! Physical comedy punctuates a scene that brilliantly illustrates the blindness of characters with respect to their own situation and behavior.

The comic hijinks continue as Lopakhin receives less than a hero's welcome upon his return. Expecting someone else to walk through the door, Varya surprises Lopakhin by hitting him on the head with Firs' walking stick. After telling the assembled group of guests and family members that the auction ended a long time ago and that Gayev is just behind him, Lopakhin complains that his head spins from Varya's blow and the suspense builds as to what happened. Gayev exits to bed without disclosing anything, but he weeps, however, and adds for emphasis: "You have no idea what I've been through!" (372). "Who bought it?" asks Madame Andreyevna. "I did," Lopakhin says simply. Liubov almost falls down and Varya takes the keys off of her belt and throws them to the floor and then leaves. Lopakhin tries to explain what happened. He beat Deriganov in a bidding war that ended at 90,000 plus the balance on the mortgage. "My God, the cherry orchard belongs to me!" he exclaims, addressing his own disbelief. He wants everyone to stay and hear what happened. "I bought the estate where my father and my grandfather slaved away their lives, where they wouldn't even let them in the kitchen!" (373). He picks up the keys that Varya dropped and calls for the orchestra to play even as he changes his own tune: "Come and watch what I do! I'm going to chop down every tree in that cherry orchard, every goddamn one of them, and then I'm going to develop that land! Watch me! I'm going to do something our children and grandchildren can be proud of" (373). The assembled audience in the ballroom, many of whom will soon be displaced by Lopakhin's aggressive plans for the future, recoils at the news.

Lopakhin abruptly turns to Andreyevna, who has curled up in her chair, and addresses her directly: "Oh, why didn't you listen to me? You dear woman, you dear good woman, you can't ever go back to the past." He seems to wish that he weren't now in his current position: "Oh, if only we could change things, if only life were different, this unhappy, messy life..." (373). For a brief moment, Lopakhin, too, lapses into the subjunctive mood and imagines an alternative course of events, perhaps a route that might have made it possible for him to marry Liubov. He had hoped, surely, that his economic rise would have made him an attractive match for her and enabled her to overlook his humble origins and class differences. Now, though, he recognizes that that can never happen. Tipsy from a little too much champagne and from the headiness of the day, Lopakhin almost knocks over a small table on his way out the door, but claims, that as the new owner, he can pay for any damages incurred. "I can pay for everything," he brags. Anya comforts her mother with idealistic phrases: "Come with me, Mama, we'll go away, someplace far away from here. We'll plant a new orchard, even better than this one, you'll see, Mama, you'll understand, and you'll feel a new kind of joy, like a light in your soul…. Let's go, Mama. Let's go!" (374). Unfortunately, it is hard to believe that this is ever going to happen given the similarity of the ending of this scene compared to, say, the end of Act 3 of *Three Sisters* in which the "come on, let's go" plea sounds highly ironic. Here, as well, Andreyevna has already stated her true desire to return to her lover in Paris without any hint that a new orchard will crop up there.

The final act, Act 4, takes place on moving day in which all the former residents of the estate must scatter to disparate parts. Liubov, naturally, heads to Paris and the place she always wanted to reside. Stage directions dictate that the scene is the same as Act 1, the nursery, except now everything has been taken down and "the place feels empty" on an October day (374). Former adversaries, Trofimov and Lopakhin, shake hands and offer parting advice to each other. Trofimov notes that Lopakhin will be "going back to your useful labors in the real world" (375). Lopakhin teases Trofimov about his many years as a student at university. As farewell advice, Trofimov warns Lopakhin not to wave his arms around too much. He says that tearing down the cherry orchard and building new summer vacation homes will not improve the world and is just "a lot of arm waving too" (376). Still, he thinks that Lopakhin has a gentle and sensitive soul and he likes him. Lopakhin offers Trofimov money, but the younger man declines the offer and launches into another idealistic diatribe:

> Look, you could give me a couple of hundred thousand, I still wouldn't take it. I'm a free man. And you people, everything you think is so valuable, it doesn't mean a thing to me. I don't care whether you're rich or poor; you've got no power over me. I can do without you, I can go right on past you, because I am proud and I am strong. Humanity is moving onward, toward a higher truth and a higher happiness, higher than anyone can imagine. And I'm ahead of the rest! [377].

Even if Trofimov doesn't "get there" himself, he says, "I'll make sure the rest of them get there." (From the orchard, the sound of axes hitting the trees can be heard). Lopakhin doesn't see eye to eye with Trofimov, but parts in a friendly manner. In contrast to Trofimov's idealism regarding the future, Lopakhin imparts his two cent's worth of wisdom: "Whenever I work real hard, round the clock practically, that clears my mind somehow, and for a minute I think maybe I know what we're all here for" (377). He ends by recalling the story of Gayev taking a job at the bank, but concludes that it will not last because Gayev is too lazy. Anya enters and tells him that the sound of the axes upsets her mother and Lopakhin agrees to put an end to it until everyone leaves.

Lest one think that Trofimov represents some kind of prophet for the new world to come, his earlier protestations of love with Anya twist heroic valuation of his character. At the end of Act 2, Trofimov steals a private moment with Anya and notes that Varya is afraid that they will fall in love. "She's so narrow-minded," he asserts. "She simply can't understand that we are above love." He speaks of the great future and enthralls Anya with his lofty rhetoric: "We are moving forward, toward the future! Toward one bright star that burns ahead of us! Forward, friends! Come join us in our journey!"

Anya avoids an uncomfortable pause by talking about the weather. She then tells Trofimov that she doesn't love the orchard the way that she did as a child. Prophetically, he tells her: "This whole country is our orchard. It's a big country and a beautiful one; it has lots of wonderful places in it" (360). After another pause, he launches into a big speech about the sins of the past, the fact that Anya's ancestors owned slaves, and that it will take many years to pay the human debt back. Swayed by the power of his speech, Anya agrees to do something about it: "The house we live in isn't our house anymore. It hasn't ever been, really. And I'll leave it all behind, I promise you I will" (361). She is "radiant" when she tells him that she loves "the way you say things!" He works himself up in another speech in which he ends by saying that he feels happiness coming, that he can almost see it, as if he were about to grab her and kiss her passionately, but she interrupts him with her observation of the rising moon. They hear Yepikhodov playing his guitar in the distance, as well as Varya's call for Anya. Picking up on the atmosphere, Trofimov concludes that the rising moon is a sign of happiness, "coming closer and closer." He dodges the opportunity to behold his own happiness by deferring to the future: "And even if we miss it, if we never find it, that's all right! Someone will!" Hearing Varya again, they steal away together to walk by the river. They avoid, however, any talk of how they really feel about each other.

The failure of that relationship to approach any kind of honest intimacy pales in comparison to that of Lopakhin and Varya. Everyone expects those two to get married and considers the prospect almost a *fait accompli*. Except for the fact that Lopakhin never actually asks her to marry him! Varya voices her concern early that it will never happen: "Everybody talks about us getting married, people even congratulate me, but there's nothing.... I mean, it's all just a dream" (337). With five minutes to go before they must leave for the train station in Act 4, Liubov encourages Lopakhin again to propose marriage to Varya once and for all: "She loves you, you like her.... I don't know why, I just don't know why the two of you keep avoiding the issue. Really!" (381). Lopakhin agrees to try and "get it over with," and even notes that there is champagne on hand for a toast. Alone, both Varya and Lopakhin know what this moment is meant to be and yet both stall, Varya out of necessity. Because Lopakhin is not forthcoming, Varya makes up an excuse to look for something in the pile of belongings and suitcases. Lopakhin does not muster the question he is supposed to ask (will you marry me?) and instead asks where Varya is going to go when she leaves even though he presumably knows the answer to this question. Then, he repeats this same pattern of questioning when, after a pause, he comments, "Well, looks like this is the end of things around here..." (382). Varya continues to examine luggage in order to occupy herself with something and avoid the awkwardness of direct eye contact. Lopakhin asserts that he is leaving for Harkov and that Yepikhodov will be in charge for the time being. When Varya questions his choice, he begins to chatter about the weather as compared to a year ago at this same time. Varya says she didn't notice that it was freezing on this morning and, after another pause, finishes the conversation, "Anyway, the thermometer's broken." Someone calls for Lopakhin from outside and he uses the interruption as an excuse to escape from the room. Varya sits down on a bundle of clothes and begins to cry.

Luibov pokes her head into the room to see how things went and quickly realizes that nothing happened. After a pause, she says, simply, "We have to go" (382). Varya quickly agrees and adds that she can get to where she's going today if she doesn't miss the train. Everyone enters the nursery with coats on and begins to pick up bags. Gayev begins to make another speech: "On this occasion, this farewell to our beloved house, I cannot keep still. I feel I must say a few words to express the emotion that overwhelms me, overwhelms us all—" (383). Fortunately, Anya and Varya shut him down and don't let him speak any more. As he stands with his sister in their house for the last time, all he can summon is "Oh, sister, sister..." (384). Again, the intensity of his feeling and emotional distress prevent him from any sort of articulate expression. Andreyevna, on the other hand, summons a last dramatic speech to add solemnity to the occasion: "Oh, my orchard, my beautiful orchard! My life, my youth, my happiness, goodbye! Goodbye! Goodbye!" Despite her claims, Liubov looks forward to what lies ahead for her life in Paris. She has worked and prepared for this eventuality. Anya and Trofimov call for them and, finally, they depart and the stage directions read: "In the silence, we hear the occasional sound of an ax chopping down the cherry trees, a mournful, lonely sound." The final proof of Liubov's indifference slowly appears in the form of Firs who has been left behind and is noticeably ill. He realizes that everyone has gone, that they have forgotten about him despite all the questions about his whereabouts vis-à-vis the nursing home. He lies down. In the distance, a sound "that seems to come from the sky, a sad sound, like a string snapping" reprises the one heard by the group at the cemetery in Act 2 (385). The repetition of the odd sound reinforces the message that characters fail to connect with each other and deal with what occurs in the here and now of daily life. Instead, they direct their lives elsewhere: to the future, to a lover in Paris, to summerhouses, progress, and mysterious sounds in the distance! And they do this as time goes by and opportunities for human interaction and daily sustenance slowly, inevitably fade away. The sound of an ax striking a tree punctuates the end.

PART 3

Strindberg
Isles of the Dead

Strindberg projects Arnold Böcklin's 1880 painting, *The Island of the Dead*, as the final image in *The Ghost Sonata*. While the painting might be unfamiliar to most people today, it was not only a favorite of Strindberg's, but also one of the most pervasive and popular images of the late 19th and early 20th centuries. On the occasion of the Metropolitan Museum of Art acquiring the painting in 1926, longtime Curator of Paintings (1909–1934) Bryson Burroughs began his announcement by proclaiming that the work was "perhaps more widely known than any other German work of art since the sixteenth century" (146). Catherine C. Fraser cites two Scandinavian novels of the time that referenced the painting and claims that the painting in 1907 (the year Strindberg wrote *The Ghost Sonata*) would have been comparable in terms of audience recognition with works by Andy Warhol or the silkscreens of Liechtenstein in the 1960s (281, 283). Böcklin actually created five different versions of the painting between 1880 and 1886. Rachmaninoff saw one of them in Paris in 1907 and, inspired by what he saw, composed a symphonic poem with the same title a year later. He was not the only famous person to feel inspired by Böcklin's work. Toril Moi reports that Freud had a copy of the painting in his waiting room; Lenin had one tacked up above his bed in Zurich; and Adolf Hitler also bought one of the originals (136–137).

Fraser is surely right, then, when she asserts at the beginning of her article, "The painting would have been familiar to those who saw the first performances of the play at the Intimate Theater in 1908" (281). That is, audiences would have recognized it if an image of the painting had actually appeared. Egil Törnqvist discovered from published reviews that in August Falck's original production a couple of doors opened at the end to reveal a landscape with fir trees in lieu of Böcklin's painting (105). Subsequent famous productions of the play eschewed Strindberg's stated ending as well according to Törnqvist. Max Reinhardt omitted the image of the isle in 1916 in favor of an open window and a sound collage that suggested a journey to the Great Unknown rather than any blessed isle (112). Olof Molander directed the first of his five productions beginning in 1942 and he, too, re-imagined Strindberg's final stage direction and chose to have the back walls open up and the Student disappear into an upstage haze. In his final production, Molander, a converted Catholic, sent the Student upstage with uplifted arms in the form of a cross toward a small black-and-white reproduction of Böcklin's painting. Ingmar Bergman eliminated the image of the painting entirely in all four of his productions that spanned almost 60 years from 1941 to 2000. The last production took place in a theatrical space that was about equal to the size of Strindberg's Intimate Theater and it used a minimal number of properties as Strindberg had advised (140).

Directors frequently ignore the stage directions of playwrights in order to create powerful images for a unique event that suits the time and place of a specific production. Charged with the duty of transposing a dramatic text from the two-dimensional page to three-dimensional reality, directors shape material in the most theatrical and compelling ways that they think possible. And, while the changes that the three great directors above made to the ending of Strindberg's great play all sound interesting, a greater principle than artistic freedom governed their final interpretations and decisions. If the image of Böcklin's painting had been faithfully reproduced according to Strindberg's stage directions at the end of the drama, an audience would see what it had already perceived during the course of the performance. Böcklin's *The Island of the Dead* shows what Strindberg's play enacts, the primary action in many of Strindberg's plays, the desire to transcend the irreconcilable struggles of daily life. Therefore, the painting gratuitously repeats what the play has already endeavored to show. *The Island of the Dead* contains many recurring elements from Böcklin's previous works and favored motifs. Burroughs notes that the artist first expressed an interest in this subject matter as early as 1864 and displayed similar elements subsequently in a number of paintings: "the rocky shore, the building inhabited or deserted, the cypress trees, and the sea, sometimes stormy and sometimes ominously quiet" (146). Burroughs details the particular circumstances of *The Island of the Dead* and how Böcklin imported these familiar tropes into a new work. A young widow visited him in Florence and asked him to commemorate her late husband. He suggested some sort of spring festival scene to lift her spirits, but she requested "a landscape over which one could dream" (146). He began immediately on two slightly different images incorporating all of his favorite and traditional elements. When the widow returned to check his progress, he explained to her: "its influence is so quiet that one is startled if there is a knock at the door" (148). One version he gave a softer appearance by increasing the number of flowers on the tombs. The Metropolitan Museum in New York City owns this version, painted on board and rectangular in shape, its width much greater than its height. The Museum of Basel in Switzerland purchased another version, paint on canvas, more austere in appearance and also more square than rectangle in shape.

The dramatic scene takes place under moonlight but several focal points glow as if at sunset. In the background looms an ominous rock formation surrounded by water. From a large recess in the center of the rock island stems a glen of tall, dark cypress trees. Several openings in the surrounding rocks, apparently manmade, suggest a sepulcher. Two figures in a rowboat in the foreground of the painting confirm this interpretation of the island. A seated figure facing away from the viewer rows the boat; the other figure, also turned away from the viewer and toward the island, stands straight up in the bow of the boat. In front of the standing figure lies an oblong box that appears to be a coffin. A strange white light illuminates all three figures. The rowboat heads to the island to inter the body. The bow points to the opening in the rock island and creates a palpable sense of movement in the painting. Water around the boat remains placid, and the gentle ripples on the surface from the oars add to the serenity of the scene. As the artist informed his patron, the quiet scene invites mourning and contemplation. But it is significant that the widow asked for an image upon which to dream because the entire scene strikes the viewer as more mythological than realistic. The somber subject of the painting, the shape of the rocks, the play of light and dark, the tranquility of the evening, the stillness of the water, and the black hole at the center provides an opaque window through which the viewer may chart a destination that is both inevitable and completely unknowable. *The Island of the Dead* affords the viewer a vantage point and an opportunity to contemplate life's endgame and the mysteries that inform earthly existence.

The painting perfectly dramatizes the end of *The Ghost Sonata* in which the final spoken lines prior to the appearance of Böcklin's work read: "You poor little child, child of this world of illusion, guilt, suffering, and death; this world of endless change, disappointment and pain. The Lord of Heaven be merciful to you on your journey..." (*Five Plays* 297). The importance of the painting, however, lies not in relation to this single work, but to all Strindberg's major dramatic works in which in play after play the protagonist longs to relieve the repetitive drudgery of everyday living. The march toward death in Strindberg is not only inevitable but ultimately a welcome destination as it provides escape from the intractably bitter arguments that entangle men and women. When Julie exits at the end of *Miss Julie*, for example, her fatal decision might seem horrible and horribly fascinating but it is a solution nevertheless to a problem for which there appears to be no other answer. Similarly, when Tekla rushes to her collapsed husband at the end of *Creditors*, his climactic death escapes the prolonged torture of her former husband's revenge plot. The death of Edgar at the end of *The Dance of Death*, after a protracted battle with ill-health but an even more protracted battle of human relationships and vacillations between love and hate that exist between him and his wife, Alice, comes as a relief and a release—especially coming at the end of a very long play in two parts. The expressionist plays and the chamber plays at the end of Strindberg's career, including *To Damascus*, *A Dream Play*, *Easter*, *The Ghost Sonata*, and *The Great Highway*, extol an explicit religious theme in which death provides solace and safe haven after having lived in the world. The same calm that permeates the quiet and contemplative mood of *The Island of the Dead* seeps into the final scenes of these plays to provide a sense of relief from the turbulent conflicts that exist between human beings. Böcklin's painting stages a visual representation of the movement toward death, the acceptance of it and the transcendence of earthly concerns that form the primary action in many of Strindberg's plays. The shrouded, upturned figures, and unfathomable darkness in the center offer a compelling vision of the new kind of drama that Strindberg tries to create.

Strindberg's best thoughts on the theater from which he drew inspiration throughout his literary career came from the same decade as Böcklin's paintings and trace most directly from the author's preface to *Miss Julie* in 1888. This short document, one of the seminal documents in theater history concerning the aims and tenets of modern drama, succinctly outlines the problems of drama in the late 19th century and then outlines how the new drama solves those same problems. In addition, the author suggests a direction for the future growth and development of drama. Perhaps not coincidentally, Strindberg's initial tone in his preface is not unlike Chekhov's Konstantin and the call for new forms of drama! It might be a stretch to say that Chekhov modeled Konstantin's speech after Strindberg, but Chekhov had read and liked *Miss Julie* and it is not inconceivable that he took the preface as a foundation for Konstantin's similar complaint against the theater. Both Strindberg and the Chekhovian *enfant terrible* rail against the staid and conservative contemporary theater. While Chekhov stretches the complaint to hit a comic note with the call for new forms, Strindberg insists that it is impossible to do anything new and that he has simply "modernized the form in accordance with demands I think contemporary audiences make upon this art" (Preface 64).

Complexity, nuance and ambiguity are the qualities that Strindberg values in terms of dramatic character and human motivation. In preparing his audience to understand Miss Julie's behavior, Strindberg posits several competing factors:

> her mother's primary instincts, her father raising her incorrectly, her own nature, and the influence of her fiancé on her weak and degenerate brain. Also, more particularly: the festive atmosphere of midsummer night, her father's absence, her monthly indis-

position, her preoccupation with animals, the provocative effect of the dancing, the magical midsummer twilight, the powerfully aphrodisiac influence of flowers, and, finally, the chance that drives the couple together into a room alone—plus the boldness of the aroused man [66].

Strindberg rebels against the virtues of melodrama in which polarities of opposites strike maximum dramatic contrast. He does not deny the theatricality of melodrama, but tries to answer the challenge by putting in play all the contradictions that exist not only between characters but within characters as well. As he writes, famously, "'vice' has a reverse side closely resembling virtue" (67).

Strindberg anticipates Brecht when he says that theatrical entertainment should be educational: "I find the joy of life in its cruel and powerful struggles, and my enjoyment comes from being able to know something, being able to learn something" (65). Strindberg, like Brecht, delved in the sciences and his dramatic works examine human behavior. It is not enough to show what happens, he argues; modern audiences "want to know how it happened." In search of the motivations and reasons for actions, Strindberg elaborates: "We want to see the strings, the machinery, examine the double-bottomed box, feel the seam in the magic ring, looks at the cards to see how they are marked" (71). Strindberg's dramaturgy seeks to identify the unseen and underlying forces that govern behavior below the surface of mere appearance. While *Miss Julie* and its accompanying preface offer prototypical documents of the realistic and naturalistic periods, the playwright insists that one cannot pretend that a theatrical event does not take place in a theater. *Miss Julie* certainly does not expose its own theatricality in the same way that Strindberg's later works such as *A Dream Play* and *The Ghost Sonata* exploit the machinery of the theater and its capacity to create dream-like illusions, but Strindberg suggests, even here, the future direction that his theater would go over the course of his career and that he would not be content to remain a realist or naturalist.

Strindberg devotes the second half of the preface to specific reforms, many of which seem charmingly antiquated and conventional today. In order to achieve greater realism, he advocates doing away with painted scenery in interior rooms and canvas doors that shake and wobble every time they open or close. He seeks to minimize the use of heavy makeup and glaring footlights; encourages actors to turn upstage instead of playing everything downstage and full frontal; hides the orchestra and the prompter's box; and confines the action to one setting in order for the environment to play upon the imagination of the audience. Strindberg also calls for the elimination of act divisions in order to keep the audience in its seat and prevent it from escaping the spell of the author-hypnotist. He argues that plays should be 90 minutes in length in order to captivate fully the attention of an audience during that span. Strindberg seems absolutely prescient with these demands and observations as plays today have largely dispensed with intermission breaks in favor of continuous action that releases an audience from a theatrical grip in less than two hours.

More interestingly, Strindberg claims that his new play combines three separate art forms: monologue, mime and ballet. Strindberg calls his "mime" the business that the cook Kristine carries out by herself in the kitchen, performing various domestic and culinary tasks. The entrance of Jean and Kristine's co-workers into the kitchen and their boisterous singing and dancing comprise the "ballet." This riotous and vulgar behavior masks and also at the same time represents the violent and brief sexual escapade between Julie and Jean that occurs just offstage. Calling this moment a ballet is not nearly as important as seeing its function as a visual analogy to what happens offstage in Jean's bedroom. The ballet functions in accord with the tenets of realism and naturalism, but Strindberg also shows the "machinery" of the play in an elegant and artistic manner. The drunken and rowdy and coarse behavior of the crowd provides an artistic representation of the violent act that remains unseen and just offstage.

By far, though, the two most influential reforms that Strindberg proposes have to do, not with play construction, but with scenery on the stage and the size of the stage as well as the auditorium. With respect to the scene design of *Miss Julie*, Strindberg claims that he "borrowed from impressionist painting the device of making a setting appear cut off and asymmetrical, thus strengthening the illusion. When we see only part of a room and a portion of the furniture, we are left to conjecture, that is to say, our imagination goes to work and complements what is seen" (Preface 73). Instead of centering the kitchen within the frame of the proscenium arch, Strindberg creates an angle off-center to create the illusion that the visible scene is only a slice or fragment of a much larger scene that extends offstage laterally into the wings and vertically into the flyspace of the theater. When Julie makes her first entrance, then, she comes from somewhere connected to the kitchen. Indeed, the chorus enters later for the ballet and effectively suggests that it has tracked Julie to the kitchen. Earlier, when Julie takes Jean out of the kitchen and back to the dance, the scenic construction suggests the proximate location of the dance to the kitchen space. As the action proceeds, the threat of outside intervention imprisons Julie and Jean. Quite brilliantly, then, the final intervention comes not from outside the door but from up above through a speaking tube when the count, Julie's father, returns to his house and begins to bark orders. Although the count never appears, his return signals the end of the battle between class and gender and reminds Julie and Jean who wields the ultimate power and authority.

Strindberg ends the preface to *Miss Julie* with a call for the most important reform of all: a small stage and a small number of seats to see this new form of drama. If the new theater is to be a laboratory in which to investigate the complexity, nuance and ambiguity of human behavior and action, then only a small physical space can serve as microscope through which an audience looks. After this new theater arrives, Strindberg allows, "then perhaps we might see a new drama arise, or at the very least a theatre that was once again a place of entertainment for educated people. While waiting for this theatre, we will just have to go on writing, preparing the repertoire that will one day be needed" (Preface 75). Strindberg hoped that *Miss Julie* would represent the new drama. The new theatrical space that Strindberg sought, however, would not come until the next century and the last years of his long and productive theatrical life. Strindberg's first venture to start his own theatre in 1889 was called the Scandinavian Experimental Theatre in Denmark but it lasted for only a week. *Miss Julie* was banned due to its subject matter and the production of *Creditors* was not received well. Only the very short *The Stronger* received good notices. *Miss Julie* finally received its world premiere in 1889 as a private showing for 150 spectators in the student union of the University of Copenhagen (Marker 12–13). It didn't become a success until Andre Antoine produced it in his small, independent theater in Paris in 1893, a triumph of stage naturalism, ironically timed almost precisely with Strindberg's stylistic break from realism and naturalism.

The Intimate Theatre in Stockholm (1907–1910) was his second and final attempt to create his own theater space to optimize his vision of drama. He and his young director, August Falck, modeled the new theater after Reinhardt's Kammerspiele Theater in Germany, though the Swedes initially had plans for a theater with 400–500 seats that far exceeded the 292 of the German theater. The structure that they acquired, however, was far smaller than Reinhardt's theater, a building on Norra Bantorget, and it ultimately held only room for 161 seats. While Strindberg advocated for a small stage in a small theater, the stage of the Intimate Theatre was extremely small, measuring just six meters wide and four meters deep. In three seasons of operation, the tiny theatre produced 24 of Strindberg's works, including four "chamber plays," of which *The Ghost Sonata* was one, that were small works designed to have an analogous effect as chamber music. Ironically, Marker and Marker conclude that the tiny theater did not have the technical capacity to produce the theatrical visions of Strindberg's new plays and were far more successful with revivals of his early more naturalistic plays such as *Miss Julie* (118). In this regard the Intimate Theatre seemed to follow in the footsteps of Antoine's Theatre Libre.

The Intimate Theater, however, while small in size, paid sumptuous homage to Arnold Böcklin by hanging a copy of *The Island of the Living* on one side of the proscenium and *The Island of the Dead*, its companion piece, on the other. Just as Strindberg advocated a shift in scenery in order to make the offstage world contingent with the theatrical space, he framed the paintings from left to right for the audience to read life's journey from life to death, and to witness the live action on the stage within the proscenium opening as an interlude between the beginning and end. In a letter to Emil Schering in 1907 that accompanied a copy of *The Ghost Sonata*, Strindberg claims that writing the play caused him to suffer but that his Religion "saved my soul from darkness." He writes: "the hope of a better life to come, and the firm conviction that we live in a world of folly and delusion (illusion), out of which we must struggle to free ourselves" (Törnqvist and Steene 107). Strindberg expands and fully realizes his vision of death as the ultimate freedom and release to a peaceful afterlife, hinted at by *The Island of the Dead*, with the juxtaposition of both paintings between which the human folly on stage plays as though it were a dream.

The Ghost Sonata ends with an image of Böcklin's painting, but Strindberg soon started another chamber play later in 1907 named explicitly *The Isle of the Dead* that he subsequently abandoned after only two scenes. He confided to his German translator Schering: "'I had begun a major Chamber Play with *Toteninsel* as a setting. The beginning was good (Kama-Loka) but I lost interest, as though I'd lost interest in life, and had a presentiment of death'" (Robinson 8–9). Strindberg's loss of interest in *The Isle of the Dead* as an independent play may also have been due to a realization that the play actually repeated the movement from life to death in *The Ghost Sonata*, as well as the essential action in most of his major plays. One of Strindberg's essays in *A Blue Book*, a multi-volume work that he had begun in 1906 and continued working on until his death, "Higher Forms of Existence: *Die Toteninsel*," explores the world that Böcklin's painting creates and talks about the inhabitants of the island in a similar manner that the Student addresses the Young Lady at the end of *The Ghost Sonata*: "They longed for the morrow so as to know more about their fate and thus be reconciled to their past, which remained the only way to peace and felicity, to recovering their faith in the goodness of God and their hope of a better world to come" (Appendix 116). Strindberg welcomes death as an escape from the toll and toil of daily existence in which human passions suspend any hope of contented equilibrium.

The battles between men and women in the early plays from 1886 to 1892, epitomized by *Miss Julie*, still his most famous play, typically end in death or, in the case of what Strindberg calls comedy, divorce. Despite the palpable attraction between the leading characters in plays ranging from *Comrades* (1888) to *The Bond* (1892) and *Playing with Fire* (1892) the action regularly dissolves any union. The most significant event in Strindberg's life was what he called his inferno crisis during which he wrote no plays between 1893 and 1897. He conducted scientific experiments, painted, explored the field of photography, and dabbled in alchemy, but he wrote no dramas during this time of intense mental disturbance and anguish. When he emerged from this tormented state at the end of the 19th century, he wrote a different kind of play, disregarding realism/naturalism in favor of post-inferno expressionism in which he depicted life onstage as if it were a dream. Beginning with *To Damascus* in 1898 and ending with *The Great Highway* in 1909, these plays present many of the same conflicts between men and women as in the realistic plays, but with an overt religious context that often explicitly presents death and the prospects of an afterlife as the welcome end to human conflicts of desire and passion. The end of worldly concerns comes as a relief, suffering represents the norm of human existence, and Strindberg depicts daily life as a dreamlike experience distorted from true reality. Reality is unreality, life is a dream, and the dreamlike world of life after death is the only true reality.

Strindberg's comedy, *Comrades* (1888), responds to Ibsen's argument for equality between the sexes and women's emancipation in such plays as *A Doll's House* (1879), *Ghosts* (1881) and *Rosmersholm* (1884) by asserting that in a true marriage between a man and a woman there must be defined roles and that the husband must be superior to the wife. In this satire of domestic life set in Paris in the late 1880s Axel and Bertha, two painters, marry as friends and lovers as well as artists. In order to boost his wife's career, as well as to test their marriage bond, Axel submits his wife's name on one of his paintings to be judged by the salon. After the salon inevitably picks her picture, Bertha lets the triumph go to her head and the economic independence that comes with the award threatens to disrupt the balance of power within the relationship. Although they had espoused equality between them, Bertha's victory places her in a superior position, economically and artistically, within the relationship, and she begins to play the part of the "man" and attempts to emasculate her husband for whom she now professes a loss of respect. Ultimately, Axel reveals that the winning painting was, in fact, his own, but he loses all of his love for Bertha. He stands in triumph at the end as he prepares to leave Bertha and meet his new mistress, whom he says he may marry as well. This new woman, however, is not his friend, but only his lover. He confides: "For I want to see my comrades at the café—but at home I want to have a wife!" (*Comrades* 169). The reactionary conservatism of Strindberg pales in comparison to Ibsen's radical critique of relationships between men and women and the possibilities for a new and progressive society. The fact that *Comrades* hints at a paternal chauvinism that still exists to this day does not make it timelessly funny.

The Captain, Adolf, drives himself mad over the course of only two days in *The Father* (1887) because he realizes that he can never prove that his child, Bertha, now a young woman, is his own. For lack of a little DNA testing, then, the tragedy unfolds in three acts as Adolf transforms from a functioning, albeit somewhat paranoid, man to a straitjacketed automaton and victim of an apparent stroke. Yet, the question of paternity, which is, in fact, not in doubt, is hardly the struggle that consumes the play and gives it vibrant life. Rather, the action plays out as a quest for power between Adolf and his wife, Laura, over the fate of their only child. Adolf wants her to move to the city and train as a teacher so that she may be able to provide for herself in the event that she does not marry. Laura, lonesome at home, wants Bertha to remain with her. To gain the upper hand, Laura, for some time prior to the beginning of the play, has insinuated through various means that her husband lacks mental stability. She sensed his weakness and plotted to provoke his rage. The question of paternity, however, is not one that she invents; she merely uses her husband's preoccupation with it to prove that he is in fact violent and irrational. If the medical authorities will declare his insanity, she will win the power struggle with her husband. Laura acknowledges the stakes of the fight with her husband in a dynamic scene that ends Act 2: "What's this whole life and death struggle for if not power?" (39). Dialogue a bit later in the same scene defines their fight as winner-take-all for their daughter's future and survival of one of them:

> CAPTAIN: In this fight, one of us must go under.
> LAURA: Which?
> CAPTAIN: The weaker naturally.
> LAURA: Then is the stronger in the right?
> CAPTAIN: Bound to be as he has the power.
> LAURA. Then I am in the right.
> CAPTAIN: Why, what power have you?
> LAURA: All I need. And it will be legal power to-morrow when I've put you under restraint [43].

Even the quest for power, though, is not the true conflict in the drama— it is simply all that is left after the attrition of all the years of marriage has taken its toll upon both combatants. Near the very end of the play in Act 3, at a point in which Adolf is helpless in Laura's hands, he beckons her to remember the best years of their union a long time ago: "When you were young, Laura, and we used to walk in the birch woods. There were primroses and thrushes—lovely, lovely! Think how beautiful life was then—and what it has become! You did not want it to become like this, neither did I. Yet it has. Who then rules our lives?" (56). "God," Laura answers simply here, but earlier she cited their own sexual nature as the root cause for their deteriorating relationship. In Act 2 she declares: "Sexual love is conflict. And don't imagine I gave myself. I didn't give. I only took what I meant to take. Yet you did dominate me.... I felt it and wanted you to feel it" (42). The quest for power is thus an illusion of power, of control, over which Adolf and Laura hold no dominion. Assertions of power ultimately confirm its absence and the futility of seeking it in a world in which human beings have no control. With regard to their own intimate relationship, Adolf and Laura realize that they cannot embrace each other completely without giving away too much of themselves and their own sense of autonomy and purpose in the world. Adolf needs Laura as his mother, friend, and lover. Laura buckles under the impossible task of fulfilling all three of the demands simultaneously. She cannot answer all of Adolf's needs; he cannot answer all of hers. They blame each other for what they lack and turn to their child, whom they both love, as a means to get their needs met through a third party and to escape the desperation that they feel regarding their partner; they use the child to make themselves feel better and to get from Bertha what they cannot obtain within the bonds of their marriage.

This struggle proves futile, and while Laura is the de facto winner in the power struggle with her husband, the Captain, resignation is the only way out for either contestant. The stroke that silences Adolf at the end delivers peace such that he has not been able to experience within the action of the drama. Appropriately, "Amen" is the last line of the play. Despite the fact that the Captain does not believe in the Christian God or any sort of afterlife, the Nurse, who has served him since his boyhood, proclaims wishfully and naively that the Captain did turn to God with his last breath. Regardless, however, the Captain does finally reach a peaceful state that validates the message in the hymn-book from which the Nurse reads at the beginning of the second act:

> A sorrowful and grievous thing
> Is life, so swiftly passing by,
> Death shadows with his angel's wing
> The whole earth, and this his cry:
> 'Tis Vanity, all Vanity!

A second verse amplifies the themes of the first:

> All that on earth has life and breath,
> Falls low before his awful might,
> Sorrow alone is spared by Death,
> Upon the yawning grave to write:
> 'Tis Vanity, all Vanity! [32].

In Strindberg's final plays, the Christian promise of a better life to come after death offers solace for a world of human suffering. Despite the naturalistic underpinnings of *The Father*, it is nevertheless possible to read the end in the beginning and look to the light that lies in the plays ahead. Having said that, though, the "vanity of life" still triumphs in Strindberg's most famous play, *Miss Julie* (1888), and also one of his best, *Creditors* (1889). In the former, the titular heroine wills her own destruction by entering the private domain of her valet. "I am going now—to rest," she announces shortly before exiting the servants' kitchen to commit suicide. Before doing so, she halts, and then adds: "But just tell me that even the first can receive the gift of grace" (113). First refers to class in this case and Jean points out, helpfully, that Julie has degraded herself so thoroughly that she is no longer the first, but the last. "And the first shall be last," Julie responds, her final line, an allusion to the biblical injunction against those of wealth and privilege, but given the transposed positions of Jean and Julie, she gains a surprising victory in death over Jean, who is left to answer the interminable ring of the servants' bell (114).

Creditors, as in *The Father*, portrays the inevitable doom of intimate relationships between men and women that break down, not in spite of love, but because of it. The young Adolf in this play is not a cavalry officer but an artist who confides to his new male friend that he fears that he has given too much of himself in love to his new wife. He confesses that he has made love to her "so passionately that I couldn't tell if she were I, or I, she. When she smiles, I smile; when she weeps, I weep" (126). Unbeknownst to Adolf, his confessor in this scene is none other than his wife Tekla's first husband, Gustav, who has come to exact revenge for losing her to another man. Despite the fact that Tekla and Adolf obviously love each other, Gustav successfully plays upon the insecurities of both in order to drive a wedge between the lovers. After first setting Adolf up with innuendo in the guise of friendship, Gustav positions Adolf in an adjoining room and attempts to seduce Tekla. Tekla does not detect the trap until it is too late and her husband makes his appearance in the room and collapses on the floor. The line between love and hate, imposed so forcefully in *The Father* and *Miss Julie*, is almost imperceptible in *Creditors* as Strindberg portrays intimate relationships as fragile arrangements.

Short and experimental, *The Stronger* (1889) departs briefly from the man/woman conflict to pit two women, both actresses, against each other in a one-act drama in which only the protagonist, a "Mrs. X," speaks, while "Miss Y" only listens and responds silently. The illusion of power plays out by revealing that the speaker is actually the weaker of the two and that her adversary dominates her by withholding speech. In the course of their chance meeting at an outdoor café Mrs. X taunts Miss Y but discovers that her rival has stolen her husband in a love affair. The question of dominance, who is the stronger and who is the weaker, returns to a familiar battle of the sexes in *The Bond* (1892). Appearances do not necessarily reflect the reality of the marital situation between the Baron and Baroness. The husband asserts: "My weakness towards you, which was the strength of my feeling, gave you the notion that you were the stronger, whereas you were only more malicious, more brutal, more unscrupulous than I" (196). They love one another, but they cannot live with one another and the play takes place in a courtroom during a divorce suit in which they attempt to part amicably in deference to their child whom they adore and wish not to harm. In this satirical dramatization of the contemporary Swedish court system, both the parents, despite their protective intentions, lose custody of their child even as they receive the dissolution of their union. Whereas *The Stronger* depicts a true, albeit surprising winner, *The Bond* presents the man and woman as equally bereft by the struggle's outcome. In the concluding lines, the Baroness bemoans her fate: "I shall wander about the roads and in the woods, so as to hide myself and be able to scream—scream myself tired against God who has put this devilish love into the world to torment mankind" (207). Only death can release the two combatants from their eternally rhythmic cycle of love and hate.

At the end of Act 2 of *Comrades*, Abel warns her friend, "You have been playing with fire, Bertha!" (146). "Isn't it possible for a man and a woman to live together as comrades without striking fire?" Bertha asks. "No," Abel says, "You may be sure that as long as there are two sexes, just as surely will there be fire." Indeed, *Playing with Fire* (1892), a long one act billed as a comedy similar to *Comrades*, focuses on a carnal triangle between a young painter, Knut, his wife Kerstin, and their mutual male friend, Axel, who shares the same name as Bertha's husband from the earlier play. A glass-enclosed verandah set up as a living room functions as a magnifying glass that intensifies the sexual heat within the room such that contact between men and women threatens to burst into passion at any moment and 21 continuous scenes in the relatively short play provide little relief from the constant pressure. The physical presence of the friend stimulates Knut's sexual passion for his wife. At the same time, he enjoys the fact that his friend also desires Kerstin and that she even seems to reciprocate his interest. After the two finally confess their love for each other and then to Knut, though, Axel refuses to take Kerstin and blames her for their moral lapse. She collapses and he runs away. The action suggests that men and women cannot be friends—the sexual threat always looms—yet marriage itself and the routines of daily life dull intimate contact, especially the sexual act. Sexual attraction invariably devolves into physical repulsion.

When Strindberg emerged from his psychological "inferno" crisis and returned to the theater at the end of the 19th century, in addition to moving back to his native Sweden from Paris, he embarked on new kinds of dramatic expressions that reflected his own spiritual journey, religious awakening, and sense of his own mortality. Beginning with *To Damascus* in 1898, Strindberg wrote over 30 plays in rapid succession during a 12-year period that ended in 1909. Many of these plays number among his very best work. Together with early great plays such as *Miss Julie* and *Creditors*, Strindberg's oeuvre exhibits staggering varieties of formal and thematic innovation and experimentation. Strindberg, to a greater extent than Ibsen or Chekhov, bridges the 19th and 20th centuries and, in that sense, is the most modern of all the modern dramatists.

Although Strindberg published the first two parts of his trilogy, *To Damascus*, in 1898, and the final part in 1904, the initial play stands on its own as an independent work in which the pattern of successive scenes begins and ends at the same locale. The title alludes to the conversion of St. Paul who, on the road to Damascus to persecute the followers of the Lord, encountered a light from heaven and heard the voice of Jesus, to whom he pledged allegiance as the true Son of God. Themes of reversal and conversion manifest in the scene design pattern of this highly autobiographical work that depicts Strindberg's psychic and physical struggles during his "inferno" period and features a protagonist named "the Stranger" who shares many similarities with the playwright: he is a famous author, but he is also infamous and has suffered greatly from the critics; he forbids his wife to read one of his books, a likely reference to *Getting Married*, a collection of essays by Strindberg in two volumes on the subject of women and men that outraged the conservative public to the extent that charges of blasphemy were levied against him; references to the Stranger's alchemical experiments; the "Lady" in the play shares characteristics of all three of Strindberg's wives; and other characters are likely patterned after people with whom Strindberg had intimate contact; and, more interestingly, the play references other works by the author. In Part III, for example, the Tempter describes a marital situation that applies perfectly to Alice and Edgar in *The Dance of Death*: "Twenty-five years of married life is not to be shrugged off—and all these years they had been feuding. Their love-life for a quarter of a century had been nothing but one long quarrel, with many petty ones in between. And still they loved each other, and expressed thanks for all their blessings through the years!" (314–315). Strindberg again depicts the indivisibility of love and hate between men and women and the debilitating effects that such powerfully entwined emotions create. The Stranger states near the end his belief that it is "possible to bring about a reconciliation between mankind and woman through a woman" (308). The conclusion, however, refutes that premise, though, as the Stranger disavows earthly passion and all human delights in favor of an ascetic existence at a monastery located high above in the mountains. The entire trilogy turns from human desires and earthly concerns to God in order to achieve solitary peace.

The conversion theme receives formal reinforcement with Strindberg's turn against realism and naturalism. No longer content to dramatize the mere surfaces of life, Strindberg attempts to demonstrate the interior life of his protagonist by creating a "station" drama akin to a medieval mystery play that shows the progression of the Stranger's spiritual journey as he gradually sheds his cloak of vanity, possessiveness, and egotism on the way to God and death and peace and spiritual enlightenment. Whereas earlier plays such as *Miss Julie*, *The Father*, and *Creditors* present relations between men and women and life on earth in general as a grisly affair, *To Damascus* hints at a way out of the human morass through devout Christianity—an emphatic turn that is wholly absent in both Ibsen and Chekhov (Varya's religious fervor in *The Cherry Orchard* is the stuff of comedy). While the drama between man and woman remains center stage in *To Damascus*, that struggle is only part of the larger theme of the trilogy in which the Stranger ultimately decides to turn away from all earthly pleasures and pursuits and cross the river to the monastic life on the other side. More sinned against than sinning perhaps, the autobiographical protagonist is still far from a perfect man and he suffers from perceived slights as much as actual ones and also performs unkind deeds as much as any other character. The conversion, then, presents a hard choice and Strindberg gives no easy answer but Strindberg emphatically shows that such a dramatic move is the only one that can offer salvation.

Crime and Crime (1899) compares revealingly with Ibsen's *The Master Builder* (1892). Both plays feature a protagonist who might be considered a stand-in for the author—Solness is an architect and Maurice is a playwright—who succumbs to the temptations of a younger woman in order to pursue personal drives and ambitions that result in the deaths of their children or child. In Ibsen, however, the action proves Solness innocent of actual wrongdoing. In fact, Hilda Wangel unleashes the inner "troll" in Solness that allows him to ascend once again to artistic heights. Ego, selfishness, drive and ambition may bring about harm to other, normal folks, but in this play it is the price of success and the human cost of being an artist. In the Strindberg play, however, Maurice does not escape from moral judgment as easily. He ruins his artistic success and personal happiness by allowing himself to wish in a fleeting moment that his child were dead. Even though it is only a momentary thought, and he truly loves the child, and even though he actually did nothing to harm the child and did not cause its death, the action of the play still proves him guilty. As the Abbé informs him at the very end, "And guiltless you were not, for we are responsible for our thoughts, our words, and our desires. You murdered in your mind when you wished the life out of your child" (276). The action of the play thus demonstrates the struggle to live humanely and justly and the impossible task of living without sin or misdeeds. Early in the play, Jeanne, Maurice's mistress, whom he forsakes in the action, asks: "Then won't there be an end to the misery even when this is over?" (214). She surely refers to "this" as life. The Abbé does not give her an answer but only requests that she come see him when she needs enlightenment on this question, suggesting that only death might grant eternal peace.

Easter (1900) stands as a refreshing anomaly among all of Strindberg's works and counters the prevailing opinion of the playwright as a grim misogynist. The need for human suffering returns as a dominant theme, certainly, but the action of the play redeems suffering and the principal redeemer is a lovely young female character named Eleonora that Strindberg created for Harriet Bosse who shortly thereafter became his third wife and with whom he was deeply in love at the time. Eleonora, who has returned to her family home from a mental institution, reminds others that suffering is necessary in order to promote consciousness of Christ's sufferings on the Cross. The action of the play takes place over three days, Maundy Thursday in Act 1, Good Friday in Act 2, and Easter eve in Act 3. Unlike so many of Strindberg's early plays that end in death, however, *Easter*, in tune with its religious calendar, ends on hopeful notes of reconciliation, forgiveness, and mercy. Formally, the six-character play is set in a single interior room for all three acts that suggests the same kind of realism of Strindberg's early plays. However, the living room is specifically designated as a verandah enclosed by glass walls, similar to the design of *Playing with Fire*, which is covered by curtains that can be opened and shut. Strindberg achieves spectacular effects with descriptions of enormous and threatening shadows projected upon the curtains by the approach of visitors from the outside. In a remarkable surprise, the looming shadow of a man whom the family has long feared returns to claim his debts, finally, in the last scene and declares that all things come around in time and that he remembers a kindness done to him when he was young and so he forgives the later wrong that was done to him. The darkness disappears and the Easter holiday produces light as the curtains open and God's light, mercy and love fill the space.

The isolated fortress of *The Dance of Death* (1901) recalls the stony island of Böcklin's painting. Edgar and Alice dwell on an island, too, that stands upon the sea. It is as if the play is set on the island that the painting represents. Indeed, as the title suggests, the play is about death, or, to be more precise, it is about the endgame of life and the imminent approach of death. In advance of their silver wedding anniversary, Edgar and Alice review their history together and lament the time wasted in each other's company with a number of bitter recriminations. Edgar collapses on several occasions, but each attack seems to be a false alarm. The portrait of a marriage that emerges is of a couple that is at once sick to death of each other but unable or even unwilling to live apart. And, despite the many awful things that they say to each other, there remains an insoluble bond between them. The first of two parts, usually presented separately on its own bill, concludes with Edgar very much alive and the couple resolved to maintain the undulating rhythms of love and hate that have sustained their relationship through the years. Part 2 is much shorter and introduces the grown children of Edgar and Alice and

Kurt, their friend and relative. Judith appears to be very much her father's daughter, strong-willed herself yet willing to do her father's bidding and marry the man of his choice. In the end, however, Judith insults her father in order to follow her heart's desire. What could have been a tragedy actually follows an ancient comic trope of an old man trying to dictate the relationships of youth. As in Ibsen's *The Master Builder*, youth wins the day. Judith's rebellion shocks her father and he suffers a stroke at the climax of the play and dies suddenly. After all that Edgar has done to Kurt and his wife, Alice, after all the insults and attacks finally subside, Alice changes her attitude toward her husband and she and Kurt begin to mourn his death. After all the years, she admits that she must have loved him and that he had certainly been worth loving ... and hating. Kurt marvels how Edgar had "fought for his own existence" in a remarkable struggle. "Peace be with him!" Alice eulogizes, to conclude the drama (453).

A Dream Play (1901) and *The Ghost Sonata* (1907), about which much more will be written separately below, number among Strindberg's greatest works representative of his stylistic rebellion against naturalism and turn to expressionism. Fantastically, the point of view in the former work is none other than the dreamer who might be either Strindberg or audience members/readers who project themselves into the action. The dream of the drama presents earthly existence as a repetitive nightmare from which there is no escape. The character of Indra's Daughter, who has descended to the planet from above, witnesses a human carnival of suffering and intones frequently the thematic mantra of the play that human beings must be pitied. Strindberg concludes his author's note prior to the dramatic prologue by comparing daily existence unfavorably to that of a dream-filled slumber. "Sleep, supposedly a liberator, is often a torturer, but when the torment is at its worst, an awakening reconciles the sufferer with reality. No matter how agonizing reality can be, at this moment, compared with a tormenting dream, it is a pleasure" (*Five Plays* 206). While *A Dream Play* dramatizes the form of a dream as an alternative state of existence but one that portrays the essential characteristics of mundane living, *The Ghost Sonata* enacts a dream-like existence in order to present the reality of life behind the façade of superficial appearances. The hero, a young student named Arkenholz, discovers that beauty and status in the house on the corner conceal a rotten and empty core of deceit and corruption. "We are not what we seem," the Mummy declares, "for deep down we are better than ourselves, since we detest our faults" (*Five Plays* 287). The old characters outlive their usefulness as good people and are ghostly, soulless relics waiting for the end. Tragically, however, life in this dead house has been sucked out of the beautiful Young Lady as well, who succumbs, at last, to "the drudgery of keeping the filth of life at a distance" (293). The Student, who had hopes of marrying the Young Lady, offers her a final benediction and a prayer of eternal peace. His final lines, and the final lines of the drama, read: "The Lord of Heaven be merciful to you on your journey…" (297). Rather than presenting an alternative reality as in *A Dream Play*, *The Ghost Sonata* purports to show how painful life really is—repetitive, sinful and miserable—and offers the prayer of an afterlife as the only possible salvation for humanity.

Strindberg wrote his final play, *The Great Highway*, in 1909 as a conscious end to his career and to his life as well. He knew that he was gravely ill and dying. He named the play after the road that went past the so-called Blue Tower in which he lived and even past the cemetery that he had picked for his burial. Metaphorically, of course, the title refers to the road on life's journey that culminates in death and leads to the gates of heaven. As in *To Damascus*, this play is a "station" drama in seven scenes that takes place along the route, including "At the Last Gate" in the penultimate scene followed by "The Dark Wood" in which the protagonist, The Hunter, again, a stand in for the author and not dissimilar to the Stranger in *To Damascus*, finally reaches his destination when he can no longer see his way. Although the play reads as a personal statement by the playwright and does not seem to create the possibility for theatrical sway in the way that *A Dream Play* and *The Ghost Sonata* might hypnotize an audience, Strindberg writes some of his best verse in this play and saves his best for last. In the final scene, facing imminent death, the Hunter concludes a long monologue with a few simple lines that encapsulate Strindberg's major themes of suffering and the desire to transcend earthly existence:

> Bless me, Your creature,
> Who suffers, suffers from Your gift of life.
> Bless me, whose deepest suffering,
> Deepest of human suffering, was this—
> I could not be the one I longed to be [*The Great Highway* 689].

Given who Strindberg longed to be, as a painter or a playwright, it is hard to believe that he actually liked Böcklin's *The Island of the Dead*. Toril Moi makes the emphatic point that at the time that Strindberg wrote *The Ghost Sonata*, Böcklin's work was under critical attack as being decidedly non-modern with its emphasis upon subject matter rather than painterly technique. Moi cites Böcklin as proof of Ibsen's mundane taste in the visual arts but goes on to show brilliantly that Ibsen stole his image of Irene in *When We Dead Awaken* straight from the upright figure in the rowboat in Böcklin's painting (137). The white figure in the rowboat, while it might have inspired Ibsen, might also have inspired Chekhov when he was writing Konstantin's little play. The still loneliness of Böcklin's painting is certainly the stuff of Konstantin's play about a world soul alone in the world in which "the weary moon in heaven lights her lamp in vain" (Chekhov, *Plays* 118). Konstantin's theory of drama, too, states, "We have to show life not the way it is, or the way it should be, but the way it is in dreams!" (116). To further show Ibsen's indebtedness to Böcklin, Moi cites allusions in *The Lady from the Sea* to another work by Böcklin (139).

But, while Ibsen perhaps had poor taste in painting and Chekhov parodied the new symbolist movement in the arts, Strindberg was a painter himself and his visual works show none of the mythological realism of Böcklin's. It is impossible to find a living figure in any of Strindberg's tortured, abstract, energetic landscapes in which he troweled paint on canvas in layers to reflect the dark turbulence and violence of the universe. Catherine Fraser tries to show the similarity between Strindberg's paintings and Böcklin's *The Island of the Dead*, but her effort remains a stretch at best. Perhaps the blackened center of Böcklin's work caused by the looming cypress trees is analogous to the voids created by Strindberg's swirling, empty landscapes, but it is more plausible to think that the subject of Böcklin's painting inspired Strindberg's imagination and that he transposed the literal message of Böcklin's visual representation into the dominant action of his plays. At the end of Strindberg's two-scene fragment, *The Isle of the Dead*, the character of The Teacher instructs his student: "You preferred plays on the stage to the stage of life; but if life is a dream, then a play is a dream about a dream, even though you treat it as if it were reality" (48). Here, then, Strindberg poses the anti-realistic modern theater in a nutshell. The theater does not reproduce reality. The stage is to life as the dream is to reality. By presenting the dream on stage, a venue that is already a dream, Strindberg presents the dream of a dream that is, in the end, the only true reality. All the trappings of the theater that are put to use in such plays as *A Dream Play* and *The Ghost Sonata* remind the audience that the what it sees is not real, but in the same way that nothing it takes for reality is real. If Böcklin's *The Island of the Dead* is a decadent piece of art that is antithetical to modern art, it nevertheless certainly inspired Ibsen, and maybe Chekhov, and perhaps even Strindberg to make modern drama in which the elements of theater, including speech, movement in time and space and language, serve as an analogue not for reality, but the substance and substitute for the unreality of existence on earth.

Creditors (1889)

> "'However, they know in their hearts that someone, someone in particular, sees them even in the dark. And that frightens them. And in their fear, the absent one begins to haunt them, looms up before their eyes, becomes a bogey-

man, a nightmare disturbing their nights of love. A creditor, knocking at the door, come to collect."

Gustav arranges to stay in an adjoining room at the same seaside resort as his former wife, Tekla, and her new husband, Adolph. After Tekla leaves for a few days, Gustav seizes the opportunity to befriend Adolph, whom he has never met, gain his trust, and attack all his insecurities as an artist and as a man. He urges Adolph to give up painting in favor of sculpture, convinces him that he cannot continue sexual relations with his wife for health reasons, and even argues that Tekla has used him for her own career advancement as a novelist and actually cares nothing for him. To prove his points, Gustav offers to spy on the couple from the keyhole in his room in order that he may judge Tekla's behavior and witness her true feelings. When she returns from her trip, she immediately senses that something has happened and that Adolph acts quite differently than he did before she left. Despite his evident love for her, Adolph cannot forget what Gustav said and he picks a fight with Tekla and demands that she leave with him later that night. He vacates the room, as per the plan and exchanges place at the keyhole with Gustav to watch him interrogate Tekla. During that performance, Adolph discovers that Gustav is Tekla's ex-husband and that she still finds him attractive. Gustav begins to seduce his former wife and torture his rival next door with each advance. Just before Tekla succumbs to his charms, though, she finally suspects that the muffled sounds from next door must be from her husband. She opens the door leading to the veranda and Adolph, afflicted with a kind of stroke, slumps in, foaming at the mouth, incapable, even, of speech. Gustav, showing only slight pity and remorse, leaves having fulfilled his revenge plot to restore his honor in the wake of public divorce and humiliation. Tekla, devastated, cradles Adolph's lifeless body.

Like *Miss Julie* written the previous year, *Creditors* is a 90-minute play with three characters in which the stage time equals that of the story time. As in the earlier play, too, Strindberg wages his battle between a man and woman in a naturalistic style that foregrounds the scientific thinking of that time, including theories of genetics and the perils of sexual excess. Whereas the former play is really a two-character play in which the third character, Kristine, remains in the background, *Creditors* presents a triangle in which the three scenes between two characters display all possible permutations: two men (Gustav & Adolph); husband & wife (Adolph & Tekla); ex-husband and ex-wife (Gustav & Tekla). This arrangement allows Strindberg to pursue his themes of love, jealousy and revenge as well as the complicated nature of intimate relationships and the incalculable debt that the present always owes to the past. The irreconcilability between men and women, however, as central as that is to Strindberg's work, is not nearly as interesting as the theatrical framework that he devises for the play that brilliantly offsets its naturalistic foundation. Naturalism as a style does not acknowledge the presence of the theatrical audience, who views the performance as if it were looking through a "keyhole" in the absent/imaginary fourth wall that spans the proscenium. In this play, however, Gustav deceives Adolph and does not disclose his full identity and therefore plays a part much like an actor in a play. In the course of the first scene, the audience, but not Adolph at this point, discovers that Gustav is none other than Tekla's ex-husband. In the second scene, Adolph fights with his wife with awareness that Gustav watches him from the keyhole of the adjoining room. He trades places with Gustav in the final scene and his rival, who is a kind of stage manager for the entire event, passionately woos Tekla with full intent to destroy his offstage onlooker. Ultimately, Adolph reenters, but not through the door, but through the veranda opening directly upstage that puts him squarely facing the theatrical audience. In this mirror image, the action reflects the audience and asks it to consider its role in the spectacle and the cost of voyeurism.

The opening scene picks up in the middle of things with Adolph's first line: "—and for all this I have you to thank," a statement that seems innocent enough at first but which later events will render as heavily ironic. Gustav, who does not identify himself by that name, smokes a cigar, while Adolph works on a wax figure upon a modeling stand. Adolph relates how he had been devastated for several days after his wife left on a trip and how he had been unable to do anything. "But after a few days I woke up, pulled myself together. My fever-maddened head cooled off. Old projects, ideas I'd nearly forgotten, popped back into my head. I felt like working, felt the itch to create again. Once again I had vision. Could see the shapes hidden in things. And then you showed up" (*Selected Plays* 1:283).[22] Alone and at a loss for something to do, Adolph nearly recovered on his own accord when his new "friend" appeared. Gustav subsequently and methodically undermines Adolph's self-confidence and plants the seed of doubt in him regarding his relationship to Tekla. At root, Tekla's mere absence upsets Adolph and he freely admits that he loves her very much: "I know it's strange, but sometimes I think of her not as somebody else but as a part of me. She's my heart and guts. In her is my will to live and my lust for life" (284–285). Adolph shows Gustav the female figure that he's been sculpting, molded from memory, of Tekla: "That woman lives in my body, just as I do in hers" (288). Gustav senses from the figure that Adolph has "made love to her passionately" and he hides his jealousy by declaring that Adolph has, according to his diagnosis, the first signs of epilepsy as a result of his sexual addiction. This happened, Gustav elaborates, because the woman managed to usurp the "prerogative of the male" (289). Gustav describes some terrible symptoms and advises that, as a precaution, Adolph should practice complete sexual abstinence for six months at least.

Adolph admits that his child by Tekla does not live with them because Tekla felt that the boy, at the age of three, began to look like her former husband. Gustav probes deeper and asks if Adolph ever gets jealous about his predecessor. Adolph does not deny it, and Gustav then assures him that he will never get rid of such thoughts: "It'll become an obsession, a discord that you can't resolve, a jarring note always ringing in your ears" (291). Adolph notices that Gustav behaves at moments exactly like Tekla, "squinting one eye, as if taking aim" (292). He notices some of the exact same vocal mannerisms as well. Gustav skirts further scrutiny by saying that perhaps they are distantly related and says: "It might be amusing to meet your wife and see for myself" (292). After Adolph muses that Tekla has never absorbed any of his expressions, Gustav seizes the opening and says merely that this is proof that she has never loved him. A woman "loves by taking," he says, and the fact that she has taken nothing from Adolph proves that she has never loved him. A woman can only do that once, with the first husband. Ironically, Gustav adds: "Your trouble is that you've never been cheated. Watch out for those who have" (292). At this point, if not before, the theatrical audience realizes the true identity of Gustav, but Adolph does not. Instead, he falls deeper into Gustav's trap when he asks him to analyze his marriage.

Gustav theorizes that shared guilt concerning the absent first husband (Gustav) brought Adolph and Tekla together: "And the more physical their relationship becomes, the more spiritual they pretend it is." Gustav guesses that they call each other "brother" and "sister" to hide the intense sexuality of their relationship and to try and hide from the absent first husband: "However, they know in their hearts that someone, someone in particular, sees them even in the dark. And that frightens them. And in their fear, the absent one begins to haunt them, looms up before their eyes, becomes a bogeyman, a nightmare disturbing their nights of love. A creditor, knocking at the door, come to collect" (293). In order to live with what they had done, Gustav postulates, they had to scapegoat the first husband. Adolph tries to justify his relationship with Tekla by saying that she improved him, whereas she did nothing for her former husband because he was "an idiot" (294). Gustav agrees, but points out that the evidence of the husband's idiocy seemed to be his failure to understand his wife. Tekla has no profundity, Gustav insists. She simply influenced Adolph because she wore a skirt. "Have you ever seen a naked woman? [...] A teenager with tits, an undeveloped man, a kid who shot up and stopped short. A chronic anemic, who spews blood like clockwork thirteen times a year" (298). Woman is no equal to man according to Gustav. What really fuels his attack, however, is the fact that Tekla left him for Adolph and wrote her first novel, a success, which depicted Gustav, a main character in the book, as an "idiot."

Gustav observes that the two men have been talking for six hours and encourages Adolph to rest in preparation for his wife's return, which the husband both longs for and fears: "She fondles me, she's tender; but there's something in her kisses that suffocates me, sucks my strength, paralyzes me" (298). Adolph begins to wish that he'd never encountered Gustav as his tormentor piles on further and diagnoses that Adolph does not have long to live. He hates him but he cannot let him go. "I'm drowning; you haul me up, and when I'm up, you hit me on the head and dunk me again" (299). Adolph recognizes that Gustav has stolen all of his vitals and left an empty shell behind. "You've turned everything to ashes—my art, my love, my hope, my faith" (299). With a final masterstroke, Gustav cruelly manipulates Adolph by asking him to look at a photograph of Tekla and to study it for what it really shows: "a flirt, with lots of makeup, and a saucy wink in her eye." It's a matter of interpretation and Gustav reads the photo for Adolph: "Look at the brazen smile. *You* never get to see that. Look at the way her eyes are prowling for some man. And it isn't you. Look at the low cut of her dress—the hair done up differently—her sleeves pushed up, the bared arms. Do you see?" (302). Adolph sees it now, but only because his supposed friend sees it for him.

The sound of a steamer indicates Tekla's imminent arrival and Adolph moves to meet her but Gustav urges restraint and instructs him how to read her actions and thoughts: "If her conscience is clear, you'll get a bawling out that will make your ears ring. However, if she's feeling guilty, she'll be sweetness itself, and coo and cuddle up to you" (303). To make absolutely certain, Gustav says he'll watch Adolph and Tekla from the adjoining keyhole and even switch places with Adolph after a while in order for the husband to watch. Gustav completely theatricalizes the scene: "I'll post myself there and keep an eye on you while you play games with her in here. And when you've had your fun, we'll change places. I'll go into the lion cage, and you'll be at the keyhole" (304). Gustav makes Adolph promise not to mention anything about him to her and they agree to meet later and compare notes about what they have seen. He tells Adolph to sit where he'll be certain to be able to see them both at the same time. Adolph is afraid of what might happen next but can do nothing now to stop the momentum.

Tekla approaches her husband directly and kisses him to begin the second section of the play. Stage directions describe her as "friendly, frank, cheerful, and charming" and Adolph is almost won over "in spite of himself" (305). He feels torn between his genuine love for her, the devotion that he thinks he ought to have, and an uncomfortable awareness that he plays a part in a dramatic scene for the benefit of the unseen but watchful Gustav. He wants to avoid both intimacy with Tekla and his weakening disposition toward her in view of his friend. Tekla notices something different about her husband and believes that someone else has been in the room. She wonders aloud who put it in his head that he could not paint anymore. Adolph tries to defend himself: "You're always suspecting somebody behind what I do and what I think." Adolph almost blurts his confession here but Tekla cannot fathom the literal truth of what he hints. Tekla voices her big fear: "I'm afraid somebody will come and take Little Brother away from me." She's not afraid of other women, but of his male friends: "the ones who put crazy ideas into your head" (307). Noticeably frightened, she desperately wants to know who has been in the room with him prior to her entrance. Adolph lies and says that only his doctor has been to see him and that the doctor told him, among other things, that he was on the brink of epilepsy. He adds that the doctor told him that they couldn't sleep together any more, either. Tekla responds: "They want to separate us. I've seen that coming for a long time." Adolph tries to allay her anxiety by saying that she cannot see what doesn't exist and asks her of what she is so afraid: "That I would get to see you with someone else's eyes? See you for what your are—and not for what I took you to be?" (308). Indeed, Adolph tries to do just that—see Tekla in a new light through the eyes of the "objective" spy Gustav behind the adjoining door. At the same time, though, Adolph tries to alert his wife to the dangers of their present situation.

Tekla says more than she knows when she warns Adolph about what he says: "Don't let your imagination run away with you, Adolph. Imagination is the monster that dwells in man's soul, Adolph" (308). Not merely paranoid, Tekla knows the high stakes to preserve and cherish a loving and intimate relationship. She perceives correctly that Adolph now acts strangely towards her. He presses on to inquire if she learned this wisdom from the "innocent youths" aboard the boat and makes clear that he has received news of her travels. Tekla is aware, now, that Adolph has had news of her travels, but she feigns not to care. Her infatuation with youth, she replies, unfazed, led her to marry him (Adolph). When Adolph counters that he would prefer to be the only youth in her life, Tekla explains, "playfully," that her heart is so big that she has "room in it for many besides him" (309). Adolph appears to melt and she invites him to embrace her and then scolds him for being jealous, but before they touch "the sound of two raps with the chair in Gustav's room" warns Adolph that he has softened and veered off course from his stern examination. He stiffens and announces that he wants to talk seriously, but Tekla takes his face between her hands and kisses him. "You damned witch! You can charm the pants off a man!" he exclaims, not without joy (309). Adolph tries to see her objectively and declares that she wears an expression now that he has never seen. He relates how Bret Harte describes an adulteress: "As a pale woman who can never blush" (310). Although she doesn't know Mr. Harte, Tekla informs Adolph that she blushes for her lover but not her husband. She infuriates her husband, but mostly because Adolph falls for her so quickly and easily: she next invites him to bite her and holds out her arms, he rushes to her and kisses her, she teases him about their compromised position should someone come in, but Adolph says he does not care. "I don't give a damn about anything as long as I have you!" (311).

The fear that his predecessor lurks to gloat over his downfall haunts Adolph, despite assurances from Tekla that she would not let that happen and her admission that she only flirts with other men in order to be liked by them. As for her ex-husband, she claims not to have heard from him in six months and that she severed all ties with him after their child died. He's living on the west coast now, she believes. Adolph confesses that he now identifies with him: "These last few days, when I've been alone here, I couldn't help wondering how he must have felt when he found himself all alone, when you left him" (312). Adolph usurped her husband's place and asks, guiltily, if she ever loved that man. She did, she says, but she grew tired of him and she says she'll never grow tired of Adolph. Unconvinced, Adolph borrows Gustav's language and casts himself in the role of the partner to whom Tekla owes a great debt for her emotional and artistic development: "And in an instant I was transformed into the troublesome creditor, who wouldn't go away. You wanted to tear up the IOU's. And to avoid going deeper into debt, you stopped dipping into my wallet; you went to others" (315). She calls Adolph an idiot, "playfully," but her term reminds him of what she called her ex-husband. Perhaps that man was not an idiot after all, he thinks! His growing sympathy for Gustav angers Tekla: "Funnily enough, even I'm beginning to feel attracted to him, now that I've gotten bored being your nursemaid. At least he was a real man. The only thing wrong with him was that he was mine" (315). Adolph launches into a long speech about the history of their relationship and how he supported her when she was down and brought her back to life into a circle of new friends and helped to restore her reputation. This would have been after her marriage failed and she was trying to succeed as an artist, a novelist, in her own right. Adolph introduced her to his friends and encouraged her and backed her and poured his very life into her: "Then I was the man, the real man, not that sexual athlete you had left but a man with strength of spirit" (317). According to Adolph, Tekla no longer loves the man to whom she owes a debt: "Sometimes I felt that what was behind it was a desire to get rid of me, the creditor, the man who knew too much about you" (317). Extremely agitated and upset, Adolph "seems to fall into a stupor," a forewarning of his delicate physical condition (319). He apologizes and requests that they talk no further. Tekla encourages him to get some fresh air before dinner, he rises in agreement, but insists that they pack and leave immediately upon his return. Tekla refuses on account of a concert that she promised to attend, they continue to argue and Adolph urges her to think about her actions while he is gone.

Tekla attempts to act indifferently when Gustav feigns his own casual entrance in the third and final scene. He politely offers to leave immediately and tells her that if he had known she would be there, then he never would have come to the resort: "I don't intend to sour your happiness by hanging around," he confides. Tekla assures him that he is welcome to stay. After the tedious argument with Adolph, Gustav's charm comes as welcome relief and she compliments his rare qualities of tact and discretion. She assures him that her husband has also expressed sympathy for Gustav as well. Ironically, Gustav comments: "Not even dislike can make a permanent place for itself in our hearts" (321). Tekla has wanted all of them, all three, to meet, shake hands and at the very least to part as friends. Gustav couldn't agree more, he says. He claims to offer kindness, support and friendship, but hatred remains in his heart and drives all of his actions.

Gustav suffered through the years since Tekla left him, he admits, but that suffering and sorrow has purified and ennobled him (322). Tekla asks for forgiveness, but Gustav assures her that he is the one who needs to ask her for forgiveness. With the next exchange, Strindberg's stage directions in the Elizabeth Sprigge translation indicate that Tekla is "fencing" when she notices that they are both crying "at our age," and that Gustav is "parrying" when he agrees that he is old, but that she has grown "younger and younger" (*Twelve Major Plays* 155). Such directions suggest that while the dialogue is complimentary and not impolite in any way, the couple remains wary of each other and attacks with kindness. They sit down and Gustav insists that she really knows how to dress, while Tekla responds that she learned fashion from him. She tells him, too, that he taught her how to think, but she could always do that, he says, then adds: "Look at you now—you've got a sharp mind. At least when you write," a statement that reveals a bit of Gustav's almost-hidden bitterness and vitriol (323). Tekla covers this potentially awkward moment by referring to the quiet circumstances in which they now relax. He was always a bit too peaceful, Gustav allows, now on the offensive, and that's why she left him to pursue a more active lifestyle among the famous. "Never a dull moment in the life of an artist, and I gather your husband isn't the retiring sort," he digs. Flirtatiously, Tekla's careless remark that follows opens the door for his next move: "Sometimes you can have too much of a good thing" (323).

Gustav makes a point of noticing that she still wears the earrings that he bought for her—and, making sure that Adolph hears—insinuates that they make her husband look like "a fool." Quickly, impulsively, Tekla blurts, "He was that to begin with" (324). When Gustav first mentioned the earrings, Tekla took one off immediately. Now, she struggles to put it back on and Gustav comes to her assistance, pinches her ear and muses: "Suppose the man of the house saw us like this!" She tells him that Adolph is very jealous. Sounds from the adjacent room prompt Gustav to ask, seemingly innocently, "Who's in there?" (324). Tekla ignores the interruption and continues to question her ex-husband about what he's doing now and how he's been getting along in the world. Still parrying, Gustav turns back her questions to ask how she fares. She inadvertently uncovers the wax figure while she thinks how to respond, and Gustav jumps at the opportunity to declare that it looks just like her, a bit embarrassing given the fact that the figure is nude. Gustav asks her whether Adolph is "prudish" as a way of finding out about him sexually and Tekla ends up admitting, "Well, he's sick now." In another blunt sexual allusion, Gustav concludes: "Well, Little Brother shouldn't go sticking his nose into somebody else's honey pot." Tekla only gently rebukes him and Gustav now asks her whether she remembers that this room is the very one that they stayed in when they were first married. She asks him to stop, but he insists that she look at him. "They look intensely at one another," the stage directions read (325). In his longest speech he tells her that he enjoyed educating her and wiping her slate clean of all previous knowledge and experience. He claims that he made her. "When I sit here like this, talking to you, it's as if I were opening a bottle of my favorite wine, from my own vineyard. My own wine comes back to me, only improved with age" (326). He discloses that he has chosen to marry again, another young girl, but, playing his cards expertly, he claims that he has had second thoughts after seeing Tekla again: "My roots are still imbedded in you. I feel it. I'm part of you, and the old wounds are opening up again" (326). Quite deliberately, he employs a metaphor of plants just as Adolph did in his long speech to Tekla.

Tekla freely admits that it has been pleasant to talk to Gustav again and to exchange ideas so easily and freely and that she envies his new wife to be. After Gustav interjects that he, too, is jealous of her spouse, Tekla stands and says they must part now, forever, but not before Gustav confronts her: "You've caught some disease from that sick soul. He's infected you with spiritual anemia. Let me breath new life into you. Perhaps it is autumn for us, but I'll make your talent burst into bloom again—like a remontant rose" (327). Taken aback, Tekla recognizes Gustav as a threat who takes "my heart and soul" (328). He replies that she hasn't got a soul, that her soul is just an illusion and he demands to know when and where they can pursue an affair. She finally relents and tells him that Adolph leaves at 8 and to come for her at 9. No sooner does she say this then she hears a din from the adjoining room. Gustav peers through the keyhole and opines that a dog must have overturned a table and smashed a carafe.

Tekla blames Adolph for her scheduled infidelity, but then she begins to reconsider recent events and piece together Gustav's plot: "The big bad wolf sneaking up on my little lamb" (329). Gustav claims that his nature and circumstances drove him to seek revenge. She accuses him of being a "vengeful bastard"; he calls her a "frivolous bitch" (331). Each has acted according to his or her nature. She asks, though, if he can ever forgive her and he claims that he has done so already. In all the years, he's never done anything to her, he says. He brushes off his current behavior as a mere trifle: "All I did was have a little fun with your spouse. That's all it took to make him crumble" (332). Tekla feels that she has nothing to reproach herself about, either: "It's providence that determines our actions; that's what Christians say. Others call it fate. Either way, it makes us innocent." Gustav agrees up to a certain point: "Sooner or later the bill collectors show up. Innocent? Yes, before God—who no longer exists. But still responsible to oneself and to one's fellow creatures." Gustav claims that he only came to restore the honor that Tekla had stolen from him. He now rings the bell to announce his departure. He is not, however, returning to his fiancée: "I haven't got one; and will never have one. And not running home. Because I haven't got a home; and don't want one" (332) He doesn't need any further atonement, he says, and then delivers a rhetorical twist of the Lord's Prayer that offers a glimpse of his bitter discontent:

> Forgive me for allowing you to tear my heart and soul to pieces? Forgive me that you dishonored me. Forgive me for being made fun of by my students every day for seven years. Forgive me for liberating you from the tyranny of your parents, for educating you and freeing your mind from old superstitions and silly old ideas. For making you mistress of my house, for giving you friends and a social position. For making the child I first met into a woman. Forgive me my debts as I forgive you yours! [333].

He instructs her to settle her accounts now with the "other" man and suggests that Tekla might find out how he felt when she left him years ago. Tekla instantly realizes the set-up now, that Adolph has watched the entire episode from the adjoining room and has heard and seen everything that transpired between her and Gustav.

Adolph finally appears in the doorway leading to the veranda: "deathly pale, a streak of blood on his cheek. His eyes are blank and expressionless, and he is frothing at the mouth" (334). A witness to what has transpired, Adolph mirrors the theatrical audience and the blood on his face indicts all those who watch and do nothing and reminds an audience that the spectacle may have amused for a night's entertainment but that it has inflicted damage upon all three characters, human relationships in general, and relationships between men and women in particular. Handiwork done, Gustav bids farewell, but stops and turns to watch Tekla run to Adolph and embrace him. Adolph collapses and Tekla "throws herself on his body, caressing him." She begs forgiveness from him but he doesn't speak and Tekla realizes that he is dead. Gustav delivers the last line: "She really does love him, too! Poor fool!" (334). Whether "poor fool" refers to Adolph or Tekla remains ambiguous. Both are victims of the fragility and volatility of intimate relationships. As for Gustav, the instigator of the action, he stands out as the greatest fool of all, unable to recover from the pain of his relationship with Tekla and destined to walk alone for the rest of his days with only proud and pathetic memories of violent retribution. Whereas Miss Julie gained a strange kind of victory over Jean even in death, no character in *Creditors* escapes the weighted debt of past entanglements and obligations.

The Dance of Death (1900)

> "The trouble is—there comes a moment when the ability to make my own world, as you put it, vanishes. And in place of that world is reality—naked, ugly reality."

A mature couple, Alice and Edgar, bicker and complain endlessly about the misery of their 25-year marriage on the occasion of their upcoming silver anniversary. They live virtually alone with only each other for company in a granite fortress where Edgar is an artillery captain on an island that protects the mainland. A former actress, Alice exhibits theatricalized behavior that revels in a good fight. They complete each other's sentences, trade insults, make jokes, and spar as if they were each aware of an elaborate game in which only they know the rules. The game playing escalates when Alice's cousin, Curt, arrives and grants them an audience of one for their competitive spectacle. The triangle of *Creditors*, featuring two men and a woman, repeats except that here Curt is an onstage presence to whom both Edgar and Alice appeal in an attempt to win the day as the most aggrieved party in a long-lived relationship. Curt reacts only to what he sees and does not take very long to conclude that the domestic situation between the couple is horrible, dire and brutal and sides with Alice against Edgar.

Underlying the severe discord, however, is Edgar's fear of death and the unknown. He boasts that his dead body will be nothing more than fertilizer for the garden, but such grave thoughts only further add to his evident unease about the imminence of his demise. He suffers a prolonged stupor at one point and later his physical collapse forces him to visit a doctor on the mainland. Although he looks ill upon his return, Edgar boasts that he has received a clean bill of health and proceeds to tear up the new will he made and inform Alice that he has instead applied for a divorce and plans, now, to marry a younger woman. Furious, and not to go down without protest, Alice reports to the military authorities that her husband has embezzled funds for years and then, in another turn, seduces Curt. Later, in an elaborate pantomime, Edgar finds himself alone and chucks a number of his worldly possessions, including whiskey decanters, boxes of cigars, packets of personal letters, out the window and into the sea below. Revealingly, he starts to throw out his wife's wreaths from her theatrical successes, but he instead tenderly folds them up in cloth and tucks them away from harm. Alone with Curt, Edgar finally admits that he is dying and does not have long to live and that, in fact, he made up stories about divorce and such with not a bit of truth attached to any of his threats.

Still in the dark, Alice boasts to Edgar about her new lover and taunts him to the point that he draws his saber in a rage. Newly horrified, Curt runs away for good. Alone together again, Edgar and Alice immediately make up and Edgar confesses the truth to his wife. Alice fears now for having telegraphed the military police, but Edgar reassures her that he never actually embezzled anything and that nothing will come of Alice's report. He confides that he had a near-death experience and received a vision of what life might be like on the other side (after death) and somewhat tenderly admits that he may have overdone his recent performance. Alice accepts his apology and issues her own for her behavior and the couple begins to plan a party for their anniversary and vows to move on together with what time is left to them.

Unlike the scene design of *Miss Julie*, which, Strindberg points out in the famous preface to that play, borrows from impressionist painting with respect to an angled perspective that suggests space beyond the parameters of the proscenium arch, the layout for *The Dance of Death* presents a typical symmetrical arrangement that adheres to one-point perspective from a central viewing position. The initial description reads: "A round room, the interior of a fortress tower built of granite and situated on an island off the coast. At the rear, a wide, arched doorway with glass doors like French windows, through which can be seen an artillery emplacement, a large gun, the parapet, the shoreline, and the sea itself" (*Selected Plays* 2:185).[23] Strindberg quite elaborately describes a deep vista that the audience can see clearly beyond the action, as if the playwright reverses the perspective of Böcklin's *The Island of the Dead* to show a world of peace and escape beyond the confines of what both Alice and Edgar describe as a kind of granite sepulcher. Whereas the painting shows a figure in the foreground rowing to the dark island, Strindberg puts his dark scene of witty struggle between husband and wife in the foreground and presents the peaceful background of sea and shoreline as a hopeful destination. Strindberg's dialogue with one of his favorite paintings creates a new perspective on the subject of death. Endless squabbling and insults hurled between Alice and Edgar suggest a life of torture and a kind of death in life. But, by the end of the play, Edgar learns something that leads him to say: "Maybe when death comes, life begins" (260). Surprisingly, things are not what they seem, hope exists, and the panoramic vista that the audience sees upstage of the primary action and battle provides a whiff of fresh air that Edgar and Alice breathe at the final curtain.

The break in the play between death and dying and life and living takes place in the fourth unit of five designated by the playwright in this full-length play. Significantly, pantomimic action comprises all the action amid no dialogue whatsoever. Again, in his preface to *Miss Julie*, Strindberg boasts about how he incorporates elements from the classical drama, including monologue, pantomime, and ballet. He designates a pantomimic scene in that play in which the cook, Christine, goes about her tasks silently in the kitchen and then prepares to go out to dance with Jean. Despite Strindberg's claims about his innovation, however, the pantomimic scene in *Miss Julie* does little more than highlight the slave mentality of a character about whom the playwright admits freely that he cares little. Here, though, Strindberg uses pantomimic action to reveal a side of Edgar's character that has not been apparent. It "speaks" to the fact that Edgar has had an extraordinary experience about which he cannot talk and reveals his innermost thoughts. The classical stage might offer the chance for monologue, even soliloquy, but the modern and naturalistic stage offers no such convention. Strindberg claims that there are ways to motivate a monologue in the modern theater, people do really speak to themselves, he says, but apparently he felt that he had no way to do that in *The Dance of Death*. Instead, Edgar develops relationships with a number of properties in the elaborate silent action that reveals his innermost thoughts and feelings. Without speaking, Edgar admits that he is dying and displays a range of thoughts and emotions as he moves about the room and picks up various things and examines them and tosses them out the window. Edgar has survived in the world, he says later, by crossing things off and moving on. This scene enacts that philosophy as Edgar dispatches with the material possessions of corporeal existence. At a crisis moment of his own mortality, he struggles to come to terms with what it means. He has always invented the world to conform to his viewpoint and according to his comforts. But, as he also says later about the experience of reconciling oneself to death, "the trouble is—there comes a moment when the ability to make my own world, as you [Curt] put it, vanishes. And in place of that world is reality—naked, ugly reality" (252).

Edgar reckons with mortality through an examination of stuff. A novelist has the advantage of describing the thoughts of a character and giving them a narrative shape that fit nicely with dialogue involving other characters. In the theater, in drama, though, the playwright must show rather than tell. Strindberg directs Edgar to pick up several objects and reveal his inner thoughts by how he handles each property. A solitary presence, Edgar has nothing to hide because he does not have to perform for any other character on stage. The material things he seemed to care about he no longer has any affection—cards, whiskey, cigars and even his glasses go right out the window. Pictures of his two children, however, he tucks into his breast pocket. Given what has transpired between Alice and Edgar, it comes as no surprise when Edgar smashes the portrait photograph of his wife and sends it out the window with the other junk. He takes her theatrical wreaths down, too, and almost throws them out as well. But he stops, does not throw them out, but instead carefully and tenderly wraps them up in a runner from the piano and sets them aside in a safe place. Action reveals character, and by these actions Edgar reveals that, despite his violent arguments to the contrary, he cares very much about Alice. The scene presents him as a man of deep feeling with deeply ambivalent feelings about death and dying that he valiantly attempts to sort and reconcile in the final turn of his life.

If Edgar reveals himself in the pantomimic scene, he wards off any possibility of being known in the previous three units. The opening scene establishes that Edgar and Alice have been married for a very long time and know each other's habits extremely well. A friendly and very funny competition between the couple opens a gambit in which they try to trump each other, as if they were playing cards, in games of wit. The following dialogue typifies exchanges in which they each vie for the last witty word:

> EDGAR: Do we have any Burgundy left in the wine cellar?
> ALICE: As I recall, we haven't for the last five years had a wine cellar.
> EDGAR: You're so disorganized, Alice. Always have been... [187].

Presumably, Edgar and Alice know very well whether or not they own a wine cellar, but Alice jokes with Edgar by suggesting that they may not have had one for the last five years! Is it likely that they owned one prior to that time? No, but Alice's hazy recollection sets up Edgar to finish his joke by insinuating that Alice may have misplaced the cellar or lost access to it in all the household clutter. If Alice had said simply that they did not have a wine cellar then Edgar's joke could not gain any traction. Even though this joke comes at her expense, Alice plays along in order to facilitate the fun between them. The subject of the wine cellar is benign, but the same pattern often occurs even when the barbs and insults carry more weight and target more serious matters. Even when they trade insults, Edgar and Alice work in cahoots.

Alice's background as an actress in the theater lends itself to a mode of discourse that befits a stage more than a living room and, while the couple complains about the repetition of daily rituals, routines and conversations, dialogue becomes more similar to that of a dramatic script. Edgar delights Alice with the following "improvisational" romp that he delivers as a witty retort:

> Haven't you noticed that we say the same things to each other every day? Just now when you made your routine comment: "At least in this house," I would have given my routine reply: "It's not just *my* house." But since I've gone through that routine five hundred times, I decided to liven things up—to yawn instead. Which can be

interpreted as meaning I'm too lazy to answer. Or it might mean: "Right you are, my pet." Or: "I've had enough" [196].

Alice applauds the performance of her husband as if he were an actor in a play. Even though the speech comes at her expense, she appreciates the skill, dexterity and inventiveness of her husband's verbal agility. He performs for her, and she does the same for him. And when Curt, Alice's cousin, arrives, whom they have not seen for 15 years, they each have another person to watch their performance. Edgar and Alice vie to win Curt's allegiance and force him to pick one side or the other, but, really, as things turn out, Edgar and Alice always play together in a baffling arrangement that Curt never figures.

The elaborate language games that Edgar and Alice play pass the time and distract attention from the underlying and pervasive theme and preoccupation of the main characters: the fear of death and dying. Aging Edgar and Alice talk about death as if it were a relief that could not come soon enough to suit them, but the frequency with which they reference the subject reflects an overwhelming anxiety about its imminence. Edgar masks his fear with a bravado that reflects a kind of godless and spiritless naturalism with his definition: "An end. Period. Then you take what's left, put it in a wheelbarrow, and use it to fertilize the garden" (187). Between Edgar and Alice, they invoke the image of the human body as fertilizer on three different occasions, a repetition that suggests preoccupation and fear of the subject, and perhaps a hope, too, that it isn't true. Edgar's outlook sounds particularly hollow when he boasts to Curt: "

> Listen, it's perfectly true that when the machine breaks down, there's nothing left but what you can put in a wheelbarrow and haul out to manure the garden. But as long as the gears are turning, you've got to use them, use your hands and feet, keep slugging and kicking as long as the parts hold out! That's my philosophy [203].

Indeed, the awful things that Edgar says and does are only so much "slugging and kicking" to prove that he remains vital, but the theatrical nature of this speech, too, reflects a tired script that he has performed many times, but that offers no reassurance to him now as the dark time grows near. Later, after Edgar collapses, Alice stands over him and jeers him with his own image of the body as fertilizer in the most highly invective speech in the play:

> Look at him! A stinking wretch of a captain who never got to be major. A scarecrow who thinks his men are trembling in their boots when they're shaking with laughter. A sniveling coward who is afraid of the dark and believes in barometers. And why all the hullabaloo over this man? For the grand finale when this bag of wind turns into a sack of shit to fertilize the garden! And second-rate shit at that! [231].

Alice's cruelty, at face value, attempts once again to assert dominance over Edgar and seal her final victory. That is only part of what's going on, however, because she might not say such awful things if Curt were not present to hear her. And, hearing her, Curt might never suspect that Alice, too, fears death, her own, perhaps, but certainly her husband's, and that she fears what life might be like without him. Curt's presence keeps her in a performative mode in which she must cover her most private and intimate thoughts and protect herself from her most powerful emotions. Does she hate Edgar as much as her language suggests? Perhaps, but it is likely, too, that she resists showing how she really feels in front of Curt and that her display of hateful contempt is only the exact opposite of what she may both feel and fear: love and compassion.

Curt, the observer, the audience's surrogate, only sees what Edgar and Alice independently and collectively want him to see—a man and woman, husband and wife, in constant and tumultuous, if not violent, confrontation. At different times, Curt seems to sympathize with Edgar; at other times he takes Alice's side. Alone with Edgar, Curt inquires: "What on earth is going on in this house? What's happening? The place smells poisonous, like old peeling wallpaper. Just coming in here makes you sick. I'd walk out this instant if I hadn't promised Alice I'd stay. There must be corpses rotting under the floorboards. The air is so full of hate it's suffocating" (207). After Edgar falls into an unconscious stupor, Alice tries to explain what has happened to them over the years: "We separated twice while we were engaged, and since then we've thought of separating every day that passes. But we're welded together, I guess, and we can't free ourselves.... Now nothing but death can separate us.... So we await death as a deliverance" (209). Alice advances the play's theme of life as a kind of death and also seems to convince Curt that both she and her husband long for death as a release from each other's grasp. She elaborates further on the antagonism that fuels their marriage: "It's a hate beyond reason. Without cause, without point or purpose. And also without end. It's crazy. You know why he's afraid to die? Because he's afraid I'd marry again" (210). Alice speculates that something more than hate has kept Edgar faithful to her through all the passing years. Spite or jealousy might motivate Edgar's desire to stay alive, but he also might want to keep living in order to remain close to Alice for as long as possible. Something that resembles love for Alice might underpin his actions. Nothing she says to Curt verifies or contradicts anything about Edgar, but Curt makes his own value judgment and issues his own definitive interpretation of events to Alice that seem to encompass the situation: "You've described your hell so realistically that there's no way it can be a metaphor, poetic or otherwise" (223).

Subsequent events prove Curt as a thoroughly unreliable witness. Indeed, his allegiance begins to shift from Alice after Edgar returns from a doctor's appointment on the mainland. Curt assumes the role of peacemaker and tries to broker a truce between the couple on the basis of the transformation that he sees evident in Edgar: "Surely you've seen the change in him. After that brush with death he's acquired a kind of dignity. He seems elevated somehow, uplifted. Maybe when he began to have thoughts about immortality, he got a new slant on life, too" (237). Curt intuits imminent death and describes Edgar's ravaged countenance to Alice as evidence: "His face is phosphorescent, as if he were dissolving. His eyes glimmer like will-o'-wisps over swamps and graves" (238). Alice plays the part of the cold one, now, and her husband's poor appearance and sickly demeanor do not fool her. Instead, she warns Curt that her husband likes to dissemble and that Curt would be wise not to believe anything that Edgar says. She studies him carefully to determine what game he now plays and indeed Edgar does surprise Curt when he springs his next trap. Betrayed, Curt seduces Alice, though it is also certainly possible to credit Alice for the seduction. At any rate, the sexual liaison between them does not last very long.

In the fifth and final unit of the play, Curt says something to Alice that echoes thoughts he voiced earlier directly to Edgar: "These prison walls must have absorbed all the crimes of the world. They reek of them. All you have to do is breathe and you get them in your system. Look at you: all you're thinking about is the theater and supper afterward, while I was thinking about my son" (250). Here, Curt stands on superior moral ground than Alice, but she confronts his hypocrisy and claims that his only real motive has been to sleep with his friend's wife. She informs Edgar that Curt is her new lover, now, and that she plans to leave with him. Curt, however, refuses, and heads for the door over protests from both Alice and Edgar:

> CURT: Go to hell! Go back to the abyss you came from!—God! I hope I never see you again!
> EDGAR: Don't leave me, Curt! She'll kill me!
> ALICE: Curt, don't abandon me like this! Don't abandon us! [257].

Curt does leave and then a strange thing happens. Left alone, Edgar and Alice immediately make up and tend to each other's needs. Edgar admits that he really is dying and that everything else he recently said was a lie. Alice confesses that she telegraphed the authorities against her husband and fears for what she has done. Edgar assures her, though, that no harm will come to them. Rapprochement between husband and wife demonstrates that the two of them were in league the entire time against Curt. They only seemed to be on opposite sides. Their cries to the contrary upon Curt's final exit amount to only so much playacting. With no one left for whom to perform after Curt's exit, they come together in what amounts to what David Mamet might call a "tell"—a sign or signal that indicates true feelings or intentions.

Edgar and Alice toy with Curt in ways that resonate with the game of "Get the Guests" in *Who's Afraid of Virginia Woolf?*, the great American play that Edward Albee wrote 60 years later. Just as Nick and Honey seem to represent the normal couple that witnesses the wacky antics of Martha and George, Curt visits the forbidding tower where Edgar and Alice live and reports on their domestic violence and marital discord. In each play an inversion occurs in which the "normal" witnesses hide secrets and motives that outdo those of the hosts. In *Virginia Woolf*, Honey reveals her fear of childbearing; in *The Dance of Death*, Curt reveals his amorous intentions toward Alice all the while posing as a better person than her or her husband. Surprisingly, the action in each play, despite all the barbs and insults that fly between husband and wife, reveals the love and abiding affection between the host couples. Each play, in its own way, is a kind of love story. Indeed, Edgar relates the charming story to Alice near the end about another couple set to celebrate 25 years of marriage in which the wife had to wear her wedding ring on her right hand because the husband had cut off her ring finger with a machete "in one of his tender moments" (261). Alice cannot help but laugh, between tears, at an image of marriage that blurs the line so sharply between love and hate.

At the heart of *Who's Afraid of Virginia Woolf?* lies a secret: George and Martha cannot have children of their own. The reality of that situation hurts them so deeply that they invest in a number of games to cope from day to day and year to year. There is no similar secret at the bottom of *The Dance of Death* and the action of the play confirms only what was there all along: an intense bond, call it love, between Edgar and Alice; and intense fear about the future and the prospect of death that looms over both members of the married couple. They do not talk about their fear, they simply know that it exists and attempt to deny it. They occupy themselves with games and dialogue and verbal ripostes to deny the presence and certainty of death but such efforts only confirm its eventuality and inevitability. The long interlude with Curt is a little dynamic play that they stage together to while away the time and stave what preoccupies their imaginations—the coming end of days.

Fortunately, though, the mere fear of death is not where the play ends. Edgar had a near-death experience in the play and lived to tell about it. Curt intimates that Edgar has undergone a transformative experience but he has no idea to what extent his statement rings true. Rather than make him more fearful of death, the experience of its long shadow gives Edgar new strength to view events and a new perspective on the time that remains for him on earth. He becomes downright detached, philosophical and even humorous at the end to Alice:

> Whether life is a serious business or a big joke is something I've never been able to figure out. As jokes go, it's rather sick. Better to take it seriously. Makes it more peaceful and pleasant.... However, just when you've made up your mind to be serious, along comes somebody who puts you on. Like Curt. Well, what do you say? A party for our silver anniversary? (261).

The end circles back to the beginning with reference to the anniversary party and this emphasis on repetition in tandem with daily routines along with resigned acceptance to fate contributes to making Strindberg's early 20th-century play quite modern. Far more than the linear development of almost any Ibsen play, the circular pattern in Strindberg points to the future of modern drama that reached its zenith, perhaps, with Beckett's *Waiting for Godot*. Consider for a moment the two similar acts in that play, the appearance of the Boy at the end of both acts, the similar dialogue at the end of both acts, and the identical exchange at the end of each:

VLADIMIR: Well? Shall we go?
ESTRAGON: Yes, let's go.
They do not move [36, 61].

A half-century earlier, Strindberg's curtain line to *The Dance of Death* reads quite similarly. Edgar voices repeatedly his philosophy about eliminating anything that he deems unwanted or unnecessary. He finishes with a flourish that presages Beckett's two tramps: "Cross out and move on. So— let's move on" (262). The drama ends here; it is impossible to know whether he and Alice move on together or not. But unlike the repetitive action in Beckett's play that reinforces a pattern of stasis and circularity, and one that Chekhov iterates, too, at the end of *Three Sisters*, Edgar's declarative statement at the end of Strindberg's play suggests a reinvigorated sensibility informed by a transformative experience that makes change possible and necessary. If the repetitive action of the play reinforces the notion of life as a kind of death, Edgar expresses a new outlook at the end and inverts the old philosophy with the following hopeful observation: "Maybe when death comes, life begins" (260). In the beginning, Alice boasted that only death would release them from the tyranny of marriage, but at the end Edgar voices optimism to Alice that death might represent a new beginning for them as though life on earth were just a prequel to an eternal relationship. As such, the end of the play does not represent a return to the beginning or even the cyclical pattern of daily life, but the possibility of a breakthrough into a different realm of spiritual existence that transcends life on earth. The entire play takes place within the walls of a military fortress that seems to imprison Edgar and Alice, but with respect to a reversed image of Böcklin's *The Island of the Dead*, the final line suggests a break through the stones into the light of blue sky and open sea.

A Dream Play (1906)

"That's what life is—going through it again and again."

Indra's Daughter descends from the clouds to see for herself and to report to her father whether or not there is justification for the great din of human complaints and lamentations on earth. She makes three principal encounters in the dream sequence. First, she discovers an officer who is a prisoner inside a castle, the interior and exterior of which provide the scenic focal point. She frees him to resume his habitual task of waiting at the stage door of an opera house for his fiancé. Every day he waits for Victoria with a bouquet of flowers, and every day she fails to open the door, a ritual that demonstrates the repetitive and futile aspects of daily existence. In the central portion of the play, Indra's Daughter meets the Lawyer who claims that all the sins of the world have rubbed off upon him. In order to guard against outside filth, he directs a woman to seal all the openings with paste, a fruitless exercise that fails to create a hermetic seal, but instead fills the inside with smoke and robs the apartment of air. Indra's Daughter's last major episode is with the Poet, whose compassion for the world of suffering measures against the self-righteousness of the mob. In this final section, the imagery turns heavily Christian and the Poet introduces references to Christ as the Saviour whom the righteous crowd crucified. In dialogue with the Poet, Indra's Daughter articulates two central conflicts that have been evident throughout the "dream": the joy of pain versus the pain of joy and the battle between the sensual (the body) and the spiritual (the mind). She concludes many times over that human beings deserve pity and she leaves the planet and returns to the heavens certain that humanity indeed suffers as a way of life, but also hopeful that humanity can evolve and turn human suffering into knowledge for self-improvement. As if to reinforce that point, the castle seems to rise from the ground throughout the play, flowering plants continue to grow and thrive around it, and the final image of the play showcases the beautiful display of a gigantic chrysanthemum as it bursts into full and colorful bloom atop the castle wall, a symbol, perhaps, for better days to come.

The "Note from the Author" that precedes the dramatic text describes surrealism as a style in a similar manner in which the Preface to *Miss Julie* outlined the tenets of naturalism on stage:

> Following the example of my previous dream play *To Damascus*, I have in this present dream play sought to imitate the incoherent but ostensibly logical form of our dreams. Anything can happen; everything is possible and probable. Time and space do not exist. Working with some insignificant real events as a background, the imagination spins out its threads of thoughts and weaves them into new patterns—a mixture of memories, experiences, spontaneous ideas, impossibilities, and improvisations. The characters split, double, multiply, dissolve, condense, float apart, coalesce. But one mind stands over and above them all, the mind of the dreamer [*Selected Plays* 2:268].

A Dream Play (1906)   169

The dreamer is none other than the playwright, Strindberg, whose dream-state consciousness projects a theatrical vision in time and space. This conceit encourages a director to stage the play with great latitude, ranging from a bare stage and minimal stage effects to the use of emerging technologies that surpass what Strindberg could have imagined at the time he wrote the play in the first decade of the 20th century. The plasticity of the play still has the capacity to excite a production team to employ new ways and means. While the famous preface to *Miss Julie* prescribes how to produce the play and confidently rattles off the playwright's techniques and innovations to achieve his desired effects, the prefatory comments for this forerunner of surrealism gear solely to the imagination of the future reader/audience/director.

Strindberg, however, does make an explicit comment regarding the tone of the play and the nature of the dream that does greatly influence any interpretation of the work:

> For him [the dreamer] there are no secrets, no inconsistencies, no scruples, no laws. He does not condemn, does not acquit; he only narrates the story. And since the dream is more often painful than cheerful, a tone of melancholy and of sympathy with all living creatures runs through the pitching and swaying narrative. Sleep, which should free the dreamer, often plagues and tortures him instead. But when the pain is most excruciating, the moment of waking comes and reconciles the dreamer to reality, which, however agonizing it may be, is a joy and a pleasure at that moment compared with the painful dream [268].

While the daughter of the Hindu god, Indra, does witness human events and pass judgments in the play, Strindberg attempts to distance himself from those same judgments. More importantly, though, he suggests that the dramatized events in his play produce abstractions of what occurs in everyday life and are therefore much more like nightmares than dreams. This is quite different from the experience of symbolism/surrealism in Chekhov's *The Seagull*, although the young playwright Konstantin also declares that we should not portray life as it is or as we want it to be but as it appears in our dreams. The problem with his play, though, as even his girlfriend, Nina, points out is that nothing happens and there are no "living people in it." A good play needs a love story, she quips. If too little happens in Konstantin's play, too much possibly happens in Strindberg's more mature and full-length work. Too much love, too much pain, too many scenes, too many episodes and events that dramatize the intense pain of everyday life, the sum of which creates a rich irony. If the naturalistic determinism of *Miss Julie* depresses an audience because of its bleak outlook on life and human nature, reality looks much better in *A Dream Play* when compared to dreams of that same reality. The hopeful, even optimistic ending of the play is only possible after the dreamer eventually awakens from his dream and discovers that everything that happened was just a dream in which nothing is real and real life, in fact, seems much more palatable and desirable than the life that appeared as just a dream. Life may be horrible, Strindberg seems to say, but it is much less horrible than the dreams of that same life!

The Officer that Indra's Daughter rescues from the castle refuses to dream at all and remains ambivalent about his captive state: "Either way I'll be in trouble. You have to pay for every joy in life with twice its price in sorrow. I hate to sit imprisoned here, but if I bought myself some joy and freedom, I'd pay for it three times over in pain and suffering" (276). Quite the opposite of the dreamer, the Officer accepts the realities and certainties of confinement as preferable to the unknown possibilities that come with striving for something better. Furthermore, he does not understand why he should have to perform the routine and often very unpleasant tasks of daily living. Indra's Daughter simply answers: "So that you'll want to get away from it." Despite life's hardship, she adds: "it's your duty to find your way to the light." The Officer counters that life has not done its duty by him and has been unjust and the next several scenes support his point of view. The first is a flashback to his home when he was a child. His father presents his mother, an invalid, with a new shawl, but she rejects the present because she sees no point in the gift since she is going to die very soon. The father asks forgiveness for all his transgressions against her, but she says that there is no need to ask because he has done nothing wrong. In a signature Strindberg moment, similar to points in *The Dance of Death* and all Strindberg's plays that deal with mature and intimate relations between men and women, the mother accepts what has transpired between them over the years as completely normal: "We've been hard on each other. And why? We don't know. We couldn't help ourselves..." (277). She beckons her son, Alfred (The Officer) for a private word and warns him that he must not go through life feeling as if he had been wronged. Yet, a moment later, she offends her husband when she gifts the shawl to her maid. Returning to an attitude of ambivalence, the mother concludes: "Oh, I give up! If you're nice to somebody, you're mean to someone else. Help one, hurt another. What a life!" (280).

Convinced that love conquers everything, Indra's Daughter hauls the Officer into a new scene that advances years and transforms into an alleyway and the stage door of a theater. The Officer, now a young man, dons a frock coat and top hat and carries a bouquet of roses that he plans to present to his fiancé, Victoria, a star of the opera company. He's been coming to this spot for seven years, he claims, and she always answers his call from her window but she never comes down and exits through the stage door. He waits endlessly and tirelessly. The Daughter observes: "For the gods in heaven a year is only a minute." The Doorkeeper parries quickly: "And for us here on earth a minute can seem like a year" (285). When the Officer next appears he "looks rather dusty and dirty," and his "roses have withered." When he enters again a short bit later his hair has turned grey and he has a grey beard. His clothes are ragged and the petals from the bouquet have all dropped. He notices the change of seasons but happily reports that autumn is his spring because the opera season is about to begin and she, Victoria, will surely come. The Daughter comments on the rapid elapse of time: "Day and night—day and night! ... A merciful providence wants to shorten the time you have to wait. The days are flying by, chasing the nights" (287). Still waiting, the Officer adopts the tone of ambivalence that he expressed in the very beginning as a prisoner in the castle: "Nothing is as I imagined it to be. You see, the thought is greater than the deed, finer than the thing itself..." (288). Intent upon finally seeing behind the stage door, the Officer exits to contact a locksmith. The seasons change yet again in his absence, and when he reappears next he is an extremely old man who totters back and forth upon his legs. He still seems content that Victoria is waiting for him, but a policeman soon arrives and forbids the opening of the door. Undeterred, the Officer plans a legal appeal.

The next scene transforms into the Lawyer's office and all the characters that gathered to watch the opening of the door in the previous scene are now prospective clients waiting to see the Lawyer and look as if they have been "standing there always" (292). The Lawyer bears all the sins of humanity, but the worst thing he does, he says, is to separate men and women through divorce: "Because it goes against nature itself, against the source of all good, against love" (293). He concludes: "I tell you it's a wretched business. Living, I mean." The Daughter agrees: "Poor souls. I feel so sorry for them." The Lawyer assures the Officer that Victoria has not left and still waits for him behind the door, and then he invites his guests to attend a ceremony at which he will receive his doctor of Law degree. The scene changes again to the interior of a church in which the crowd from the preceding scene now appears as ushers with wands, dancers with laurel wreaths and the rest of the assembled congregation. Just prior to conferral, however, the crowd disperses and leaves the discredited Lawyer alone. Why, the Daughter rhetorically asks: "Because you spoke up for the poor, put in a good word for the criminal, lightened the burden of the guilt, sought to pardon the condemned? ... What wretched people! They're not angels, are they? Still, I feel sorry for them" (295). She looks in a mirror and sees the world as it should be, because, as is, it is the wrong way up. The world of appearances is a copy, a "mad world" (296). Since the Deans of the Faculties will not crown the Lawyer with a wreath, the Daughter presents him with a crown of thorns and begins to play the organ, from which singing voices rather than music cry to God to be merciful.

The stage darkens and the Lawyer hears the tears of mankind falling on the ground: "Sighing ... wailing ... moaning" (297). He claims that the only joy in life is love (also the bitterest!). In response, Indra's Daughter tests him with a proposal for marriage. "Suppose we get bored with each other?" he asks, but she perseveres. Married life, unfortunately, suffocates both of them. The very next scene presents the crushing poverty of their dreary domestic situation in which an unknown amount of time has already passed. Despite their struggles, the Lawyer maintains that neighbors envy them because they still have food, albeit mostly cabbage that the Daughter hates. She clamors for a little beauty in the house, even a flower that they cannot afford, while he wishes for the kind of beauty that costs nothing: a disciplined tidiness in the home. They agree that marriage is very difficult if not impossible: "We'll live together and make each other sick. Your pleasure—my pain; and vice versa," the Lawyer analyzes, a sentiment that echoes the Officer's mother from earlier in the play. "We poor souls, I feel sorry for us," the Daughter concludes, having exchanged empathy for personal experience (302). The Officer, middle-aged and prosperous, now reappears and asks the Daughter to escape with him. She readily agrees and leaves her home strewn with hairpins. The Lawyer discovers the pins and reads in them a metaphor for married life: "There are two prongs but one hairpin. Two making one.... A lock that holds when it's open" (305). Like the door to the room, he says. "When I close it, I open the way—for you, Agnes [the Daughter]!" (306). He leaves and closes the door on the scene.

The Daughter and Officer stand as they were previously as the scene changes around them to reflect an exterior landscape. Fairhaven appears in the background, a beautiful wooded shore, and a strait can be seen in the middle distance. In the foreground, a quarantine station contrasts with the background, its terrain resembling that of a landscape after a forest fire. Stage directions indicate that people receive treatment on "machines that resemble instruments of torture" (306). This place is called Foulstrand and the Quarantine Master points out that the sick people live here, including the gluttonous rich who have surfeited and stuffed themselves: "Look at the fellow on the rack. He's eaten too much *pâté-de-foie-gras*, and drunk so much Burgundy he's got knotted feet" (307). Another one "lying on the guillotine—he's drunk so much cognac, we've got to straighten out his spine by putting him through the mangle." The healthy people live over on Fairhaven, but Foulstrand is the home of all the guilty sinners: "on this side everyone's got some sort of problem he wants to hide." A third important character, the Poet, enters and prepares to take his mud bath, a ritual that prompts a wry comment from the Quarantine Master that the Poet spends so much time with his thoughts up in the air that he rejoices in the mud as pigs do. The Poet claims, though, that the mud hardens his skin and that as an artist he no longer feels the sting from gadflies. Taking in the entire scene around him, the Officer exclaims: "What a strange world! All contradictions!" (309). "Ecstatically," the Poet proclaims that man was made from clay, that art is made of clay, that domestic tools and pots and pans are also made from clay, and that clay in its liquid form is called mud. The Poet accuses the Daughter of not being able to see what is happening on earth, not being able to see the injustices here on the ground because she sits too high up in the clouds.

The Officer next welcomes He and She, a romantic couple, to the quarantine station. They arrive in a boat from Fairhaven with their arms wrapped around each other. The Officer describes them: "There's real happiness, boundless bliss, the ecstasy of young love!" (311). Such young love cannot last, as they pull the lovers in to Foulstrand. The horrible surroundings at the quarantine station repulse the young couple and the Poet regards what's happening to them as a crime against love: "Let the lovers be. Meddling with true love is a capital crime.... Why does everything beautiful have to be dragged down, dragged through the mud?" (312). The lovers don't understand what has happened to them, but the Q. Master explains that it is not a matter of anything they have done to cause such misfortune: "You needn't have done anything to have to suffer the little vexations of life." "Happiness never lasts," cries She (313). They enter the shed where the sulphuric flames bleach her blue dress white and drain her skin of color. He and She emerge from the shed with pale faces. Seeing them in distress, the Officer admits, comforts him a little because he still misses Victoria, but he is still able to reason: "It can't make me happy to see you suffer" (314). The Daughter comments: "Almighty One, listen to them! Life is cruel! Poor lost souls! Take pity on them!" (315).

The scene reverses perspective such that the Daughter and Officer now stand in Fairhaven, the strait remains in the midground, and Foulstrand can be seen in the distant and shadowy background. Viewing a bright and cheerful dance, the Daughter declares: "This is vacation land! Everybody's resting and happy! No work for anybody—parties every day—everybody's dressed in their fines clothes—music and dancing even before lunch!" (315). She wonders aloud, though, why three young women remain aloof and watch through a window while a fourth, "Ugly Edith," sits alone at an open piano. The Officer explains that Edith has sat alone for hours without receiving a single invitation to dance, while the other three young women are all servants who are not allowed to participate in the festivities. "What a cruel game!" the Daughter comments (316). Edith begins to play Bach in competition with the music inside and gradually folks emerge from inside to watch and hear her play, including a Naval Officer who grabs another young woman and leads her away. Stage directions read: "Edith breaks off playing, rises and follows them with her eyes, her face registering her heartache. She remains standing as if turned to stone" (317). Later, the Daughter reports that Edith weeps after the Naval Officer proposes marriage to her rival and prepares to sail away. Incredulous, the Daughter inquires: "You mean there isn't a single happy person in this paradise?" (320). The Officer affirms that there is as they watch another couple enter together. Clearly happy, the husband explains to his wife that he wishes to die at love's peak rather than its inevitable valley. He reasons further: "I'm afraid of happiness. A mirage, made to lure us on" (321). They exit toward the sea together. Once again, the Daughter voices her refrain: "What a cruel world! And the poor souls who live in it."

The Lawyer reappears to convince Indra's Daughter that repetition is the worst evil of earthly existence and that everything that one has to do again and again falls under the onerous name of duty: "Everything you shy away from. Everything you hate to do and have to do! It means doing without, giving up, denying yourself. It means everything unpleasant, disgusting, and painful" (324). Duties are only enjoyable, he says, after they are completed. "What's pleasant is sin," he says. That, naturally, is punished: "If I have a good time, the next day I have a bad conscience and suffer the torments of hell. Success just sets you up to be knocked down." "That's what life is—going through it again and again" (325). The Daughter claims that she is ready to go back [home, to the clouds, to her father] but she wants to see the door opened first so that she might know the secret behind it. Before she leaves, she hears a distant cry of lamentation that the Lawyer says comes from the doomed on Foulstrand. They cry so loudly over there because of their proximity to Fairhaven: "Because the sun is shining *here* [on Fairhaven], because there's music *here* and youth and life *here*. That's why they feel their misery so much more deeply" (326). After the Daughter suggests that they must set them free, the Lawyer allows that someone already tried that once long ago: "Someone once came to set them free. They hanged him on a cross." The righteous killed him, the same group that denied the Lawyer his degree.

The scene transforms again, this time to a Mediterranean resort with villas and a Casino and terrace. In the foreground stands a white wall over which hang orange trees with fruit. Below the wall is a large heap of coal and two wheelbarrows. The Daughter comes out on the terrace and announces: "This is paradise" (326). As if in response, one of the Coal Heavers says, "This is hell." The Daughter asks them whether they have done something to deserve their fate. They have committed crimes, they admit, but, unlike the rich folk playing games at the casino, had the misfortune of getting caught. Furthermore there is no place for them to go, because everything has been bought and is owned by someone. The Daughter asks the Lawyer why someone doesn't do something to improve conditions for people, and he responds tersely: "all who want to make the world better end up in prison or in the madhouse" (328). Either the righteous ones put them there, or their own despair at the hopelessness of the situation drives them mad. The Lawyer adds that rich people always believe that there are "unknown reasons" for the unfortunate state of things in which the few exploit the multitude. A lady crosses the terrace with a gentleman who tries to work up an appetite for dinner, an endeavor that provokes snickers from the Coal Heavers. A child sees the blackened workers and screams. The Lawyer assures the Daughter that it is not the people who are bad and unjust, but the system under which they live.

The scene changes once again to its most exotic locale, Fingal's Cave, where billows roll gently in and a red bell-buoy rocks upon the waves. Music of the winds and the waves pervades. The Daughter interprets the music into words that she translates into verse, addresses to her father, and reads aloud to the Poet:

> The earth is not clean,
> life is not kind,
> man is not evil,
> nor is he good.
> People live as best they can,
> one day at a time.
> Living in ashes and dust,
> they breed and die:
> ashes to ashes, dust to dust.
> Feet for plodding
> were they given,
> not wings for flying.
> So the dust covers them.
> Is the fault theirs
> or yours? [332].

In dialogue with the Poet, she defines poetry as something akin to the very play in which she plays a part: "Not reality. Something more than reality. Not dreams, but wide-awake dreams" (334). She says that she has stayed on Earth too long and can no longer fly back to heaven. She is "earthbound." Before she goes, she agrees to read the words of the Poet, the work of a dreamer, a "petition on behalf of humanity, addressed to the ruler of the world, and drawn up by a dreamer" (335). His protest questions why mankind was born in an animal state. Indra's Daughter sympathizes with his lament and agrees to translate the Poet's words into an acceptable form worthy of immortal ears. The Poet sees someone walking upon the water and identifies the figure as the one whom the righteous crucified because "He wanted to set all men free" (339). "It's a strange world!" exclaims the Daughter. Next, the Poet describes an apocalyptic scene: "The sea is rising. Darkness is falling. The storm rages." *The Crew shriek*. "The sailors scream in terror when they see their Saviour ... and now ... they're jumping overboard—afraid of their Redeemer" (339). The Crew shriek again. "Now they're screaming because they're about to die. They scream when they're born and scream when they die!" (339). The waves continue to threaten them and the light begins to change. It is not a ship that they see. At first, the Poet describes it as a tower, a modern Tower of Babel. The Daughter corrects him: "If you want to storm the walls of heaven, besiege it with your prayers" (340).

The Daughter and Officer return to the alley behind the opera house and a crowd assembles once again at the stage door to glimpse what lies behind the door. When they do not find anything, they accuse the Daughter of swindling them. She assures them that they are correct in their perceptions of nothing behind the door, but adds that they have not properly understood what they have seen. Once again, she tells the Poet: "Poor lost souls. I feel sorry for them" (346). She encourages him to escape with her to the wilderness where they will be beyond the reach of the righteous crowd and where she can safely reveal the answer to the mystery. The Lawyer intervenes by reminding her of her responsibilities toward their child. The agony she feels, the Lawyer reminds her, is "the pangs of conscience" (347). When the Lawyer tells her that she can only stop these pangs by doing her duty, she questions what to do when there are clearly at least two duties to perform. "You've broken my heart in two and it's pulling me both ways," she confesses (348). The Poet reveals how he has suffered the pangs of conscience by following his vocation, the highest duty of all. "They call me disloyal, a stinker. And a fat lot of good it does me to hear my conscience tell me, 'You did right,' because the next moment it's telling me how wrong I was. And that's life for you." The Daughter beckons all of them to come with her out to the wilderness and, reasoning that the assembled followers are all her children, leaves her biological child behind in the care of another.

Outside the castle, blue monkshood, aconite and other flowers cover the ground. A giant chrysanthemum bud crests the top of the castle and candles illuminate all the windows. The time draws near for Indra's Daughter, with the help of fire, to ascend into the ether. She wonders why mankind is so afraid of death with all the prophesies of the afterlife. She does understand now, however, that it is not easy to be human. She finally reveals the secret of the universe as confirmed by the emptiness behind the door: "…the world," she says, "and its inhabitants and life itself are nothing more than phantoms, mirages, images in a dream" (350). The existential problem for humanity roots in the simultaneous desire for the spiritual and the physical and the inability to reconcile one with the other: "Constant strife between the anguish of joy and the pleasure of suffering, the torments of remorse and the delights of sensuality" (350). The Daughter removes her shoes in the final ceremony and tosses them in the fire, and thus purifies the dust and clay of the earth from her feet. Other characters from the play enter one by one and make similar contributions of their dear possessions to the fire. As the Daughter speaks her last lines in verse, the flames in the castle grow larger until fire consumes the castle. In the middle passage of her last speech she reveals all that she has learned about her time on earth among human beings:

> Now, now I know what it means to live;
> I feel the pain of being human.
> You miss what you never wanted;
> regret even misdeeds never done.
> You want to leave, you want to stay;
> your heart's drawn and quartered, torn apart
> by conflicting wishes, indecision, doubt [353].

After she goes into the Castle the flames leap, the music swells and a wall of human faces appears: "questioning, sorrowful, despairing." As the flames soar, the flower bud on the roof of the castle bursts into a giant chrysanthemum.

While Strindberg's dream play projects a world that is much more intensely unpleasant than everyday life, Indra's Daughter makes clear that the world we call reality is itself a dream. The play then projects a shadow of a shadow to show that what lies beyond life, the afterlife, offers true peace. To be human is to strive, to love, to fight, to grow, blossom and to wilt like the dominant images of flowers in the play. "Why do flowers grow up from dirt?" The Daughter asks the Glazier outside the castle in the play's initial scene. "They don't like to be in the dirt, so they hurry up into the light as fast as they can—to bloom and die" the Glazier responds (275). A metaphor for life, humans aspire to grow from the mud of the earth and into the light. The gigantic chrysanthemum, final image of the play, bursts and blooms with breathtaking awe and beauty. And, while the colorful bloom lasts only temporarily, the rich earth promises to foster growth in the next renewed growing cycle. Much more than in his previous naturalistic plays and more explicitly than in *The Dance of Death*, Strindberg presents the strife and turmoil and unavoidable conflicts and worries and duties and responsibilities in *A Dream Play* that human beings desperately try and fail to transcend, yet hints that the unending struggle can fertilize future generations.

The Ghost Sonata (1907)

> "They all look like ghosts.... This has been going on for twenty years—always the same people, always saying the same things."

A young student, Arkenholtz, wanders one morning to a public fountain after having rescued a family from a fire the previous night. He did not arrive at this spot by accident. For some time, he has watched from afar the beautiful young woman who lives in the corner apartment and imagined that life would be complete, even perfect, if he could marry her. An old man sitting on a green bench outside the building, Director Hummel, watches the young man's every move with great interest. He has been watching the young man for a long time, too, and he has arranged this rendezvous. Later identified as a stealer of souls, Hummel strikes up a conversation with Arkenholtz with the intent to convince the young man to do his bidding. He already knows that the young man is the son of a man whom he destroyed in a legal battle years ago. He claims that the father owed him a great deal of money but says that all debts will be considered paid if the young man performs a simple task: to lead the way for Hummel's subsequent entrance to the apartment. Hummel describes in detail all of the inhabitants of the building, including his ex-wife and former fiancée, and how they have conducted their affairs unscrupulously, hypocritically, illegally, and immorally. With his new status as hero from the previous night, Arkenholtz, according to Hummel, will gain access to the building as an honored guest and gain audience with his heart's desire. Hummel arranges for him to sit next to the Young Lady and her father at the opera that afternoon as a way of introduction.

In the second scene, Hummel follows the student into the apartment and proceeds to confront all the inhabitants with the lies of their lives. He disturbs them with information that he has gathered against them over many years. The tables turn, however, when the character known as The Mummy reveals that the ghostlike existence and interactions of the apartment dwellers serve as conscious acts of penitence and retribution for their many sins. Hummel, too, has his own lies and hypocrisies, the Mummy points out, and his desire to inflict cruelty and exact revenge makes him much worse than any of the assembled guests at the supper. Faced at last with his immense and dire human failings, Hummel follows the directive of the Mummy and enters her closet to hang himself, after which she calls for the death screen to announce another victim.

In the final movement, the scene shifts to the Hyacinth Room in which the Student courts at last the beautiful young woman whom he has longed to meet. He declares his love and desire to marry her, but she cannot consent because, she says, she does not have long to live. The repetition of everyday living, cleaning, washing, cooking and eating has drained her life. The obese and nasty cook, who hovers ominously at the doorway, extracted all the nutrition from the food and replaced all the wine in bottles with colored water. Convinced by all that the Young Lady says, the Student recognizes now that hardship and pain dictates life on earth and that all good souls must look to the next life for rest and peace.

In *A Dream Play*, the playwright cast himself as the dreamer and staged his own imagination: characters came and went, appeared and disappeared, scenery transformed almost instantaneously from one setting and locale to another, moment to moment action lacked coherent narrative but hooked together thematically and repeated throughout the play. The surreal aspects of *The Ghost Sonata* work quite differently. The dreamer is not the playwright, but a character within the dramatic fiction. Initially, the Old Man, Mr. Hummel, appears to be the protagonist as he directs the action and seems most interested in encountering the inhabitants of the apartment. Indeed, Hummel dominates the entire second section of the play. Ultimately, however, he, too, disappears, and the Student, Arkenholtz, gains the final word in the last scene with the Young Lady. Arkenholtz admits that he is a "Sunday Child" and therefore special; and the opening scene establishes his unique vision that hints at special powers, which prove necessary in the course of the play as he discovers that the world of outward appearances is not aligned with the world of reality.

Unlike *A Dream Play*, too, the scene appears to be the realistic exterior of an urban environment. The focal point of the design depicts the corner of a façade of a modern house, showing the ground floor that terminates in the Round Room, above which a balcony extends from the first floor. The stage directions further suggest a perspective that places the corner apartment in the mid-ground of the scene: "The corner of the house with the round room also faces a side street that runs upstage" (*Selected Plays* 2:361). Left of the round room, the Hyacinth Room runs upstage along the side street. Various windows with drapes and curtains as well as the balcony make the inhabitants of the apartment visible to the audience. Downstage of the apartment forms another "street" with a bench in the foreground of the stage picture upon which the Old Man sits at the beginning of the play. The theatrical audience views the activity in the house from the same vantage point as the Old Man.

Strindberg conceived the play in three scenes or movements to accord with the musical form of the sonata: exposition, elaboration and recapitulation. Hummel introduces the action in the first scene that takes place entirely on the street in the downstage part of the stage. The second scene takes place inside the Round Room, in which Hummel leads the charge against the people whom he has known all his life, but discovers to his ultimate peril that things are not as they appear. The final scene occurs in the Hyacinth Room and adopts a wholly different key, and yet, too, the Student, Arkenholtz, discovers that the world differs greatly from the one that he had imagined. As the play moves in time through its three movements, then, it also moves in space from downstage to upstage, as if the characters and by extension, the audience, were to move deeper into experience/reality and through the layers of illusion covering the world. Despite the apparent realism of the scene design and the local street scene, the progression from outside to deep inside the house and from downstage to upstage probes an investigation of the world of appearances.

The Student enters to begin the play and goes to the public fountain directly opposite from the Old Man on the other side of the stage. He pours a drink of water and tries to engage a Milkmaid, who joins him there, in conversation. She does not speak, but only gazes at him in horror. The Old Man, Hummel, observes from his perch on the green bench and wonders why the young man speaks aloud apparently to no one. He does not see the Milkmaid, whom the initial character list describes as an "apparition." He reacts "in horror" when the Student asks: "Didn't you see the milkmaid I was talking to?" (370). Hummel's servant confides later to the Student that his employer fears nothing in the world except for one person, whom the Student guesses correctly, is none other than the young Milkmaid. He surmises that something must have happened in the past, perhaps in Hamburg. In the final moments of the first scene, the Student recalls when he saved a person from drowning once on a Sunday morning in Hamburg. The Milkmaid makes her final appearance with this revelation, Hummel can see her this time, and she waves her arms as if she were in water and stares fixedly at Hummel, a silent accusation that he once drowned a young girl or was at least responsible for her death.

Hummel feigns that he is blameless and innocent of any wrongdoing and seeks the help of the Student, rather, to redress all the wrongs that have been done to him. He instructs: "Just do as I tell you and you won't regret it. I want to see you happy—rich, respected. Your debut last night as the courageous rescuer is the beginning of your fame. From now on your name is your fortune" (367). He needs the young man to serve as his arms and legs in order to gain access to the corner apartment. He explains: "You see that I'm a cripple—some say it's my own fault—others blame my parents—personally I blame it all on life itself, with all its traps—in avoiding one you fall right into the next one" (366). Hummel asks him if he'd like a job, Arkenholtz says yes, and Hummel immediately instructs him to place an order for a specific seat at the matinee of *The Valkyrie* that would place him next to the Colonel and his daughter.

After securing his ticket, the Student admits that he has always been drawn to the apartment: "I went by here yesterday, when the sun was glittering on the panes—and dreaming of all the beauty and luxury there must be in that house" (367). He wondered aloud to a companion while gazing at what it would be like to live there with a beautiful young wife and two kids and a lot of money. Indicating that he was watching him at the time, Hummel tells the Student that he is very fond of the house as well and that he, in fact, knows everyone who lives in it. At 80 years old, he knows everyone, he says, and it is natural for him to take an interest in "human destinies." The drawn blinds of the Round Room allow Hummel to identify the Colonel as the man whom the Student will sit next to at the opera in the afternoon. Amazed, the Student equates the scene to that of a fairy story. "My whole life, my dear young man, is like a book of fairy tales," Hummel counters, "but although the stories are different, one thread ties them all together and the same leitmotif recurs constantly" (368). He does not name his theme of revenge, but turns attention back to the interior of the apartment and a marble statue of the Colonel's wife as a young woman. He advises his new young friend that although "we can't judge other people," she left him once, he beat her, and she returned to marry him a second time, and that at present she sits "in there right now like a mummy, worshipping her own statue" (368). The Hyacinth Room is where the daughter lives, Hummel adds, and she will return soon.

Hummel requests the Student to wheel him into the sun because he's terribly cold. "When you never get to move around, the blood congeals. I'm going to die soon, I know that. But before I do, there are a few things I want to take care of.—Feel my hand, just feel how cold I am" (371). He grabs the Student's hand and refuses to let go. "—I have an infinitely long life behind me—infinitely long—I've made people unhappy and people have made me unhappy, the one cancels out the other. But before I die, I want to make you happy." The Student cannot tolerate the grip of the Old Man. "Let go, let go of my hand—you are drawing all my strength from me—you're turning my blood to ice—what do you want of me?" Hummel begs his patience and says that he will soon be able to see and understand everything as the Young Lady approaches. Overcome by her beauty, the Student begins to weep because he reasons that his attraction to her is hopeless. Hummel assures him that he can help: "But I can open doors—and hearts—if only I can find an arm to do my will. Serve me, and you shall be a lord of creation" (372). "Am I to sell my soul?" the Student asks, fearful of a Faustian bargain. Hummel lies and assures him that he must sell nothing. He has taken all his life and now, he says, he has the urge to give. He wants the Student to be his heir rather than his own son whom he calls a "good-for-nothing." He encourages the Student to pursue the Young Lady so that he can watch and enjoy life at least from a distance.

The action of the play, however, examines life at close range as the second scene moves inside the house and into the Round Room. From that vantage point, the Young Lady can be seen reading a book through a door leading to the Hyacinth Room and the back of the Colonel is visible through another door leading to the Green Room, both future destinations for subsequent scenes as the play explores every aspect of the interior life of the house. Johansson, Hummel's servant, in discussion with Bengtsson, the Colonel's manservant, expresses his delight upon gaining entry: "It's always been my dream to get into this house" (379). Bengtsson understates the case when he informs him that the inhabitants are a bit out of the ordinary and he describes the gathering as the "usual ghost supper": "They drink tea, without saying a word, or else the Colonel talks all by himself. And they chomp their biscuits and crackers all at once and all in unison. They sound like a pack of rats in an attic" (380). He continues: "They all look like ghosts…. This has been going on for twenty years—always the same people, always saying the same things." The mistress of the house is crazy and lives in a cupboard because she can't bear the light. She looks like a mummy and sounds like a parrot—carried away by her own imagination. "Well," Bengtsson explains, "when a house grows old, it turns moldy and rotten, and when people are together too much and torment each other too long, they go crazy" (381). The woman known as The Mummy acts crazy primarily because she cannot reconcile herself to the fact that her daughter, the beautiful Young Lady in the Hyacinth Room, is very ill and unlikely to live very long. Bengtsson points out the Japanese screen in the room as the "death-screen," brought out when someone is about to die. Overwhelmed by all this information, Johansson exclaims: "What a horrible house…. That poor student thought that when he entered this house he would be entering paradise" (382). From outside of the house in the opening scene the residents appeared to live a magical life. From inside, however, as the two servants establish in the expository scene that opens the second scene, things are not what they seem and are far worse, in fact, than anyone could imagine.

Hummel successfully leverages the Young Man's appeal to the Colonel and Young Lady to push his way into the house. While he explores the room and gazes at the statue, the Mummy sneaks up behind him and surprises him, calls him "Jacob" and introduces herself as "Amelia." Recognition of her up close horrifies Hummel. Amelia cloisters herself, she says, so that she doesn't have to be reminded of how she used to look and how she looks now. Hummel tells her that he has come to see his child, whom the Mummy points out now sits in the Hyacinth Room. She tells him that she told her husband, the Colonel, the truth once but he didn't believe her, even though the revelations were a "terrible crime" that falsified his noble name. She and Hummel, however, committed a greater crime and she emphasizes that Hummel deserves most of the blame. Hummel refuses to accept responsibility for what he did and shifts the blame to the Colonel: "Your husband started it all when he stole my fiancée from me! I was born unable to forgive until I have punished! I've always looked upon it as an imperative duty. And I still do!" (384). The Mummy warns him that he will die "behind that screen" if he tries to hurt the daughter or her father (the Colonel). Hummel pays no heed and brags: "Be that as it may. But I'm a bulldog. I never let go" (385). He reveals his plan to attend the ghost supper and for the Student to marry the Young Lady. Horrified at the prospect of all being together, the Mummy exclaims: "Oh God, why can't we die? If only we could die!" She explains why they have stayed together all through the years: "Our crimes and our secrets and our guilt bind us together! We have split up and gone our own ways an infinite number of times. But we're always drawn back together again…" (386).

With the Colonel's approach, the Mummy implores Hummel to spare her husband.

After having secretly bought all the Colonel's unpaid promissory notes, Hummel claims ownership of everything in the house. The Colonel tries to save face by pointing to his "family escutcheon" and his good reputation, but Hummel quickly produces a document that proves the Colonel's family name has been extinct for a hundred years. Taking the Colonel's signet ring, Hummel informs him that he is not entitled to call himself a colonel, either, since it was only a temporary title that expired long ago. "Do you know who you are?" Hummel wonders. If the Colonel were to take off his wig, look at himself in the mirror, take out his teeth, shave off his mustache, unlace his metal stays, then he might recognize himself as a certain lackey, "a cupboard lover." For now, Hummel upholds the illusion so long as the Colonel obeys him. The Colonel also wonders who Hummel is: "I've seen your eyes and heard your voice before," he claims. "Never mind that," Hummel warns. "Be silent and do as you're told" (388).

Hummel gathers the old people in the Round Room in order to confront them with all of their crimes: the Mummy, the Colonel, his old fiancée, and the baron, with whom the Mummy once had an affair. Hummel suggests that they not serve tea since no one wants it and that they should sit quietly: "I prefer silence ... in which one can hear thoughts and see the past. Silence cannot hide anything—which is more than you can say for words" (390). Periods of silence break up his long speech in which everyone looks at each other or away from each other. Hummel asserts that everyone knows who he is and what he wants and why he is here. "Nature herself has planted in man a blushing sense of shame, which seeks to hide what should be hidden. But we slip into certain situations without intending to, and chance confronts us with moments of revelation, when the deepest secrets are revealed, the mask is ripped from the impostor and the villain stands exposed..." (391). He continues with his assault: "In this estimable house, in this elegant house, where beauty, wealth, and culture are united.... *Long silence.* All of us sitting here, we know who we are, don't we? ... I don't have to tell you.... And you know me, although you pretend ignorance." He next announces that the Young Lady in the Hyacinth Room is his daughter and that he has come to rescue her because she has lost the will to live "withering away because of the air in this house, which reeks of crime, deception, and lies of every kind." He expresses his desire for the Student to marry her and asserts that he has come to right the wrongs of the past. "That was my mission in this house. To pull up the weeds, to expose the crimes, to settle all accounts, so that these young people might make a new beginning in this home, which is my gift to them!" During the silence, he stops so that all may hear the sound of time passing, the tick-tick-tick of the clock in the room.

In a stunning reversal, the Mummy finally erupts in a long speech that begins: "But I can stop time in its course. I can wipe out the past, and undo what is done. Not with bribes, not with threats—but through suffering and repentance" (392). She approaches Hummel: "We are poor miserable creatures, we know that. We have erred, we have transgressed, we, like all the rest. We are not what we seem to be. At bottom we are better than ourselves, since we abhor and detest our misdeeds." Jacob Hummel, on the other hand, is worse than the rest of the assembled miserable sinners because he, unlike them, pronounces judgments and is worse than he seems to be: "a stealer of souls." He stole her with false promises; he strangled the baron with debts he could not pay; he stole the Student with lies about what his father owed Hummel. The Old Man crumples up more and more in his chair as the Mummy proceeds. The Milkmaid makes a final appearance in the hallway door, though only Hummel sees her and he "shies in terror" (392). Bengtsson comes forward to reveal that he knew Hummel in Hamburg and that he committed his most hideous crime there: he lured a young girl out on the ice to drown her because she had witnessed him commit another crime. The Mummy passes her hand over Jacob's face and tells him that this portrait shows the real Hummel. She instructs him to rise and enter the cupboard where she has "sat for twenty years, crying over our misdeeds," and then orders him to hang himself with the same rope that he has used to strangle others (393–394). She calls for the death-screen and concludes: "It is finished.—May God have mercy on his soul" (394). All say "Amen" and the scene switches to the adjoining Hyacinth Room where the Young Lady plays her harp and the Student delivers a recitation:

> I saw the sun.
> And from its blaze
> There burst on me
> The deepest truth:
>
> Man reaps as he sows;
> Blessed is he
> Who sows the good.
>
> For deeds done in anger
> Kindness alone
> Can make amends.
>
> Bring cheer to those
> Whom you have hurt,
> And kindness reaps
> Its own rewards.
>
> The pure in heart
> Have none to fear.
> The harmless are happy.
> The guileless are good [394–395].

In the Hyacinth Room, deep within the family apartment, the perspective shifts and shows both the Colonel and the Mummy through the door that opens to the Round Room. A large Buddha sits atop the stove and hyacinths fill the room. The Student claims he loves this type of flower above all others: "its stem rising straight and slender, like a young maiden, from the round bulb, which floats on water and sends its white rare roots down into clear, colorless nothingness" (395). He loves all the colors, especially the "blue as morning mist, deep-eyed blue, ever-faithful blue." He has loved them since childhood, more than gold or pearls, yet the fragrance also overpowers his senses and causes him pain. The hyacinth represents an image of the Cosmos with bulb as earth, the straight stalk as aspiration to rise out of the earth, and the six-pointed star-flowers at the top as heaven above. Referring to the Buddha in the room, he adds: "That's why Buddha sits there with the bulb of the earth in his lap, watching it constantly to see it shoot up and burst forth and be transformed into a heaven. This poor earth shall become a heaven. That is what Buddha is waiting for" (396). Ecstatically, the young couple describes how snowflakes, stars and shallots all manifest analogous properties to the hyacinth, and the Student joyfully claims that they have given birth to new thoughts that now wed them together.

Not so fast, the Young Lady interjects: "Time—testing—patience" are required (397). She says that she must review the dinner menu with the Cook and that boring routines such as this one have sucked the joy of life from her. As if their love puts them above such mundane and repetitive tasks as eating and cooking and cleaning, the Student naively asks: "What have we got to do with the kitchen?" The Young Lady claims that the Cook "belongs to the Hummel family of vampires. She's eating us up…" She cannot fire her because she recognizes that the Cook punishes the family for its sins: "We've got her for our sins. Can't you see that we are pining and wasting away?" The Cook prepares food everyday, but she extracts all the flavor and nutritional value from the meals: "She boils the beef until there's nothing left of it and serves us the sinews swimming in water while she herself drinks the stock. And when we have a roast she cooks all the juice out of it and drinks it and eats the gravy. Everything she touches loses its flavor. It's as if she sucked it up with her very eyes. We get the grounds when she has finished her coffee. She drinks the wine and fills up the bottles with water" (398). The Cook embodies only one of the trials and tribulations that the family must endure. The family must execute the housemaids' work as well. The room in which they sit, for example, is the "room of ordeals" because, although beautiful, it is always cold and the fireplace always produces smoke. The writing table wobbles and the Young Lady must fix its stability every day: "Every day I lay a piece of cork under that foot, but the housemaid takes it away when she sweeps, and I have to cut a new piece. The penholder is covered with ink every morning, and so is the inkstand, I have to clean them up after her, as regularly as the sun goes up" (399). She continues to detail the litany of daily travails: to wake up in the night to pull down the window that the housemaid has left open; to tie the cord on the damper to the stove that the housemaid has torn off; "to sweep up after her, to dust after her, and to start the fire in the stove after her—all she does is bring in the wood!" (400). After the Student has quite heard enough, the Young Lady still reminds him that labor must always come first: "The drudgery of keeping oneself above the dirt of life." Despite having money and two servants, the Girl insists: "Living is such a nuisance, and I get so tired at times." She reminds the Student that life would be even more difficult if there were a nursery and a child. The Student calls a child "the dearest of joys," while the Young Lady counters that a child is also the costliest. "Is life really worth so much trouble?" she asks. The Student tells her: "There's nothing I wouldn't do to win your hand" (400). The Girl tells him that he cannot ever have her. Stunned, the Student questions why she dropped her bracelet earlier for him to pick up and retrieve. She didn't drop it, she replies—it simply slipped off her wrist when she became too thin from lack of food.

The Young Lady tries to keep the Student from saying anything further by claiming that only inmates in an asylum say everything that they think. The Student agrees with her, adding that his father ended up in a madhouse after making a big speech: "Then something loosed the trigger, and in a long oration he stripped naked every single person there, one after another. Told them of all their deceits. And at the end, exhausted, he sat down right in the middle of the table and told them all to go straight to hell" (403). He ended up in the madhouse and died there. The Student begins to suspect that things are not what they seem to be: "Something's rotting here. And I thought it was paradise when I saw you come in here for the first time" (403). Only in his imagination, he says, can the world fulfill its promise. He begs the Young Lady to play her harp again, but she says nothing and he plucks the strings himself but the instrument makes no sound. Echoing his earlier statement about beautiful flowers having too strong a fragrance for his senses, he now recasts the image in more dangerous, oppositional terms: "Tell me, why are beautiful flowers so poisonous, and the most beautiful the most deadly? Why? The whole creation, all of life, is cursed and damned.... Why would you not become my bride?" (404). His eyes fully open, he cannot call that which is evil good, or what is ugly beautiful. In the opposition between good and evil, he turns to Christianity: "They say that Christ harrowed hell. What they really meant was that He descended to earth, to this madhouse, jailhouse, charnel house. And the inmates crucified Him when He tried to free them. But the robber they let go. Robbers always win sympathy.... Woe! Woe to all of us! Saviour of the World, save us! We are perishing!" (404). "Drooped" as if she were a dying flower, the Young Lady rings the bell and calls for the death-screen.

The Student offers a benediction of peace in the play's final moments: "And you, my darling, you beautiful, innocent, lost soul who suffers for no fault of your own, sleep, sleep a dreamless sleep. And when you wake again ... may you be greeted by a sun that doesn't scorch, in a home without dust, by friends without faults, and by a love without flaw" (404–405). The strings of the harp begin to play and the Student repeats the poem that he recited/sang at the end of Scene 2. After a faint moan behind the screen, he concludes: "You poor little child! Child of this world of illusion and guilt and suffering and death—this world of eternal change and disappointment and never-ending pain! May the Lord of Heaven have mercy on you as you journey forth" (405). The room disappears and an image of Böcklin's "The Island of the Dead" appears in the distance and music seems to come from the island: "soft, pleasant, and melancholy."

Conclusion

Strindberg's idealization of eternal life after death does not differ very much, in the end, from Chekhov's subjunctive mood. In the plays of both dramatists, characters do what they possibly can to avoid consequences in the here and now, what, say, Ibsen's characters confront, in favor of the dream of a better future. In each case, they miss opportunities to form meaningful new relationships or strengthen intimate bonds with others with whom they already regularly engage. It is as if they heed the warnings of the Ibsen protagonists' will to power and respond with an extreme withdrawal, physical and emotional, in the opposite direction.

If there is a model for heroic action in this book, however, it belongs to Nora in *A Doll's House*. She uncovers the lies of her life and takes decisive action to figure the truth and to find her place in the modern world. The other Ibsen protagonists in this study, however, hurt others with their powerful assertions of the way things are that also hide ulterior motives. Gregers Werle, for example, says that he pursues the truth, but he blindly wrecks the entire Ekdal family in the process of what really amounts to his attempt to salve his guilty conscience about abandoning his mother. Similarly, Hedda Gabler's idealization of Eilert Løvborg is really a denial of intimacy with him and Solness' guilty conscience, despite his lengthy protestations to the contrary, stems from his refusal to help other people in his employ and selfish need to exploit them for his personal gain and aggrandizement. While Nora tries to see her world clearly and discovers by the end that it is very different from what she had imagined, the protagonists of *The Wild Duck*, *Hedda Gabler* and *The Master Builder* attempt to make the world conform to their personal visions of it—with disastrous results.

Unlike Gregers, Hedda or Solness, Nora attempts to move from an idealized vision of life that includes a happy home, a handsome husband, romantic love and plenty of money to a reasoned and reasonable assessment that calls for individual respect, equality in relationships between men and women and a new morality based upon love and kindness for others. That is what

Nora looks for in the final confrontation with her husband that ends when she walks out and slams the door. If she had only discovered such things earlier, perhaps she would have married Dr. Rank? Indeed, her friend Mrs. Linde does seize a second chance at happiness and makes an unlikely match and "true marriage," based upon trust and honesty, with Nils Krogstad. If only characters in other plays could see each other similarly: Arkadina would heal her son's wounds; Vanya and Sonya would relish each other's company in the beautiful rhythm of nature on the family farm; Masha would run away with Vershinin; Madame Ranyevskaya would subdivide her estate according to Lopakhin's plan; Adolf and Tekla's marriage would survive Gustav's revenge; Edgar and Alice would dispatch Curt quickly; the Student would not succumb to Hummel's ploy in *The Ghost Sonata*; Hedvig would not die in *The Wild Duck*; Hedda would not repeat her mistake with Løvborg; and Solness would mentor Ragnar as his successor.

The *magic if* would settle all conflicts—and effectively kill the drama. Unresolved, the plays remain the thing, then, to catch our conscience and prompt a reawakening.

Notes

1. My dissertation advisor, Alice Rayner, first mentioned these lines to me as an introduction to dramatic theory and criticism.

2. Toril Moi's description in *Henrik Ibsen and the Birth of Modernism* includes an excellent image of Christian Krogh's 1893 portrait of Strindberg that Ibsen purchased in 1895 (108–109).

3. See Karlinsky 357–358. Chekhov indicated that he was sending a copy of the play in his letter to Gorky on May 9, 1899. Chekhov, according to Karlinsky's notes, had read the play ten years earlier shortly after Strindberg published *Miss Julie*.

4. In order to remain consistent throughout the book, I have elected to use the modern transliteration of Russian names and therefore will refer to the author as "Konstantin Stanislavsky" in the body of the text rather than "Constantin Stanislavski."

5. See Karlinsky 357–358. In the same letter quoted above to Maxim Gorky, Chekhov expresses frustration with the performances of the actress playing Nina as well as Stanislavsky in the role of Trigorin.

6. I retain the hyphen in quoted material from Robbins's and Hapgood's translations, but in all other instances I refer to the "super objective" rather than the "super-objective."

7. The spine of the play, according to Clurman, is vocabulary for the director in the way that Stanislavsky motivates the actor with "through-action" or "super-objective" in *An Actor Prepares*.

8. See, for example, *Brand* in which the titular hero proclaims what could be the mantra for protagonists in all the prose plays to follow:

I require All or Nothing.
No half-measures. There is no forgiveness
For failure. It may not be enough
To offer your life. Your death may be required also [53].

The inability to bend or compromise expressed by the all or nothing attitude, is also essential to Ibsen characters who, detailed in quite different ways in the plays to follow, attempt to impose their will upon the world: Nora, Gregers, Hedda and Solness.

9. I have deliberately chosen "vital contradictions" as a phrase in honor of the late Professor Michael Manheim, inspirational mentor and author of *Vital Contradictions: Characterization in the Plays of Ibsen, Strindberg, Chekhov and O'Neill* (Bruxelles: P.I.E.-Peter Lang, 2002).

10. Goldman refreshingly and unapologetically valued content over form. In her introduction to Ibsen, she observed: "It is, therefore, not a little surprising that most of the interpreters and admirers of Ibsen so enthusiastically accept his art, and yet remain utterly indifferent to, not to say ignorant of, the message contained in it" (5).

11. See, in particular, Moi's readings of individual prose plays in chapters 7–10 and the epilogue, pp. 228–324.

12. See Antonin Artaud, *The Theater and Its Double*, 1958, translated by Mary Caroline Richards (New York: Grove Press, 1979), p. 25.

13. Nora's hoped-for miracle in *A Doll's House* regarding her husband actually occurs at the end of *The Lady from the Sea* as Wangel proves willing and capable to change and accept his wife, Ellida, as a free partner in marriage.

14. Ibsen's verse plays, including *Brand, Peer Gynt*, and *Emperor and Galilean*, comprise the Romantic phase in Brustein's schema; the eight prose plays ending with *Hedda Gabler* represent his modern phase.

15. See Brustein 73–75. *The Master Builder*, with its self-reflexive portrait of the artist, emerges as Brustein's favorite Ibsen drama.

16. "Free and Clear" was actually a tentative title of Miller's play at one time.

17. *Complete Major Prose Plays*, with translations by Rolf Fjelde, is no longer in print. I have dropped Fjelde's title, *A Doll House*, in favor of the traditional English of *A Doll's House*, but have remained otherwise faithful to his work and cite his and Templeton's specific works with his title. The three other plays included in the first volume of *Four Major Plays, The Wild Duck, Hedda Gabler*, and *The Master Builder*, receive extended analysis in the pages to follow and therefore all subsequent references to these plays will refer to the Signet Classics edition.

18. The dates in parentheses refer to original production dates at the Moscow Art Theatre. *The Seagull* was the fifth production of the MAT. It had failed at its initial venue at the Alexandrinsky Theatre in St. Petersburg two years earlier in 1896. All three of Chekhov's subsequent major plays premiered at the MAT.

19. In addition to Chekhov's previously cited letter to Maxim Gorky (Karlinsky 357–358), see Donald Rayfield, *Anton Chekhov: A Life* (New York: Henry Holt, 1997). Chekhov's future wife, actress Olga Knipper, wrote Chekhov about the production of *Uncle Vanya*: "You rightly distrusted Stanislavsky playing Ivan [Vanya]" (498). Of a rehearsal of *Three Sisters* that Chekhov attended, Rayfield records that "Stanislavsky was thrown by Anton's diffidence" (518). Stanislavsky played Gayev in *The Cherry Orchard* and considered the play a tragedy, not a comedy, and certainly not almost a farce as the playwright conceived (580, 582).

20. All future references to Chekhov's plays will be to this volume of Schmidt's translations.

21. See Brietzke, pp. 86–91.

22. All subsequent references to *Creditors* in this chapter are to Volume 1 of this edition.

23. All subsequent textual references to *The Dance of Death, A Dream Play*, and *The Ghost Sonata* are to Volume 2 of this edition unless noted otherwise.

Works Cited

Aristotle. *Aristotle's Poetics*. Introduction by Francis Fergusson, translated by S. H. Butcher. New York: Hill and Wang, 1961.
Artaud, Antonin. *The Theater and Its Double*. 1958. Translated by Mary Caroline Richards. New York: Grove Press, 1979.
Beckett, Samuel. *Waiting for Godot*. 1954. New York: Grove Press, 1982.
Bogard, Travis, editor. *The Unknown O'Neill*. New Haven: Yale University Press, 1988.
Brecht, Bertolt. "Theatre for Pleasure or Theatre for Instruction." *Brecht on Theatre: The Development of an Aesthetic*. 1964. Edited and translated by John Willett. New York: Hill and Wang, 1992.
Brietzke, Alexander K. *Nothing Is But What Is Not: Chekhovian Drama and the Crisis of Representation*. Diss., Stanford University, 1993.
Brustein, Robert. *The Theatre of Revolt*. 1964. Chicago: Elephant Paperbacks, 1991.
Burroughs, Bryson. "The Island of the Dead by Arnold Böcklin." *Metropolitan Museum of Art Bulletin* 21, no. 6 (1926), p. 146. JSTOR, www.jstor.org/stable/3254675.
Chekhov, Anton. *The Plays of Anton Chekhov*. 1997. Translated by Paul Schmidt. New York: HarperPerennial, 1998.
Clurman, Harold. *On Directing*. 1972. New York: Fireside, 1997.
Creditors. By August Strindberg. New version by David Greig. Directed by Alan Rickman. Performances by Tom Burke, Owen Teale, and Anna Chancellor. Brooklyn Academy of Music, Harvey Theatre, Brooklyn, New York, April 2010.
The Dance of Death. By August Strindberg. Adapted by Mike Poulton. Directed by Joseph Hardy. Produced by The Red Bull Theater. Performances by Daniel Davis, Laila Robins and Derek Smith. Lucille Lortel Theater, New York City, April 2013.
Dumas, Alexandre, fils. *La Dame aux Camélias*. In Stanton, pp. 105–164.
Fraser, Catherine C. "Visual Clues to Interpreting Strindberg's *Spöksonaten*." *Scandinavian Studies* 63, no. 3 (1991), pp. 281–292.
Frye, Northrop. *Anatomy of Criticism*. 1957. Princeton: Princeton University Press, 1973.
Gilman, Richard. *Chekhov's Plays: An Opening into Eternity*. New Haven: Yale University Press, 1995.
_____. *The Making of Modern Drama*. 1972. New Haven: Yale University Press, 1999.
Goldman, Emma. *The Social Significance of Modern Drama*. 1914. Introduction by Harry G. Carlson. New York: Applause, 1987.
Gombrich, E. H. *Art and Illusion: A Study in the Psychology of Pictorial Representation*. 1960. Princeton: Princeton University Press, 1984.
Hornby, Richard. "Ibsen Triumphant." *Hudson Review* 56, no. 4 (Winter 2004), pp. 685–691. JSTOR, www.jstor.org/stable/3852968.

Works Cited

Ibsen, Henrik. *Brand. Ibsen Plays: Five.* 1986. Translated by Michael Meyer. London: Methuen Drama, 2000.
———. *The Complete Major Prose Plays.* Translated and introduction by Rolf Fjelde. New York: Plume, 1978.
———. *Four Major Plays.* 1965. Translated by Rolf Fjelde, vol. 1. New York: Signet Classics, 1992.
———. *Letters and Speeches.* Edited and translated by Evert Sprinchorn. New York: Hill and Wang, 1964.
Johnston, Brian. *The Ibsen Cycle: The Design of the Plays from "Pillars of Society" to "When We Dead Awaken."* Rev. ed. University Park: Penn State University Press, 1992.
Karlinsky, Simon, editor. *Anton Chekhov's Life and Thought: Selected Letters and Commentary.* 1973. Translated by Michael Henry Heim. Berkeley: University of California Press, 1975.
Kataev, Vladimir. *If Only We Could Know! An Interpretation of Chekhov.* Edited and translated by Harvey Pitcher. Chicago: Ivan R. Dee, 2002.
Magarshack, David. *Chekhov the Dramatist.* 1952. London: Methuen Drama, 1980.
Mamet, David. "Notes on *The Cherry Orchard.*" *Writing in Restaurants.* New York: Penguin, 1986.
Marker, Frederick, and Lise-Lone Marker. *Strindberg and Modernist Theatre: Post-Inferno Drama on Stage.* Cambridge: Cambridge University Press, 2007.
Meyer, Michael. *Ibsen: A Biography.* New York: Doubleday, 1971.
Moi, Toril. *Henrik Ibsen and the Birth of Modernism.* Oxford: Oxford University Press, 2006.
O'Neill, Eugene. "The Nobel Prize Acceptance Letter." In Bogard, pp. 426–428.
———. "Strindberg and Our Theatre." In Bogard, pp. 386–389.
Pinter, Harold. "Writing for the Theatre." *Complete Works: One.* 1976. New York: Grove Press, 1990.
Pitcher, Harvey. *The Chekhov Play: A New Interpretation.* 1973. Berkeley: University of California Press, 1985.
Rayfield, Donald. *Anton Chekhov: A Life.* New York: Henry Holt, 1997.
Robinson, Michael. Introduction. *The Pelican & The Isle of the Dead*, by August Strindberg, translated by Robinson. Birmingham: University of Birmingham, 1994, pp. 7–33.
Scribe, Eugene. *The Glass of Water.* In Stanton, pp. 33–104.
Shakespeare, William. *Hamlet. The Riverside Shakespeare.* Edited by G. Blakemore Evans et al. Boston: Houghton Mifflin, 1974.
Shaw, George Bernard. *The Quintessence of Ibsenism.* 1904. New York: Dover, 1994.
Sofer, Andrew. *The Stage Life of Props.* Ann Arbor: University of Michigan Press, 2003.
Stanislavski, Constantin. *An Actor Prepares.* 1936. Translated by Elizabeth Reynolds Hapgood. New York: Theatre Arts, 1982.
———. *My Life in Art.* 1924. Translated by J. J. Robbins. New York: Routledge/Theatre Arts, 1991.
Stanton, Stephen S., editor. *Camille and Other Plays.* Introduction by Stephen S. Stanton. New York: Hill and Wang, 1957.
Stoppard, Tom. *Rosencrantz and Guildenstern Are Dead.* New York: Grove Press, 1967.
Strindberg, August. Appendix. *The Pelican & the Isle of the Dead*, pp. 114–117.
———. *The Bond. Twelve Major Plays*, 176–207.
———. *Comrades. Seven Plays by August Strindberg.* 1960. Translated by Arvid Paulson. New York: Bantam, 1972.
———. *Creditors. Twelve Major Plays*, pp. 120–172.
———. *Crime and Crime. Twelve Major Plays*, pp. 209–276.
———. *The Dance of Death, Part 2. Twelve Major Plays*, pp. 409–453.
———. *The Father. Twelve Major Plays*, pp. 7–57.

———. *Five Plays.* Translated and introduction by Harry G. Carlson. Berkeley: University of California Press, 1983.
———. *The Great Highway. Twelve Major Plays,* pp. 637–689.
———. *Miss Julie. Twelve Major Plays,* pp. 74–114.
———. *The Pelican & The Isle of the Dead.* Edited and translated by Michael Robinson. Birmingham: University of Birmingham, 1994.
———. Preface. *Miss Julie. Five Plays,* pp. 63–75.
———. *Selected Plays.* 1986. Translated by Evert Sprinchorn. Minneapolis: University of Minnesota Press, 2012. 2 vols.
———. *To Damascus, Part 3. Eight Expressionist Plays.* Translated by Arvid Paulson. New York: Bantam, 1965.
———. *Twelve Major Plays.* 1955. Translated by Elizabeth Sprigge. Piscataway: Aldine-Transaction, 2009.
Styan, J. L. *Chekhov in Performance: A Commentary on the Major Plays.* Cambridge: Cambridge University Press, 1971.
Szondi, Peter. *Theory of the Modern Drama.* 1965. Edited and translated by Michael Hays. Minneapolis: University of Minnesota Press, 1987.
Templeton, Joan. "The *Doll House* Backlash: Criticism, Feminism, Ibsen." *PMLA* 104, no. 1 (January 1989), pp. 28–40.
Törnqvist, Egil. *Strindberg's "The Ghost Sonata."* Amsterdam: University of Amsterdam Press, 2000.
Törnqvist, Egil, and Birgitta Steene, editors. *Strindberg on Drama and Theatre.* Translated by Törnqvist and Steene. Amsterdam: University of Amsterdam Press, 2007.
Valency, Maurice. *The Breaking String: The Plays of Anton Chekhov.* Oxford: Oxford University Press, 1966.
———. *The Flower and the Castle.* 1963. New York: Octagon, 1975.
Vaughan, Stuart. *Directing Plays: A Working Professional's Method.* New York: Longman, 1993.
Williams, Raymond. *Drama from Ibsen to Brecht.* Oxford: Oxford University Press, 1969.

Index

The Abyss 83
An Actor Prepares 5, 78
Albee, Edward 16, 165–66
anagnorisis (recognition) 27
Antoine, Andre 137
Aristotle 6, 27
As You Like It 25
Augier, Émile 22, 26

Beckett, Samuel 18, 81, 167
Bernhardt, Sarah 83
A Blue Book 138
Böcklin, Arnold 131–32, 137–38, 146, 148–49, 160, 167, 187
Bodeen, Dewitt 26
The Bond 138, 143
Bosse, Harriet 146
Brand 13, 22, 32, 36
Brecht, Bertolt 18, 20, 135
Brooklyn Academy of Music 13
The Brothers Karamazov 5
Brustein, Robert 3, 21–22, 28, 34
Büchner, Georg 3, 24
Building a Character 78
Bull, Ole 24
buried secret 2, 23, 24, 26, 29–42, 68, 72
Burroughs, Bryson 131–32

Camille 83–85, 95
chamber plays 137, 138
Chekhov's Plays: An Opening into Eternity 80, 81, 97–98
The Cherry Orchard 2, 6, 8–11, 15, 17, 78, 80–81, 88–89, 91–92, 121–30, 145, 189
Chestnut Theatre 25
Christiania (Oslo) 25
Clurman, Harold 5
comparisons between dramatists 3–5, 27–28, 81–82, 91, 110, 134, 139, 145–49, 169–70, 188–89
Comrades 138, 139
consequences of action 1, 19–20; *see also* dramatic action; dramatic aspirations of Chekhovian characters; "magic if"; super objective; worldviews of the artists
Covent Garden 25
Creating a Role 78
Creditors 11, 12, 13, 15, 17, 134, 137, 141–42, 143, 145, 149–59, 189
Crime and Crime 145

La Dame aux Camélias see *Camille*
The Dance of Death 11, 13, 15–18, 134, 145, 146–47, 159–67, 170, 177, 189
Death of a Salesman 38
de Musset, Alfred 24
Dietrich-Grabbe, Christian 24
Directing Plays: A Working Professional's Method 94
A Doll's House 13, 14–16, 21–22, 27, 28, 29, 31, 33, 38–48, 55, 139, 188–89
Donmar Warehouse 13
Dostoevsky, Fyodor 5, 79, 103
Drama from Ibsen to Brecht 23–24, 25
dramatic action 2, 5, 19–20; *see also* consequences of action; dramatic aspirations of Chekhovian characters; "magic if"; super objective; worldviews of the dramatists
dramatic aspirations of Chekhovian characters 17, 78–81, 84, 87, 90–92, 94, 117–18; *see also* consequences of action; dramatic action; "magic if"; super objective; worldviews of the dramatists
A Dream Play 12, 13, 18, 134–135, 147–148, 149, 167–77, 178–79
Drury Lane 25
Dumas *fils*, Alexandre 22, 26, 83
Duse, Eleonora 83

Easter 146
Emperor and Galilean 13, 22
An Enemy of the People 4, 22, 27, 32
An Enemy of the People (Miller) 19
English Restoration comedies 24
exposition in Ibsen 27, 48–49
expressionism 5, 12, 134

Index

fable 13–14
Falck, August 131, 137
The Father 4, 11, 139–41, 142, 145
female roles in 19
five parts of the joke 94
The Flower and the Castle 23
Fraser, Catherine C. 131, 149
Freud, Sigmund 131
Frye, Northrop 14, 112
The Fumes of Life 83
the future in Chekhov 99, 104–05, 113–15, 118, 120–21, 122, 124, 127–29

Garbo, Greta 83
Getting Married 144
The Ghost Sonata 2, 12, 13, 16, 18, 31, 131, 133–35, 137–38, 147–49, 177–87, 189
Ghosts 4, 7–8, 21, 22, 27, 33–34, 59, 139
Gilman, Richard 3, 25, 26, 29, 80, 81, 97–98
The Glass of Water 26
Gogol, Nikolai 24
Goldman, Emma 22
Gombrich, E.H. 24
Gorky, Maxim 4
The Government Inspector 24, 107
The Great Highway 134, 139, 148
Greek drama 24, 39

Hamlet 1, 25, 88–89, 95
Hebbel, Friedrich 24
Hedda Gabler 2, 3, 4, 13, 15, 16, 21, 28, 34, 41, 57–67, 74, 110, 188–89
Hegel, Wilhelm Friedrich 8
Henrik Ibsen and the Birth of Modernism 22
Hettner, Herman 25
"Higher Forms of Existence: *Die Toteninsel*" 138
Hitler, Adolf 131
Hornby, Richard 21

Ibsen Museum 3–4
If Only We Could Know! An Interpretation of Chekhov 79
The Importance of Being Earnest 30
influence on American playwrights 18–19
Intimate Theater 131–32, 137
The Island of the Dead (Toteninsel) 131–34, 137–38, 148–49, 160, 167, 187
The Island of the Living 137
The Isle of the Dead (Strindberg play) 138, 149
An Italian Straw Hat 24
Ivanov 87–88, 91

John Gabriel Borkman 3, 22, 27, 35–36
Johnston, Brian 8

Kammerspiele Theater 137
Kataev, Vladimir 79, 90
King Lear 25

Labiche, Eugène 24
The Lady from the Sea 13, 33, 34, 68, 70, 74
Leikin, Nikolai 83
Lenin, Vladimir 131
Lermontov, Mikhail 79
Liechtenstein, Alfred 131
Little Eyolf 13, 22, 35
Long Day's Journey Into Night 18
Ludlam, Charles 83

Magarshack, David 124
"magic if" 19, 77–78, 79, 82, 101, 189; *see also* consequences of action; dramatic action; super objective; worldviews of the artists
The Making of Modern Drama 3, 25, 26, 29, 97
Marker, Frederick 137
Marker, Lise-Lone 137
Markevich, Bóleslav 83
The Master Builder 3, 13, 15, 16, 22, 27, 34–35, 36, 59, 67–76, 145, 147
melodrama 1, 20, 95, 135
metadrama 18, 33
Metropolitan Museum of Art 131–33
Meyer, Michael 3, 4–5, 21, 24, 26
Miller, Arthur 18–19, 38–39
Miss Julie 2, 4, 11–12, 13, 15, 133–37, 138, 141–43, 145, 150, 160, 169; preface 2, 134–37, 161, 168–69
modern drama 1, 7, 134, 167; aspects 2, 5
Das Moderne Drama 25
Modjeska, Helena 83
Moi, Toril 22, 131, 148–49
Molander, Olaf 131
Molière, Jean-Baptiste Poquelin 24
A Month in the Country 24
Moscow Art Theatre 4, 78, 94
The Museum of Basel (Switzerland) 133
My Life in Art 4, 77, 82

Norwegian Theatre at Bergen 24–26
Norwegian Theatre of Christiania 25–26
The Notebook of Trigorin 19

Oedipus 8
O'Neill, Eugene 18
Ostrovsky, Alexander 24

A Peculiar Position 26
Peer Gynt 13, 22
peripeteia (reversal) 27
Phenomenology of Mind 8
pièce bien faite *see* well-made play
The Pillars of Society 1, 22, 27, 30–31
Pinter, Harold 114
Pitcher, Harvey 124–25
Playing with Fire 138, 143, 146
Pushkin, Alexander 79, 86

The Quintessence of Ibsenism 22

Rachmaninoff, Sergei 131
Rayfield, Donald 83
realism 5, 144, 169
Red Bull Theater 13
Reinhardt, Max 131, 137
Rickman, Alan 13
Ridiculous Theatre Company 83
Romeo and Juliet 25
Rosencrantz and Guildenstern Are Dead 1
Rosmersholm 3, 27, 33, 59, 139
Royal Shakespeare Theatre 21

Sardou, Victorien 26
Scandinavian Experimental Theatre 137
Schering, Emil 138
Schmidt, Paul 83
Schopenhauer, Arthur 79, 103
Scribe, Eugène 22, 23, 24, 25, 26, 29
The Seagull 4, 6, 8–11, 15, 17, 19, 78–83, 89, 90, 92–101, 106, 189; play-within-play 2, 15, 83–87, 98–100, 169
Shakespeare, William 1, 24, 25, 88
Shaw, George Bernard 22
The Social Significance of Modern Drama 22
Sofer, Andrew 28
Sprigge, Elizabeth 156
The Stage Life of Props 28
Stanislavsky, Konstantin 4, 5, 6, 19, 77–79, 82,
Stanton, Stephen 26
station drama 144
Stoppard, Tom 1
"Strindberg and Our Theatre" 18
The Stronger 142–43
Styan, J. L. 125
super objective 5–7, 16–20; *see also* consequences of action; dramatic action; "magic if"; worldviews of the artists
superfluous man 87–88
surrealism 12, 168–69
Suvorin, Alexi 87
Szondi, Peter 3

Templeton, Joan 22
The Theatre of Revolt 3
Theory of Modern Drama 3
Three Sisters 2, 6, 8–11, 15, 78, 79, 80, 81, 85, 90, 111–21, 122, 125–27, 167, 189
To Damascus 134, 139, 143–45, 148
Tolstoy, Leo 5
Törnqvist, Egil 131
"true marriage" 29, 32, 33, 34, 47, 48, 54–55, 189
Turgenev, Ivan 24, 88, 96

Uncle Vanya 8–11, 15, 17, 28, 78–80, 89–90, 101–11, 112, 119, 189
University of Copenhagen 137

Valency, Maurice 23, 124–25
Vaughan, Stuart 94
Le Verre d'eau see *The Glass of Water*
Vishensky, V.I. 5
vital contradictions 14
von Kleist, Heinrich 24

Waiting for Godot 81, 167
Warhol, Andy 131
well-made play 2, 24, 26–29
When We Dead Awaken 3, 4, 13, 22, 36, 37, 68
Who's Afraid of Virginia Woolf? 16, 165–66
The Wild Duck 4, 14–17, 27, 29, 32–33, 47–57, 68, 188–89
Wilde, Oscar 29
Williams, Raymond 23, 25
Williams, Tennessee 19
Women's Rights League (Ibsen's banquet speech) 2, 21, 37–38
worldviews of the artists 5–6, 78, 188–89; *see also* consequences of action; dramatic action; dramatic aspirations of Chekhovian characters; "magic if"; super objective
"Writing for the Theatre" 114

www.ingramcontent.com/pod-product-compliance
Lightning Source LLC
Chambersburg PA
CBHW032059300426
44116CB00007B/813